MID-VICTORIAN WALES

THE OBSERVERS AND THE OBSERVED

MID-VICTORIAN WALES

THE OBSERVERS AND THE OBSERVED

by

Ieuan Gwynedd Jones

CARDIFF
UNIVERSITY OF WALES PRESS
1992

British Library Cataloguing-in-Publication Data

A catalogue record for this book is available from the British Library.

ISBN 0–7083–1148–2 hardback
ISBN 0–7083–1166–0 paperback

Paperback cover design by Design Principle, Cardiff
Typeset by Megaron, Cardiff
Printed in Great Britain by Biddles Limited, Guildford

For
Glanmor Williams,
historian, teacher and friend

Contents

Illustrations

Foreword

Four of these essays have appeared in print before. The first is the Annual Gwyn Jones Lecture for 1985, and I am grateful to Professor Gwyn Jones for so readily agreeing to its republication in this form. The second was given as a lecture before the Honourable Society of Cymmrodorion and published in the *Transactions* of the Society in 1984, and I thank the editors for permission to include it in this collection. The third originally appeared in *A People and a Proletariat: Essays in the History of Wales, 1780–1980* (London, 1980) edited by David Smith, and the fourth in *Morgannwg*, XXXIV (1988). I am very grateful to Professor Smith and Dr Alban for their kindness. The fifth, and most substantial of the essays, has been written for this collection.

All five essays aspire to understand the course of social change in Wales in the central decades of the nineteenth century, and to aim to do so, in so far as this is at all possible, from within the communities which experienced them. This is a tall order, for nothing is more difficult than to enter into a world that is past — even more difficult than the attempts of social anthropologists to enter into the unfamiliar, but real and living, cultures of primitive peoples. Like them the social historian has to master a new language, but unlike them he cannot be an active participant in the use of that language. He can only listen and try not to assume that the words and usages he reads are identical with those he uses in his own common speech. This approach to the past is even more difficult when it is the world of the common people which the historian seeks to understand. At least with them there can be no pretence that their world is ours, in the sense that the world of the educated and sophisticated can perhaps be more readily entered into. Welsh social historians are peculiarly fortunate in being able to approach the common people through their religion and the literary culture their religion created. The periodical literature of early and mid-Victorian times, and the institutions they devised for the transmission of this culture, provide the means of entry into their world. Literary quality apart — and some of the writings deserve to be better known and evaluated — the magazines of the period are an incredibly rich source and historians ignore them at their peril. I have quoted as generously as space permits from a number of these publications, on some occasions adding similar (or contrasting) references in the notes. The translations are my own and aim to convey the feeling as well as the sense of the original.

But the task is to understand not only what the common people made of the world they experienced, how they understood it and accounted for it and their place within it, but also how they interpreted it to others and, above all, how they reacted to the observations of others from different or alien cultures. A steadily increasing stream of people from outside came into the country and observed and recorded what they saw. Some were sympathetic, especially those who had some notion that they were confronted by a culture very different from their own. Others were deeply antipathetic and impatient of people whose ways of life did not accord with the values of their own. The historian must understand these observers too, their prejudices and preconceptions for, ironically, it sometimes happens that it is these which point the way to the reality which both the observers and the observed failed to see. Hence the concern of some of these essays, especially the first and the fifth, to understand, as it were, both sides of the social equation. By contrast, the fourth essay looks at one small, traditional society in order to show how the members of its many disparate parts were, in respect of their own particular communities, both observers and observed, and how the image of the whole which they ultimately projected was all the richer for the diversities it comprised.

In their different ways, all the essays are concerned with the development of politics in Wales at this crucial time in its history when the political process in the country at large was on the verge of transformation. The politicization of the people is a major theme in this collection, and it is argued that the quality of the political life experienced by Welsh people generally in the last quarter of the century was the product of the self-understanding of the generation covered in this volume.

I take this opportunity to thank again the many friends and colleagues from whose kindness and patience I have benefited so much over the years. I owe a particular debt of gratitude to my son, Alun, who has contributed more than he imagines to my understanding of past societies.

My gratitude to the staff of the National Library of Wales and the Hugh Owen Library cannot be measured. Their expert cooperation, so readily and cheerfully given, has often been beyond the bounds of duty, and I am very grateful to them all.

The book owes more than she would herself acknowledge to the patient and meticulous editing of Ceinwen Jones of the University of Wales Press, and I thank her most cordially.

Finally and especially I wish to thank my wife for her unfailing help and encouragement. Throughout our lives together it is she who has carried the heat and burden of the day, and I am the beneficiary.

Abbreviations

ARLGB	Annual Reports of the Local Government Board
ARMOPC	Annual Reports of the Medical Officer of the Privy Council
ARRG	Annual Reports of the Registrar-General
DNB	*Dictionary of National Biography*
DWB	*Dictionary of Welsh Biography down to 1940*
GBH	General Board of Health
GCH	*Glamorgan County History*
GRO	Glamorgan Record Office
ICBS	Incorporated Church Building Society
LBH	Local Board of Health
Minutes	*Minutes of the Committee of Council on Education*
NLW	National Library of Wales
NLWJ	*National Library of Wales Journal*
PP	*Parliamentary Papers*
PRO	Public Record Office
SDF	Social Democratic Federation
WHR	*Welsh History Review*

1

The Observers and the Observed

I am not aware that the Great Western Railway ever ran excursions to Merthyr Tydfil or Nant-y-glo: you will look in vain for these places in *Holiday Haunts*. But it was not uncommon in Victorian times for the curious to visit the iron towns to see for themselves the wonders of technology and to contemplate some of the more unpleasant and perhaps puzzling features of contemporary industrialization even as in earlier times they had come to enjoy the natural beauty of those selfsame places. To take an extreme example, in 1852 you might have joined a party at Bristol for 'a run on the rails and a few days amongst the furnaces of south Wales', staying at Neath *en route* in order to visit the Briton Ferry Lunatic Asylum and attend the Lunatics' Ball.[1] Such diversions, I am fairly sure, must have been exceptional, and certainly the irony of prefacing a visit to 'the Paradise of Cinders' with a reminder of madness and abnormality was not unconscious. More normal was the visitor's eye for the bizarre and the brutal, for ignorance and immorality, for the dirty and the disgusting, and his ear for the barbarous language of the natives. These, as often as not, were the qualities that some Cardiff people, ignoring what lay on their own front doorsteps, found in their own back yard; and from a greater distance the inhabitants of Bala believed that Merthyr was to Wales what Coventry was to England or Gehenna to Jerusalem.[2] Just as offensive, but betraying a different sensitivity, was the 'Great Pandemonium' metaphor with its echoes of Milton's Hell which was found modelled in the fiery, cavernous tips surrounding the ironworks and the limestone quarries higher up in the hills. Others turned to science and found their metaphors, perhaps more prophetically, in the new technologies. 'Great condensations of

This print from an American newspaper of *c*. 1855 advertised Vernon
House at Briton Ferry as a 'Private Nursing Home for Mental Patients'.

manufacturing populations' was how the geologist Conybeare (who
was also Dean of Llandaff) put it; people as factors in, and the
products of, chemical reactions.[3]

The ignorance and puzzlement betrayed by the language was
expressive of the novelty with which outside observers and the
inhabitants of these places alike were faced. The industrial
settlements were without precedent. Their emergence had been
sudden, and their future was so problematic that a different
language seemed to be required to describe them. Evanescence
rather than continuity was what was most characteristic of them,
impermanence and instability where men expected to find stable
institutions and a continuous tradition. And yet, these were the very
places that were laying claim to be the most religious urban area in
Britain, and could display the evidence in stone and mortar and facts
and figures for all to see. 'O Gymru, pa le mae dy debyg wlad dan y
nef?' ('O Wales, where is thy like under the sun?').[4]

There is a palpable difference between, on the one hand, what observers from outside, whether they were casual and adventitious or purposeful and systematic, saw, or thought they saw, in the communities growing up in the south Wales coalfield, and the quality of life experienced in them by their inhabitants. In this paper I want to explore some aspects of this area of difference in order to try to understand more fully the social realities underlying the appearance of things. I shall seek to do three things: first, to look at what the observers seemed to be saying, and why, secondly, to ask whether it is possible to see the social realities from the point of view of the people themselves, and finally, to suggest that perhaps we in our very different culture are too ready to accept the evidence of the first, and too ill-equipped to listen to what the second have to say about themselves. This is a difficult task but it is balanced by the honour of being invited to give this lecture and the sheer pleasure of being associated in this way with Gwyn Jones. The observers I have in mind fall into three overlapping categories defined as much by the motives and the intentions governing their observations as by the contents of their writings. The first I call the moralists, the second the social scientists, and the third the reporters. These are very rough categories; they are not distinct or exclusive, for it was the extent to which they overlapped or were interdependent which resulted in the creation of a kind of orthodox view by the middle of the nineteenth century of what the iron and coal communities of the south Wales coalfield were like. Together they created an image of society. The purpose of my categories is to separate out some of the main constituents in this image.

Easily the most influential of the moralistic observers were the religious ones — especially, though by no means exclusively, the clergy of the Established Church. In the early decades of the century what the bishops of Llandaff proclaimed that they saw was chiefly a growth of Dissent and sectarianism. For example, Bishop Richard Watson, the 'Christian Whig', that veritable monument to clerical abuse, went on an extensive visitation of his diocese in 1809 'over the mountains from Neath', the route of our Bristol excursionists, to a place where no bishop had ever held a visitation before, Merthyr Tydfil. He wrote:

> In my time, this place had grown to become, from a small village, a great town containing ten or twelve thousand inhabitants, occupied in the fabrication of iron; and I thought it my duty not only to

confirm the young people there, but to preach to those who were grown up that I might, if possible, leave among the inhabitants a good impression in favour of the teachings of the Established Church, when compared to those of the sectarian congregations into which the people were divided.[5]

Unlike Richard Watson, who, as a liberal theologian, did not believe that an Arian, a Socinian or an Arminian, from principle, should not be saved, and more importantly, who believed that all forms of Christianity produced a uniform morality, his successors in the see were deeply alarmed by what they saw as the growth of infidelity among a largely illiterate and uncultivated people. This was the view of Bishop van Mildert, who spent the unusually long span of eight years in Llandaff before moving to Durham. Dissent, unlike the Anglican Church, could provide no defence against evil and disaffected men who were openly or covertly endeavouring to subvert the constitution and destroy the social order. Infidelity bred disloyalty, sedition was the product of scepticism, and blasphemy led inevitably to treason. These fearful correspondences had not been made in Wales yet, for the Welsh were happy in being protected from what he called 'metropolitan influences' by their language, but the fanaticism of 'schismatic itinerants' was but a preparative of what would surely come about in the diocese if the voice of the Church could not be more effectively heard.[6]

His successor, Charles Sumner, who stayed in the diocese just long enough to be translated to Winchester — exchanging Llandaff's £900 per annum for Winchester's £12,000 (everything suffers in translation, except a bishop) — shared these views, but he seems also to have doubted the ability of the Church to provide for a population that ebbed and flowed, collected suddenly and as suddenly dispersed. And if, as was evidently the case, 'instances of gross and flagrant crime were of extremely rare occurrence', the credit of this morality, he thought, could scarcely be imputed to the Church.[7] Whether these perceptions of the ambiguities in the moral state of the diocese survived his one and only visit to the coalfield is doubtful. Shortly before he left for Winchester in 1827, he visited Dowlais to consecrate the Iron Company's new church and to induct Evan Jenkins into the living, and on the way back, some six or seven miles on the road to Cardiff, he bade Jenkins goodbye with the words, 'I leave you as a missionary in the heart of Africa'.[8] If it were beyond the power of the Anglicans to provide churches in sufficient numbers in the right places it was not impossible to provide a kind of 'mission-clergy' to settle in the coalfield to inculcate a correct social and political morality in those benighted places.

I have expatiated about the observations of the two bishops because they seem to me to typify the pre-Reform establishment morality of their times. While both were alive to the political tensions in society, to the revolutionary ferment which elsewhere in the country accompanied industrialization and urbanization, both seemed to think that the Welsh language insulated Welsh communities from the infection of revolutionary ideology, and both feared Dissent not so much for its theological dogmas, which were no different by and large from their own, as for its tendency, by an excess of enthusiasm and through its pernicious doctrines on the nature of Church government, to weaken the bonds which held society together. Dissent did not necessarily bring about revolution; it merely made it more probable that the advocates of radical change would succeed in sowing discord among communities already disaffected by worsening economic and social conditions. Possibly behind these notions was a perception that Dissent or Nonconformity was less monolithic than might appear, that some of the denominations, notably the Methodists, were close allies of the Church insofar as they upheld the same norms of political behaviour and for the same reasons. It would be natural and realistic in those early decades of the century to assume that underlying the differences was a common religious culture.

What changed all this and brought to the forefront a new social and political morality were the upheavals of the 1830s in Britain and the realization that the potential for revolution existed in the coalfield towns and villages. The events of that decade have been brilliantly narrated and analysed by Gwyn A. Williams and David Jones, and I do not propose to add to what they have written.[9] During and after that decade the society of the coalfield came under increasingly close scrutiny, and what was found sharpened the apprehension of the establishment of what was held to be a necessary congruence between right beliefs and proper conduct. Hence the proliferation of inquiries by Church and State into the 'morals', that is the behaviour, public and private, of the various communities in the mining and manufacturing districts. Most of the royal commissions and select committees of the time such as those on the employment of women and children in mines, into poor law, and especially on education, included evidence collected in south Wales; the Education Inquiry of 1846 ('Brad y Llyfrau Gleision') was specifically on Wales; and from 1840 onwards there were the annual reports of the Education and Factory Inspectors, many of which had reference to Wales. All this material was published in the form of Parliamentary Papers, sometimes with epitomes intended for wide circulation, and in the case of Tremenheere's Reports circulated gratis among managers, owners, agents of the various works, and the local establishment. Recently it has been argued, not entirely convincingly, that this material emanating from government was designed to obscure the fact of the existence in south Wales of a revolutionary proletariat.

I must now draw attention to some aspects of the role of the Church in this activity. First, the chronology of church building, which can be taken as a fairly reliable index of establishment concern, shows that Wales was not particularly a preoccupation of central government and of the hierarchy in the first two decades or so of the century.[10] None of the £1 million voted by Parliament in 1818 for building new churches, and only a minuscule part of the additional grant of £500,000 in 1824, came to Wales, and none to south Wales. This was not due to ignorance, but was the result of political calculation, namely, that the threat to public order originated mainly, or was invariably to be found, in very large towns and cities of which there were none in Wales. After the Merthyr Rising of 1831 and the march on Newport in 1839 the authorities looked at towns of lesser size, but more significantly at districts, areas rather than places. It was this that brought Seymour Tremenheere to Wales.

Secondly, the underlying problem for the Church in this diocese was different from that in populous English dioceses. In the eyes of the Church what characterized the English manufacturing towns and cities was 'spiritual destitution', that is, the religious equivalent of pauperism. The more destitute individuals and places were, the more open they were to the infection of insubordination and sedition. Religious destitution of this kind could scarcely be said to have existed on any significant scale in the coalfield even in van Mildert's time, and although provision may have been less ample in towns than in the countryside, it could never have been less than adequate.[11] But as we have seen, it was a provision made by

Nonconformists and mainly by old Dissenting denominations. This was a fact either ignored or explained away by the hierarchy, and when, as increasingly became the case, it could no longer be ignored, it tended to be deplored as something worse even than spiritual destitution. Some of the reforming bishops reluctantly accepted that Nonconformity probably did exert some good influences on society. Bishop Ollivant, for example, was of the opinion 'that had it not been for the exertions of dissenting bodies, our people must have been consigned to a practical heathenism, and left in ignorance . . . having no hope in the world'.[12] But it is astonishing how, in published reports, magazine articles, petitions to ecclesiastical and philanthropic societies, the majority of clergymen described the region as deprived of adequate provision, the people as a consequence ignorant, depraved, barbarous, and the communities where they lived uncivilized. 'Blackest Africa' indeed! The classic work of this kind, it needs scarcely to be said, was the 1847 Report of the inquiry into education in Wales. This was a kind of compendium, or digest, of the attitudes of the establishment to the communities growing up so rapidly outside the sphere of influence of the Church. The aim of the Report was to demonstrate a need and to justify the adoption of forms of educational provision designed to return a people to their old allegiances. Henceforward, propagandists for particular kinds of education deliberately devised for their effectiveness as instruments of social control in England and Wales could refer to this authoritative work, and refer to it they did. Its significance for social historians is that more completely than almost any other source it shows the extent to which different social classes adhered to different forms of religion, but also the extent to which even before 1847 there had developed a perception that the clergy were the servants of one class against another. This is a theme to which I shall return.

The second category of observers I have called 'the social scientists', and included in this category are the reports of salaried or specialized inspectors on specific aspects of social conditions such as working conditions and especially public health. In addition to these were the annual reports of the Registrar-General which began in 1839 and which included statistical studies of the age structure of the people and of the unfolding patterns of mortality. The difference between this category and the first one was in the main not the presence in one and the lack in the other of an element of propaganda, for persuasion and enlightenment, the creation of a public opinion favourable to reform by legislation, was the *raison d'être* of the Factory and Public Health movements. In this respect, utilitarians and evangelicals alike looked to Parliament and hence ultimately to the creation of an informed electorate. The main difference lay rather in the quality of the observation. The inspectors of the Board of Health were often scientists or men with technical qualifications of a high order. They included geologists, chemists, engineers, managers and, above all, medical men. In a way they were all amateurs. They had to develop techniques of objective investigation and of effective communication, and it is notable how quickly and efficiently they built up a great body of knowledge concerning matters of sanitation, housing, nutrition and medical diagnostics.[13]

One of the great objectives in the public health movement was to draw up a kind of geography of disease in Britain, and, having done this, to establish the connection between disease and environment, including food, housing, the nature and conditions of labour, and sanitation. It was this and increasing evidence of deteriorating conditions that brought the inspectors to south Wales, and their cool, statistically sophisticated reports are the first that we can rely upon confidently for a depiction of the main factors in the quality of life of the inhabitants of the valleys. With these reports, supplemented with other information from central sources and the localities themselves, we have left the windy area of rhetoric and ideals and holy moralities and have entered a world of ascertainable facts. Also, whereas the moralists tended to seek out the worst features of a place, to inflate them and use them to illustrate some religious or moral ideal, the social scientists tried to report things as they were, without apportioning blame or moving outside the realm of rational explanation. For example, an investigation into bronchial illnesses in the iron towns, undertaken on account of the exceptionally high mortality rates from diseases of the chest, broadens out into observations on the ventilation of mines, on some of the characteristic features of house building, and the life-style of work people. An inquiry into the awful mortality rates of children develops into, among other possible factors, a careful and sympathetic observation of the nursing habits of mothers 'devotedly attached to their offspring'. The ravages of tuberculosis and of diseases of malnutrition prompt questions regarding the movements of commodity prices, the curve of wages, the regularity of work, patterns of unemployment and feeding customs at work and in the home. The great inquiries of Dr Edward Smith on the food of the labouring poor in the early 1860s provided comparative statistics in terms of the chemical constituents of food, and supplied a 'minimum quantitative standard of subsistence' which could be applied not only to the nutrition of working-class families in the towns but also with considerable accuracy to that of the migrant labourers without whose replenishment the local populations could scarcely have survived for more than a few decades. The language of Sir John Simon as he comments on the significance of Edward Smith's report is very different from that of the moralists:

> It must be remembered that privation of food is very reluctantly borne, and that, as a rule, great poorness of diet will only come when other privations have preceded it. Long before insufficiency of diet is a matter of hygienic concern, long before the physiologists would think of counting the grains of nitrogen and carbon that intervene between life and starvation, the household will have been utterly destitute of material comfort: clothing and fuel will have been even scantier than food — against inclemencies of weather there will have been no adequate protection — dwelling space will have been stunted to the degree in which over-crowding produces disease . . . even cleanliness will have been found costly or difficult and every self-respectful effort to maintain it will represent additional pangs of hunger. The home too will be where shelter can be cheapest bought; in quarters where commonly there is least fruit of sanitary supervision, least drainage, least scavenging, least suppression of public nuisances, least water-supply . . . least light and air.[14]

Necessarily also the social scientists observed and described the structure and functioning of local government in the different places they visited. It astonished these observers that towns of the magnitude of Merthyr or Brynmawr and other towns of the iron-belt should be 'as destitute of civic government as the merest rural village'. This was a novel form of destitution perhaps more dangerous to social order in the end than so-called moral destitution. 'I am no longer surprised at the violent and apparently purposeless outrages which have occasionally broken out in South Wales,' reported Dr Holland in 1853. 'In Lancashire similar causes have produced similar results, but here the cause is more aggravated and the effect more violent: as Blackburn is to Merthyr, so is a Lancashire riot to a Newport rebellion.' And they observed that the groups or classes in society which possessed power exercised it mainly for their own benefit, to tax and to punish. 'Tyranny is always better organized than freedom.' Along with a lack of formal democratic institutions they found that the towns were bereft of civic buildings or public halls, that there were no places in which to hold decision-making meetings. Such observations led them to inquire into the social structure of the towns and they marvelled, but duly recorded in sober language, the extreme simplicity and rudimentary character of their class structure. They noted the absence of an integrated, self-conscious, educated middle class and likewise the almost entire lack of a residential gentry. How power was distributed or disposed in such communities was of the highest importance: in virtually every town on the coalfield democratic forms in local government had to be imposed by legislation upon minorities for the good of the majority. But as I shall show, democracy itself was a very familiar concept for the majority who were being denied its benefits.[15]

So, existing alongside, and rarely harmoniously with, the highly coloured and deeply prejudiced views of observers whose main motives were to censure and admonish and to inculcate obedience, was this growing body of largely objective information which was, and is, amenable to analysis and criticism. The observers in the first category drew attention to themselves or to their creeds and the institutions they served. Those in the second directed attention away from themselves and on to the object in an empirical and positivistic way. The first had the effect of arousing emotions of shame or humility in the people described, and fear and aggression in the establishment groups by whom they were confronted. The second succeed in deepening our understanding, and the emotion they arouse in us is pity.

Yet there were whole areas of life — corporate life, family life, the lives of individual persons — that lay outside the brief and perhaps the abilities of the social scientists to examine or describe: religion, for example, folk culture, rites of passage, the experience of work at the point of production, sickness and unemployment, the poverty cycle as an experience, music and entertainment, poetry and the things of the mind. What external observer, however free of the assumptions of his own culture, could hope to describe these? To the best of my knowledge only one person attempted such a socially comprehensive depiction of society in the south Wales coalfield in the middle of the nineteenth century, and that was the author of the so-called 'Letters on Labour and the Poor' which appeared weekly in the *Morning Chronicle* early in 1850, and which have recently been reprinted by Cass and edited by Jules Ginswick.[16]

The thirteen 'Letters' were part of a huge project launched under the inspiration of Henry Mayhew, whose work on the London poor was to have been part of the project, 'to give a full and detailed description of the moral, intellectual, material and physical condition of the industrial poor throughout England' and Wales. The correspondent for Wales was extraordinarily well-informed and thorough, and there is no doubt that his series of articles equals, or even surpasses, the official investigations 'for impartiality, authenticity and comprehensiveness'. He was taken around the Dowlais and the Cyfarthfa ironworks, he went down a mine, and spoke to miners and colliers at their work and in their homes. He spent a great deal of time with the Iron Company surgeons — one of whom was also the Medical Officer of Health for Merthyr — with lawyers, Poor Law officials, Anglican ministers (but not Nonconformist ministers), the Dowlais cashier, and one of the two booksellers. His enquiries were based on full and accurate information about industry and industrial relations based on the latest official information, and he was expert in his knowledge of the law. His articles have the additional advantage of being highly readable. Angus Bethune Reach, if he was the author, was the first sociologist of Wales.[17]

And yet, for all their wealth of information, their live descriptions of men and women and children at work and at play, their vivid and memorable street scenes, and their rare sympathy, the *Morning Chronicle* articles remain the record of an outside observer, reportage of a high order but limited. Its limitations are precisely in those areas of community and among those strands of social relations the understanding of which is vital to the apprehension of the whole. The author observed the working classes at work or at leisure, never on their own terms as a fellow worker, but always as interlocutor, always in the company of a manager or an agent. He did not understand Welsh, and must therefore have communicated either through an interpreter or not at all. Some would have understood his speech but have been dumb in his language. Unlike

Henry Mayhew, for whom the dimension of consciousness was all-important and who had perfected a technique of interviewing and a verisimilitude of speech which should adequately reflect it, the author seems to have been content to use a set form of questions and to have recorded the answers in a stereotyped manner. Idiosyncrasies of speech, local idioms and what must have been a new language compounded of English words forced into a Welsh syntactical structure are not to be found in his report, and without them whole areas of consciousness are missing. We are given valuable and memorable images of society and of the working class as a component in it, but the image is two-dimensional and flat.

Moreover, for all his sympathy for and understanding of the plight of the ironworkers, colliers, miners and the pauperized, of the pit-girls shovelling coal or piling ore, and of the door-boys and 'pygmy-colliers',[18] and the oppressive sense of injustice and exploitation that darkens the mind, the writer's social and perhaps political prejudices are not so very different from those of Seymour Tremenheere. The context of his visit in 1840 was Chartist unrest, the cholera epidemic, and a growing militancy among the Aberdare colliers. Chartism was suspected of being more powerful than at any time since 1839, and endemic disease (perhaps more than the recent epidemics) had sharpened the edges of class difference. He was anxious to identify in Merthyr the main areas of class antagonism, and to propose measures which could be applied locally and nationally to encourage harmonious industrial relations. Like Tremenheere he looked to the industrialists and coal-owners and to the middle classes to adopt paternalistic policies with regard to the lower classes. But the working classes on their part must adopt the psychology of self-help, embrace temperance, and give up their radical ideologies. Hence his vision was flawed, and though we see deeper through his eyes and observe some of the relations in the communities with great clarity, it is a partial view of the social realities of the coalfield that we are given.

It is inevitable that even the best of outside observers will be partial, for every observer carries within him his own distorting glass. Prejudices and preoccupations, emotions of admiration or fear or hatred come between him and the object. Self-interest, pride, ideology, perhaps greed, blind him to qualities and facts which are of the essence of the society being observed. Even the social scientists whose objectivity I have stressed were children of their age, and the scientific methods they brought to their enquiries unquestionably reflected their ways of seeing the conditions they described. When miasmatic theories of infection held sway, were not smells and bad ventilation more to be feared than malnutrition in the causation of disease? We can never be certain to what extent observations from the outside correspond to the reality.

There are two avenues that will lead us into a deeper and more complete understanding of the coalfield communities. Both lead us *into* the society and, by seeking to understand the values which governed the behaviour of people, enable us to observe the communities from within. The first we can call the inferential approach: what can we infer about them from the priorities or the relative importance they evidently attached to institutions of their own creation? The second approach is the literary one, the critical study of the literature produced at all levels of sophistication, and the valuation placed upon it by society as a whole.

Of the institutions of their own creation the largest, most prestigious and most influential were religious ones. There are some features of these institutions that the people at the time stressed and which we must grasp. First, their magnitude and, especially in industrial south Wales, their uniqueness. Nowhere in Britain would you find an industrial population in an area of new development so well provided with places of worship. By the middle of the century there were about 300 such in the towns and villages between Blaenafon and Hirwaun, and together they provided accommodation for about three-quarters of the entire population. These are relativities, of course, but the equations were consciously drawn and the comparisons were made by the people themselves: they claimed it as their own achievement.[19]

Secondly, there is the remarkable regularity of sustained growth for about forty years after the point of take-off which occurred in the two or three years after 1816, a period when the rate of growth exceeded that of population growth. The trend-line of constant growth, however, concealed another feature of cardinal importance, namely, an underlying ebb and flow within the regularity, years of relative decline followed by years of rapid growth. People were fascinated by these changes. They recognized that there was a relation between population change, the strength and place of origin of in-migration and levels of economic prosperity and these variations in growth rates. 'Tlodi a chyfyngder oedd wrth wraidd y

South Wales industrial landscape, c. 1825–6; oil on canvas by Penry Williams (c. 1798–1885). (National Library of Wales)

dywygiadau hyn'('Poverty and distress were at the root of these revivals'), wrote Henry Hughes about the revivals of 1817 to 1822.[20] But most characteristically they elaborated theories of revival to explain them — that pulse-like beat is what they saw as the relation of God with his people. They observed the relation between public calamity, notably cholera and other epidemics, and religious revival and they found in it the hand of providence and they inferred from it a morality of grace and of retribution.

Thirdly, this religious expansion was largely confined to the Nonconformist denominations and, further, the different denominations contributed unequally and differently to the pattern of growth. In the industrial parishes of Monmouthshire the Baptists were the leading denomination, with the Independents a good way behind, followed by the Wesleyan Methodists and the Welsh Calvinistic Methodists. In Glamorgan the pattern was similar but diversified by Unitarian and Mormon congregations. In this context it is important to stress that it was an expansion of denominations, and that sectarianism was scarcely to be seen within the broad patterns of growth. This again was a unique feature and a cause for rejoicing. The explanation for this lay in the fourth feature I wish to emphasize, namely, the classical and mature orthodoxy of the denominations. Their Protestantism, like that of their fore-fathers, stood four-square on the Bible as the revealed Word of God, on salvation by faith, on the priesthood of all believers, and it was rooted in a sense of history. No one who has studied the theological controversies which blazed between and within the denominations at the end of the eighteenth and for twenty years or so into the nineteenth century can doubt the truth of this. Religious adherence was about belief, whatever else it was about and from the well-nigh universal moderate Calvinism of the intellectual leaders of Welsh religion profound consequences were to flow. Religion in these communities was not a divisive force, any more than competition in a free economy need be divisive: it was a unifying one. The chapels that looked out over the narrow streets of dwellings at the meeting-houses of different and possibly rival denominations shared a common architectural style, and what they had in common was more important than what they disagreed about. They proclaimed not divisiveness but a fundamental harmony based on the essential of belief. To claim that this quality of believing was universal in the sense that every individual believed equally would be foolish. Maybe about a half of the population attended places of worship, and of these only a small number would be believers in the full sense of the word. And even for these, one suspects, the vestiges of the ancient beliefs and customs which they and their fathers had brought with them from the countryside enjoyed a spontaneous validity which orthodox Christianity may have lacked. The ghost of Calvin stumbled where 'Y Ladi Wen' walked with assurance. There was also a kind of counter-culture of the pub and street-corner, of sport and whippets, and there still survived an active tradition of critical thought about society and politics which had nothing to do with the denominations. But it was this substantial minority of the population which established the moral universe within which the vast bulk of the population lived. Here, as in Wales, generally, but remarkably in the iron and coal communities, was the maturest example of a mass religion, of popular religious Dissent, to be found in Britain. The politicization of this religion, the bringing to political ideas and philosophy the same clarity and discrimination, the same conviction and the same commitment as was brought to religious ideas, and the replication in secular life of the democratic forms adopted in religious organizations, would result in the sweeping away of the old politics and the creation of an informed electorate in a mature radical democracy.

Finally, and as a postscript to this argument about the denominations, it is remarkable that the inhabitants of these communities were happy to give this precedence in their esteem to their religious institutions. Some of their other institutions were so closely identified with religion as to be quasi-religious. Others, such as the friendly societies, which were numerically probably stronger than the chapels and churches put together, and which typified as it were the respectable secular side of community life, developed an image of themselves as embodying the religious morality proclaimed in the chapels.[21] With other working-class organizations, notably the trade unions, the connection was more ambiguous, but it existed nevertheless. It was not an organic connection and it was full of tension because in the crucial area of class interest and militancy there was a fundamental clash of moralities. While the unions depended upon the denominations for publicity through the press and pulpit, and while they looked to the ministers for technical advice on organizational matters, there was a kind of alliance and working arrangement. The colliers' unions of the 1850s and the early 1860s could not have been successful without the Welsh press, which was largely owned and controlled by the ministerial interest. But equally the cause of religion could not have succeeded without the colliers. Both sides were recruiting from the same communities: for a generation or so both had more to lose than to gain from a disruption.

The second avenue into community is the literary one. Literature was a quintessential part of the culture of those communities. This was so because of the Protestant nature of its religious base, and the high levels of literacy that prevailed reflected the old, necessary connection between reading and salvation. But what had started as a religious duty had quickly developed into a rich and life-enhancing movement of self-education, not of necessity circumscribed by the demands of religion narrowly defined. When people educate themselves they do not accept curricula handed down authoritatively from on high: they decide for themselves. Hence when the press had been freed in the middle of the century from the shackles of repressive governments anxious to control such choice, and books, magazines and newspapers had become cheaper, and the railways had speeded up communications, there was a tremendous explosion of publishing to satisfy this ready-made reading public. Every sizeable town had its printer/publisher, its booksellers and binders, and Aberdare became one of the main publishing centres in Wales.[22] The authoress of a kind of poor man's Mrs Beeton entitled *Coginiaeth a Threfniadaeth Deuluaidd (Cookery and Home Management)*, published in 1887 by the National Eisteddfod, took it for granted that about 13 per cent of the total costs of setting up a home (£3.80 out of a total of £35) for a young married labouring couple with a net income of 75p per week would be spent on books and subscriptions to magazines. As one would expect, the list of books she recommends is heavily religious and theological, but it included Thomas Charles's great *Geiriadur Ysgrythyrol (Biblical Dictionary)*, various classics in translation, a herbal, books on general knowledge and *Uncle Tom's Cabin* in translation. It was assumed that the family would take a weekly newspaper chosen on the basis of religious conviction and political affiliation. No doubt this represented the ideal rather than the reality, but the ideal, if nothing else, is expressive of commonly accepted aspirations.

This literary culture came to be institutionalized in the

eisteddfod. I mean not the 'National Eisteddfod' which early in its history fell a prey to aggressive middle-class respectablity, but the small, local eisteddfodau associated with chapels and friendly societies and even with industry. Their roles in the communities seem to have been far from simple. They embodied the cultural traditions of the country and the neighbourhood: they were designed to sift out intellectual and artistic excellence at the most basic of levels and to reward it: they provided platforms for utterance and audiences to listen, and above all they existed to publish. In the normal course of events, prize poems and essays appeared in volumes of transactions — the familiar 'Cyfansoddiadau Buddugol' or 'Cyfansoddiadau Arobryn', usually with engaging titles, such as *Garddy Gweithiwr* or *Blodau y Rhos* or whatever — and if not, they were likely to appear in weekly newspapers or in magazines. In this way small cultural communities came to be absorbed into a larger cultural field and to be subjected to powerful influences from outside.

The wider cultural field was both historical and contemporary. These iron and coal towns were all of recent growth. But the eisteddfod, so it was believed, was as old as the nation, and it is remarkable how this institution which, even in its revived form in the early part of the century still retained its aristocratic forms of patronage, had become transformed into a democratic and popular movement. Not the least of the consequences was the interest in history that this engendered, the history of Wales and of the wider world and its literature, and histories of the localities themselves. And lest we arrogantly assume our intellectual superiority it is worth remembering that the great Thomas Stephens, the Merthyr chemist, wrote all his major works for the eisteddfod — *The Literature of the Kymru* (1849), *Madoc*, and *Orgraff yr Iaith Gymraeg* which he wrote with Gweirydd ap Rhys, the author of *Hanes Llenyddiaeth Gymraeg* (1883), written for the Cardiff eisteddford, and of many other works of scholarship.

No eisteddfod was complete without a historical topic in the prose (and sometimes the poetry) section, and though the essays produced were seldom if ever of the intellectual grasp and critical maturity of Thomas Stephens, their existence testifies to the desire of the people to understand their present in the context of the past. The writing and publication of parish, town and county histories, of histories of industries, of religion and chapels, and above all, the huge number of *cofiannau* (biographies) is indicative of the growing consciousness of the communities of themselves as communities. This consciousness made articulate by these very special agencies, given expression by writers who belonged to the same class as those for whom they wrote (the local histories written and published in the valleys in mid century were written by colliers, ironworkers, coal agents, cobblers, tailors, chemists and ministers), was a social reality long before these communities fitted themselves up with the paraphernalia of public life and buildings of a civic kind. Indeed, it preceded the coming of democracy itself. And because the medium of communication was Welsh, the local patriotism that the eisteddfodau generated and nourished was locked into a deeper patriotism, love of one's country. There is nothing parochial about the parish histories they wrote. Dafydd Morgannwg (David Watkin Jones of Hirwaun, collier, coal agent), author of that wonderfully rich, beautifully composed *Hanes Morgannwg*, and of works on Welsh prosody and grammar, thought that there was a tendency to believe the lies of strangers because they came from London, but to ignore the truth because it was written in Welsh.

It is as certain that the eisteddfod contributed fundamentally to the making of a working-class consciousness. The most important constituent of this must always be a common understanding of the nature of society and a shared experience of one's situation in it. There is no greater error with respect to the past of the communities of the coalfield than to believe that the eisteddfodau supplied a mush of sentiment to obscure the hideous realities of excessive labour and abominable social conditions. On the contrary, even more numerous than historical topics for prize essays were what we can call 'sociological' topics, in verse as well as prose, for example: 'The Truck System', 'Social Justice', 'Wages', 'Safety in Mines', 'The Aged Worker', 'The Lock Out', 'Housing', 'Strikes', 'The Working Classes and Literacy', 'The Best Means of Improving the Morals of the Age', 'The Sunday Schools and Education', 'The Family', 'Health', and many an exercise on temperance and self-improvement. Some topics were totally abstract and philosophical, for example 'Logic', 'The Concept of Liberty', and an outstandingly well-informed and mature work on 'Ethnology' ('Cenedlyddiaeth') which a certain Benjamin Griffiths wrote in 1873 and published in a revised and expanded form in 1882, with a syllabus of the essay appended in English, 'Er mwyn cyfeillion yn mhlith y Saeson' ('For the sake of our English friends').[23] Very popular were topics to do with the Welsh language and its literature, and always the argument recurs that the Welsh language, because of its age-old, organic connection with liberty is the working man's best defence against oppression. To track down these essays one has to work through periodicals such as *Yr Adolygydd* and *Y Traethodydd*, *Taliesin* and the weekly newspapers — *Y Gwron (The Hero)*, *Seren Cymru (The Star of Wales)*, *Y Gweithiwr (The Workman)* and the *Gwladgarwr (Patriot)*, as well as the *Aberdare Times* and other newspapers, and in them one can trace how closely the choice of topic reflected not only the preoccupation of the age with morality and religion, but also with current affairs, the economic system and industrial relations. There is no space to offer an analysis of these, but it is an inescapable conclusion that this was one of the most important ways in which these working-class communities came to terms both with their past in a rational and informed way and with their present condition also. Thus a Welsh Nonconformist radical view of society was formed, expressed and absorbed into the consciousness of the industrial working class.[24]

I want finally to emphasize that this was a Welsh-language culture and that it formed the bed-rock which underlay the familiar culture of the valleys even after the language, which was its main constituent, had retreated. The second half of the century, especially in its last decades, when this Welsh-language culture was at its strongest, was also the time when a profound language shift was taking place as the tide of English immigration became stronger and the influences of English culture more pronounced. The processes of population change were complex, and the tensions set up in consequence were very complicated. It was not the case that an indigenous Welsh people were being overwhelmed by immigrant English people: for the iron and coal towns were being peopled almost simultaneously by immigrant Welsh and immigrant English, and the proportions varied from place to place and from time to time even in the same valley or within the same town. Consequently there were wide differences of opinion as to what was happening, and it was this ever-changing linguistic mix which stimulated an almost obsessive preoccupation with the question of the two languages, and endless discussions as to how the communities and the organized groups within them and the families who constituted them should cope. Was it possible to have a bilingual society with different domains of public and private life apportioned to each language? Was it conceivable that Welsh could continue to be the language of religion and devotion, of literature and poetry, leaving to English the world of business, technology, science and the visual arts? Should one be realistic and prepare for the inevitable? Or was it not the case that all the available evidence showed the Welsh language and its institutions to be stronger than ever before and not likely to succumb?[25]

No one who reads the heavy magazines which circulated in the valleys can mistake the agony which the discussion of these questions entailed. Nor is the reader likely to miss the degree of sophistication which was brought to the discussion. Not our sophistication, but theirs! They recognized and admired the achievement of science, of engineering, and of the new technologies: were they not a part of these advances, and were not Welshmen in the van in some of them? Nor did they think primarily in nationalistic terms, and their patriotism was non-exclusive. What is unique about it is their way of thinking about language change in terms of public and private morality. The ineluctable consequence of replacing Welsh by English, or even of giving English parity with Welsh, would be to corrupt the communities which had been so carefully built up by Welshmen. It is not that they were unaware of the immoral features in Welsh life: on the contrary, they were their own severest critics — though what they wrote was for the community alone and not for strangers! William Edwards of Quakers Yard, whose *Traethawd ar Hanes Plwyf Merthyr* was published in 1864, explained that he had omitted to record anything that would tend to mar the image of the place on the grounds that no reasonable reader could possibly be interested in such matters. He is not the only historian to have done so: others have relied exclusively on such matters. What would be endangered by a dominant English presence were the institutions by and through which the industrial communities had been civilized. These, as we have seen, were religious or quasi-religious ones and the agencies, such as the press and publishing, associated with them. This is why, from as early as 1852, the main denominations established chapels for the immigrant English (mortgaging their own future in so doing), founded magazines for them, and translated their Welsh religious and theological classics for them. They hoped by providing the institutions to provide also the spirit, and in doing so to protect what was the most precious creation of the Welsh people. For all its magnanimity and idealism such a policy was shot through with contradictions, and it diverted much-needed financial resources from aspects of the community where the Welsh language was most endangered, in education and in the family, to areas where there was no hope of success. It was said of the fourteen English causes founded in this way by Welsh people that at least twelve of them consisted of 'Welsh congregations speaking English'.[26] But one can understand why a people who believed themselves to possess a language which was a defence against the very evils which outsiders thought to be highly prevalent among them, and to have devised institutions of a very distinctive, even unique kind, should want to protect what they themselves had built. They had not originated by government decree, they had come into existence despite the efforts of the authorities to prevent them, and they owed but little to industrial patronage. Had they not the right to be proud of them?

It is becoming increasingly difficult, and must become more difficult still, to translate the culture of these communities into our own language. It is not easy to grasp their complexity, to feel the tensions within them, to experience change as they experienced it, because we are so ill-equipped to do what I conceive to be necessary, namely to observe without condescension the behaviour of people through the institutions they devised for themselves, and to listen to what was being said. With the secularization of our culture a whole world of reference has gone, and what vestiges of organized religion remain are a positive hindrance to understanding the religious sensibilities of our fathers. The Welsh language spoken and written by the generations I have in mind is rapidly receding into incomprehensibility even for those of us who still speak the language. We have to learn to read Victorian Welsh in the same way as we have to learn to read Elizabethan English: it is more remote from us than is Victorian English from present-day English. Likewise the literary forms beloved of our fathers make the culture that produced them even more inaccessible. Welsh prose-writers did not in general cultivate the novel except somewhat shame-facedly, and in obscure corners of magazines and weeklies (although there was far more novel-writing than one might suppose), and this means that a whole dimension of contemporary observation is not to be had or can only with great difficulty be recovered.[27]

Yet it is vitally important that those middle generations should be recovered and made intelligible to our own. They had achieved great things. They had created communities in places and in circumstances to all appearances utterly antipathetic to such efforts, and they had embodied in institutions of their own devising their own highest ideals, and not those prescribed for them by authority. Above all, they had shaped a moral universe which was a constant reproach and a growing challenge to the industrial society in which they found themselves. These were the crucial generations in their history, for these were the generations of workers who did not succumb to the dehumanizing, brutalizing forces in industrialism, who did not allow themselves to be reduced to serfdom or slavery, and who in the midst of the horrifying conditions described by the social scientists consciously created a rich and life-giving culture. These generations witnessed also not so much the transformation of an old Welsh culture into an English culture — such sharp polarities as English *or* Welsh, pub *or* chapel, bear little correspondence to the realities — but rather the formation of a new culture. I count it my great good fortune to have known the main constituents of that new culture at their most vital and to have been reared in a colliery village to the western side of the Vale of Glamorgan, where Welsh and English existed side by side and where it was possible to absorb the best of both. It was still doggedly, stubbornly Welsh in some of the institutions I have been talking about, and it seemed for a while strong enough, resilient enough, to defy the gloomy prognostications of the pessimists, even as it had done for a century or more. It was excitingly, richly English in the intellectual and literary culture of the Workmen's Hall: it was consciously working-class, utterly loyal to its union through the terrible years of the Depression, and it was proudly democratic through and through. I can think of no greater theme for Welsh historians, no nobler task than to understand the making of that culture, and no richer duty than to make such an understanding, as a necessary component in our own culture, the essential key to understanding ourselves. 'There is Nothing maketh a Man Suspect much, more than to Know Little.' That was true of the excursionists I started with and many of the outside observers I have talked about. It need not be true of us if we equip ourselves to know our past from within.

2

The People's Health in
Mid-Victorian Wales

When, in December 1857, Dr John Lewis of Maesteg forwarded a petition to the General Board of Health for putting the Public Health Act of 1852 into operation in the district, he felt obliged to add a postscript apologizing for the dirty and soiled condition of the paper it was written on. If the petition were accepted and the Health Act put into operation in the industrialized parts of the Llynfi valley all the inhabitants would benefit, but the dirty, 'hoary handed sons of toil' who would benefit most and on whose co-operation the whole enterprise largely depended had little direct influence on the affair.[1] It is upon this class of person, the working classes, the ordinary men, women and children who constituted the vast bulk of the population, that I wish to concentrate in this paper and my object is to try to examine the conditions under which they lived and the state of health which was their common lot. This is a task less easy than it seems: it is not the ordinary, labouring populations of the country that leave records which historians can subsequently use to reconstruct their lives: they are largely anonymous and leave few memorials and it is strange, when one considers the material remains of our civilization, the palaces and assembly halls, the factories and roads and bridges which are the most obvious relics of their physical activities and of their skills, that we know so very little about them. It is these dirty smudges on a petition that are evidence that at one time a formal declaration setting out what was thought to be their view had passed through their hands, that they had considered it and, if they were properly within their rights, that they had signed it.

Hence, it is not movements of an official kind, nor the activities of pressure groups, nor the conflicts and manœuvrings of politicians in Commons or Lords or political clubs that I am mainly interested in; nor yet the beginning of politics at the local level — politics at so early and primitive a stage in their development that the necessary public meetings often had to be held in the long rooms of pubs, in chapel vestries and in schoolrooms. These, since they refer to the coming of democracy at the level of the common people and to the formulation of policy and making of law at the highest levels, are of the utmost importance in the history of our country, but in this paper they will be subordinated to an attempt to uncover something of the experience of the common people and to see whether we can know anything about their reactions as individuals, as groups and as communities to the most momentous changes that any society up to that time had experienced.

In any discussion of this topic it is important to bear in mind that there was not one, monolithic country called 'Wales', one uniform people, in the middle decades of the nineteenth century. These were the decades when variety and difference in the social composition of the country first became obvious. This was the age of growing dissimilarities between different parts of the country, of change-ableness, of discontinuities, of the dissolution of ancient and traditional ways of thought and modes of living, when the spoken language of the people differed quite substantially from place to place and when all forms of it were being displaced by English. When we talk of 'Wales' in mid-Victorian times we need to be more cautious in our definitions than some historians tend to be. The old order changeth, yielding place to new, but if the mountains, unchanging as Ceiriog saw them, sacred as Islwyn envisaged them, remained, they too were being tunnelled into, their very contours changed, their woodland coverings stripped and their valleys transformed by new peoples with new needs and new techniques for satisfying those needs.

Precisely how various were these differences will become evident in the course of this paper, for my aim is to do three things: first, to look at patterns of health, diet, housing and labour in the country as a whole; secondly, to ask how and why such patterns had come to be and how far the conditions of life of the masses were interrelated and, operating together, constituted the efficient cause of the ill health of the people; thirdly, I shall suggest what their significance may have been in the political and cultural development of Wales in these central decades of the nineteenth century.

The Victorians believed that the most reliable index to the salubrity of a place, whether a rural parish or an urban one, was its mortality rate, preferably an average rate taken over a period of years long enough to establish regularities and to show unusual changes or aberrations. A death rate of 23 per 1,000, which was the average for England and Wales, was taken as a kind of 'natural mortality rate', the index of the sanitary state of a place, and since it was given a legislative authority in all public health legislation after the first Public Health Act of 1848, it was an index which achieved a kind of authority such as no other such statistic had ever before achieved. The average index for Wales, being the mean for the twenty years between 1841 and 1860, was 22 per 1,000.[2] Obviously these averages concealed great variations and were open to many objections, statistical and sociological, which opponents of the Sanitary Movement were not slow to make. It was pointed out, for example, that there was no such thing in the world as a national rate of mortality, and that degrees of insalubrity depended on numerous conditions other than the gross death rate; for example, the class of manufacturers dominant in a place, the geological formation of the surrounding terrain, the elevation of a place, the nearness of a river, and so on.[3] The variations in the Welsh rates were very wide, ranging from 17 per 1,000 in Builth and Knighton to 29 in Merthyr. The Registrar-General's published Reports for 1841–50 would seem to show the same kind of pattern of mortality as in England, with 8 of the 48 registration districts being above the national average. These were all mining or manufacturing districts, and included (in increasing order of mortality) Neath, Cardiff, Pontypool, Newport, Abergavenny, Crickhowell and Merthyr. Merthyr had the unenviable distinction of having a rate not much lower than the ten worst districts in England and Wales together and was thus on a par with the rookeries of St Giles in the East, Whitechapel, Southwark, Manchester and that abode of death, Liverpool.[4]

But to conclude from these statistics and from this arbitrary and very rough and ready index that the pattern of health in Wales was simple and straightforward with only a small number of urban places disturbing an even pattern of relatively low mortality would be to miss critically important social factors. Some statisticians, William Farr and Joseph Fletcher among them, speculated as to whether there were ethnic patterns of mortality and, fortunately for us, Farr justified the preparation of separate figures for Monmouthshire and Wales on the experimental principle that their publication would enable students at some future time to determine whether there were any differences in the diseases of places chiefly inhabited by Celtic peoples.[5] The mortality statistics were gathered by the local Registrars of Births, Deaths and Marriages as established by the 1836 Civil Registration Act, and the registration districts for which they made quarterly returns consisted of groups of parishes in at least one of which there was a town of more or less substantial size containing the Union Workhouse. This simple geographical fact could conceal enormous anomalies. For example, the District of Llandilo Fawr had a death rate of 19 per 1,000, but the town of Llandilo had a death rate of 27.3.

This leads me to a consideration of a set of facts of the highest importance in the social history of Wales, namely, the great variety of communities that it contained. For the purposes of the administration of the various laws relating to public health, places were either rural or urban, but exactly what constituted an urban area was never closely defined. It did not refer 'to a universal, clearly identifiable category of settlements, institutions or conditions'.[6] How to define urban areas was not a quibble because any place coming under sanitary law needed to be defined, and on the definition would depend the kind of administration and the specific powers and regulations to which that place would be subject. The 1851 Population Census identified in England and Wales 580 'towns of various magnitudes, either market towns, county towns, or cities', and if the country consisted of 'detached houses, . . . villages . . . and small towns without markets'[7] — a very imprecise definition by most criteria — then the population of town and country were about equal. By the 1861 census about one-third of the population of Wales was reckoned to be urban, meaning by this that they lived in corporate towns, or parliamentary boroughs, and places that were urban districts for the purposes of local government, and by various other rough-and-ready calculations and estimates. For example, three-quarters of the population of a parish, however deeply rural, which bore the name of a town contained within it, or of a registration sub-district if it looked urban, would be classed as urban.[8] On these kinds of estimates the only county with more than half of its population urban was Glamorgan. Pembrokeshire, Monmouthshire and possibly

Traditional country workers' cottages near Carmarthen.

Montgomeryshire were held to be about one-third urban, and Anglesey, Caernarfonshire, Flintshire, and Radnorshire about one-quarter urban. Merely to mention this last county as being urban to the extent of 27.9 per cent of its total population exposes the fallacy in the method of classification adopted: it was urban simply by virtue of its ancient parliamentary boroughs, most of which were defunct corporations, decayed villages wholly identified sociologically with their surrounding countryside. What was true of Radnorshire was true of all other counties in which industrialization and urbanization were as yet underdeveloped or not yet constituting the predominant sector in the economy. Urban and rural statistics have therefore to be taken with a grain of salt and we have to devise definitions which will reflect the great diversity of communities that existed.

Any classification of the kinds of settlements whose sanitary conditions we are seeking to understand should include, firstly, towns defined as such legally and constitutionally, having long histories, possessing charters which conferred on them certain powers of self-government independent of the jurisdictions of the surrounding countryside. Closely associated with these were boroughs by repute or by prescription whose liberties were ceremonial and nostalgic, defunct as to function, pretentious as to status. Most of the towns and boroughs in the first category were recognizably urban also in the sense of having distinct and thriving socio-economic bases which distinguished them from their hinterlands. They had high densities of occupation, they were built-up, they had developed in response to changing economic and commercial forces. They had developed industries and grown suburbs on their outskirts and the social differentiation which had become characteristics of their structures had come to be expressed spatially as their middle classes and bourgeois networks moved to the more salubrious and exclusive fringes while the working classes moved in to occupy their old commercial centres, creating slums where once there had been elegance. In all these towns such social differentiation, expressing itself in spatial separation, was a fundamental characteristic of their topologies. Swansea, Newport, Cardiff, Neath, Caernarfon and Pembroke were examples of such places.[9]

But there were other places, 'towns of adventitious character' as the 1851 Census Report called them,[10] which were urban only in respect of their economies and of the density of their population. They had no long histories, they were undefined in respect of their physical boundaries, they had no systems of government distinct from that of the parish and the county, they were not dependent upon adjacent towns for anything and in effect dominated their immediate hinterlands even more effectively than most of the old municipal towns. Above all, their social structures conformed to no known pattern. Such new places were Merthyr Tydfil and its string of iron town neighbours, and Aberdare, Pontypridd and the Rhondda. It was these places, undefined and inchoate, starting as 'condensations of people', as 'colonies in the desert', having no past, unsure of a future, possessing no more than *ad hoc* institutions, that were in the forefront of the movement for sanitary change, for disease and ill health (as the Victorians came to understand them) were most typically associated with these urban places. As someone remarked in 1875, '. . . fod yn Bethesda Marylebone yn ogystal â Lerpwl' (Bethesda as well as Liverpool has its Marylebone).[11]

There is one aspect of the death rate in Wales to which I must refer before examining the causes of such high mortality rates and that is the horrifyingly high infantile death rates. For England and Wales together the ratio of deaths to 1,000 live births was 150 from the time when civil registration began until 1850 when it rose during the next decade to 156 per 1,000 live births. In Wales the ratio remained fairly constant throughout the century at around 120.[12] These figures are grossly underestimated because of the inefficient registration systems, the old parochial system of registration existing side by side with the new civil one, and most demographers accept that there was an under-registration of 10 per cent in the first decade of registration and of about 6 per cent in the 1850s.[13] Nor should it be forgotten that the infantile rate was to live births: no one knows the extent of still-births and of births in *de facto* marriages which were by definition illegitimate and unregistered.[14] The catalogue was indeed appalling. Taking as examples the registration districts of south Wales we find that in 1861 more than one-third of all deaths were of children.[15] Again it must be stressed that this is an average and that in town centres and slum areas in towns, large and small, the infantile death rate was very much above the average, though it was noted at the time that there was no arithmetic correlation between areas of high crude death rates and high infantile death rates. For example, the average death rate of persons of all ages per 1,000 living in Merthyr Tydfil in the decade 1851–60 was 28.62 and of infants below the age of one year 184.4. In Nottingham the comparative figures were 26.66 and 222.6.[16] But though there was no exact correlation it was an unquestionable fact that the infantile death rate was almost always highest where the general mortality was highest, and this was invariably a characteristic of urban areas, of towns and of mining and manufacturing areas. To give one example from Merthyr again, the death rate from all causes in the decade 1846–55 was 33.2 — a figure which is higher than the figure above, because it includes the year of the cholera. But in these same years, of the 1,900 live births registered (no one can tell how many were not registered) nearly 20 per cent died under one year, 15 per cent under 3 years, and more than 5 per cent under 5 years. As Dr Kay, making an inspection on behalf of the General Board of Health, reported in 1854, 'More than half of the funerals that take place in Merthyr Tydfil are those of children under 5 years of age; and more than one-fourth of infants under 1 year.' And he added that this was only marginally lower (0.2 per cent) than Liverpool, the worst sanitary town in the country.[17] There must be, concluded Dr Greenhow in his 1861 Report, in places like Merthyr and Abergavenny 'influences especially injurious and fatal to young children'. But what these influences were no one could tell, though it is interesting to note that Dr Greenhow and other observers remarked that the child-rearing customs in south Wales differed from those in the midland factory towns and that infants in the south Wales industrial towns were killed not through neglect but by the attachment of the mothers to their children. 'Devotedly attached to their offspring, over-solicitous rather than neglectful, accustomed to carrying their children around with them in shawls without taking account of sudden changes of temperature on the infants, and prone to cover them up in their cots in hot, stuffy rooms.' Certainly, the high proportion of children who died from respiratory and so-called 'nervous complaints' or 'convulsions' would seem to support the views of Dr Greenhow.

Of the precise causes of mortality in different parts of the country we cannot be certain. Not only was nosology, even at its most professional levels, relatively unsophisticated, but also diagnostic techniques were as yet unaided by scientific methods of pathology and, until 1882, there was no reliable understanding of the micro-organisms responsible for diseases and their transmission; in addition, the medical profession itself was under no constraint, until 1874, to register precise diagnoses of the cause of death.[18] Nor were the relatives or other persons connected with the deceased under a legal obligation to obtain a death certificate for the use of the registrar. Dr Hunter, when he examined the registers of the St David's District in 1864, discovered that of 500 entries only 15 had been certified by a doctor, and that the inhabitants of the district were perfectly aware that the registrar had no power to compel the certification of the causes of death and would refuse to go a mile out of their way to obtain it.[19] Death from consumption was very common in those parts of south-west Wales but its incidence may very well have been inflated by the use of the word dialectically rather than diagnostically. There were many other terms often given as the cause of death that were vague and confusing and of little or no use to the first medical officers of the Privy Council and, later, of the Local Government Board. These men, with their new scientific methodologies and their avowed aim to establish the causes of disease, both physical and environmental, were impatient with words such as 'convulsions' or 'fever' given as the registered cause of death. It is permissible also to wonder to what extent the reports published by William Farr in the Annual Reports of the Registrar-General on the causes of death and the distribution of diseases, or indeed the reports of scientific work under the direction of Dr John Simon for the Local Government Board, may have been intelligible to the bulk of the medical men in the country. Of the 23 physicians in 1854 only 5 were under forty years of age and hence likely to have been recent graduates, and the official return made no distinction between surgeons and apothecaries of whom there were a total of 456 in Wales — 193 in north Wales and 263 in south Wales.[20] All the Poor Law unions were obliged to employ medical men but they were part-time appointments and miserably paid for the enormous areas and often huge numbers of people for whom they were responsible. For example, J. L. Roberts was given a stipend of £40 for the district of Aberdare with its population of over 15,000, William Evans £100 for the whole of Ystradyfodwg, which included the Rhondda valleys. The 13 medical officers of the five Cardiganshire unions shared the princely sum of £399 between them, to which certain small extras could be added for additional duties.[21] They were expected as a matter of course to pay for their own transport and the necessary staff for their upkeep. Not until the 1875 Public Health Act were medical officers required to be registered doctors, and there may therefore have been some justification for the doubts as to whether the registered causes of death during this period could be regarded as accurate.

Nevertheless it is possible, using contemporary documents, to construct a pattern of sorts, or at least to generalize as to the state of health of the bulk of the Welsh people in early Victorian Wales. The first important observation to make is that throughout this quarter of a century between 1847 and 1872 the problem of the health of the people was perceived as being almost entirely an urban one, so much so that the definition of 'urban' was as much on the basis of the types and intensities of diseases as on what would normally be regarded as 'urban' features. All the important legislation of this period focused on the facts of urban disease and proposed machinery, more or less effective, for dealing with it. Thus, there was the Town Improvement Clauses Act of 1847 along with other similar legislation of the same session which enabled such local authorities as chose to do so to lay down water supplies and main drainage schemes and to control nuisances. All this rather piecemeal legislation culminated in the Public Health Act of 1848 which was an emasculated form of the kind of machinery which Edwin Chadwick and his supporters had been advocating since the great *Report on the Sanitary Condition of the Labouring Population of Great Britain* of 1842 and the Royal Commission on the Sanitary State of Large Towns and Populous Districts of 1844 which had largely confirmed the findings of the earlier inquiry. What the First Public Health Act did was to create a General Board of Health and to empower local authorities where such existed, or, where they did not exist, to set them up by democratic procedures, to establish local boards of health to manage sewers and drains, wells and supplies of water, refuse and sewerage systems, the control of slaughterhouses, and the removal of nuisances, to control housing unfit for human habitation, and to provide burial grounds, recreation parks, public baths and other amenities. Such local boards of health had the right to raise loans sanctioned by the General Board of Health on the security of the rates to finance all this activity. The General Board of Health was dismantled in 1858 and, although the new legislation of that year was still permissive, the transfer of power to the Privy Council did not essentially weaken its impact. In any case a great deal of legislation, dealing especially with the environmental condition of towns and urban areas, was passed in the course of that decade, all of which was consolidated in the Sanitary Act of 1866 which was the first Public Health Act in which compulsory clauses were dominant.[22]

An essential feature of all this legislation and of the administrative orders by which its social objectives were achieved was the collection of information regarding the sanitary state of places and the health of their inhabitants. This information was of several kinds. First, there were the inquiries, so typical of the reformed Parliament, which preceded legislation and upon which legislation was based. Examples of this are Chadwick's classic report of 1842 with its masses of evidence and statistics, and the various commissions and select committees which likewise published the evidence on which their recommendations were based. The legislation itself, however, was productive of further evidence and insofar as it was not necessarily evidence deliberately called for and therefore possibly biased, the facts and opinions elicited under the terms of the Acts are often qualitatively more reliable and useful. In addition, the 1848 Health Act and all subsequent modifications of it instituted a system of inspection by the department's own experts. These reports were invariably published, but in any case exist in manuscript.[23] Between 1848 and 1872 seventy Welsh places came under the Health Acts, and thirty-one places were inspected between 1849 and 1858. The analysis which follows is therefore based upon these primary sources. Finally, the Department itself initiated investigations which were published in the annual reports of Medical Officers of the Privy Council (after 1872 of the Local Government Board) on a variety of topics but mainly on the distribution geographically and socially of different classes of diseases, especially the relation between certain diseases and industrial pollution and the environmental causes of high mortality rates, and the immediate causes of epidemics or prolonged endemic conditions of various diseases.

The general impression regarding the sanitary state of the places, urban and so-called rural, which applied for the adoption of the 1848 Health Act, either by petition of one-tenth of the owners of property and ratepayers or by reason of the death rate being above the norm of 23 per thousand, is of conditions that were almost universally bad and in some places appalling. Petitioners complained of bad drainage, insufficient or non-existent sewerage and suchlike matters, the lack of adequate supplies of clean water, and the universal prevalence of nuisances. In the earliest of these petitions, particularly those emanating from densely populated areas, there is a distinct note of alarm, if not hysteria, for everywhere the impetus behind them was the existence in the country of cholera. The history of the cholera epidemics of the nineteenth century in Wales has been studied by a number of historians and here I need only emphasize that although the main epidemics were few in number (1831–2, 1849–50, 1854 and 1866) and of diminishing intensity their existence was never entirely forgotten.[24] The similarity of some of its earlier symptoms with those of diarrhoea or dysentery sharpened the apprehensions of people to the constant proximity of disaster and helped to spread abroad the sanitary idea. Judging by the correspondence between local and central authorities and the awakened intelligence of the people as reflected in what they read and wrote, cholera was not soon forgotten but, on the contrary, remained a horrific memory and terrifying warning. Likewise, the anti-contagionist or miasmatic theories of the central authorities concentrated attention on filth and dirt, and on the devising of ways and means of carrying away and otherwise disposing of the unpleasant and dangerous products of urban life.

The costs of the public works which were undertaken in most places were very great — so great indeed that most authorities shrank from the financial obligations they were being asked to shoulder. The General Board of Health, between 1848 and 1858 when the Local Government Act came into force, sanctioned the sum of £2,956,178, and between 1858 and 1871 another £7,363,366.[25] The capital invested in Wales for sewerage, drainage and water supply between 1848 and 1871 was £1,194,750, the sums sanctioned ranging from £100 or so to £50,000.[26] For example, Pant-teg in Monmouthshire borrowed £500 in 1865 for sewerage, Lampeter £550 in 1866 for a waterworks and a slaughterhouse, while Bangor raised £7,800 for drainage and other improvements over a period of about seventeen years, Cardiff £94,000 in roughly the same period, and Merthyr Tydfil a total of £172,600 between 1857 and 1871. Swansea raised £204,599 between 1853 and 1868. Of course, the sums raised depended upon and bore a statutory relation to the rateable values of the places: the burden on the ratepayers of small urban districts was every bit as heavy and, some would argue, the benefits were less obvious for them than for the inhabitants of the big spenders, the industrial towns and the mining and manufacturing regions. It was this which turned sanitation and questions of environmental conditions into issues of politics.

Before proceeding to discuss these political implications I wish to turn to a brief consideration of two other factors in the development of public health during those decades. Both are well documented and both deserve a more extended treatment than can be offered here. The first is housing and the almost insoluble problem of overcrowding. There were several detailed and well-documented reports on these topics in the 1860s, one, by Dr Julian Hunter, in 1864 on the house accommodation of the rural labourer[27] and another by the same inspector in 1865 on the Housing of the Poor Parts of the Population in Towns, particularly with regard to the existence of dangerous degrees of overcrowding and the use of dwellings unfit for human habitation.[28] Both these investigations were undertaken with a view to projected amendments to the Health Act of 1858, especially with respect to distinguishing between defects in the sanitary regulations themselves and the degrees to which they were being put into operation. Dr Hunter's first report dealt with the colliery districts of Monmouthshire which, he thought, took their character from the conditions common to the colliers' life in all parts of England, especially the north of England, but which were 'worse in respect of cottage accommodation than any I have seen elsewhere', except where there were also chemical, metallurgical and tin-plate works near the villages. In Pontymister, near Machen, he found seven houses having only one external door and one window — and that on the side of the door. There was a ground floor only consisting of a kitchen and two rooms 7ft. × 7ft. 6in. which were used either as bedroom and pantry or kitchen or which doubled as both. In these seven houses lived 14 adults and 24 children. There were many other such abominable dwellings, all of them damp, most of them in multiple occupation, and in some groupings of them 'an ominous absence of children'. Basaleg, Risca, St Woollos and Malpas were similar places, all of them containing dwellings of extreme wretchedness and overcrowding. At Caerleon the worst parts of the town were crowded while houses with gardens, privies, pumps and two bedrooms stood empty because the people could not afford 2*s.* per week rent. Further down on the banks of the Severn at Caldicot, where there was a wire-drawing works which had recently been moved from Tintern before any houses had been built for the workers thus forced to move, Dr Hunter visited 13 houses containing 19 bedrooms in which lived 48 adults and 20 children. Where the wire-drawers lodged were 7 adults in 2 bedrooms, 6 adults and 4 children in 2 bedrooms, 5 adults and 3 children in 2 bedrooms.

Attempts were being made in some Monmouthshire parishes to check the flood of population by demolishing cottages. This had been the policy in Clearwell and in Trelech, but the people had, as it was being said, 'unconsiderately refused to be cleared with the houses' so that it was a common phenomenon to have a rising population in places of reducing accommodation. In the county as a whole in the decade 1851–61 there had been a decrease of 3,118 houses (or 4.41 per cent) and an increase of persons of 16,497 (or 4.87 per cent).[29]

Twenty years later Dr Thomas Jones Dyke, the Medical Officer of Health for Merthyr, was describing exactly the same kind of dilapidation and overcrowding as being all too typical of his town.[30] He thought that possibly one-sixth of the houses had been built at the end of the eighteenth and beginning of the nineteenth centuries. They had no through ventilation and were built on and against the earth or rock. Many were two-bedroomed houses and in those early days 'they all inhabited one room, but sometimes the lower room was large enough to hold a bedstead in the corner'.[31] Conditions in the expanding industrial towns of north Wales, in the slate-quarrying towns, in the lead-mining villages of Flint and the colliery districts of the Denbighshire coalfield were no better, and often the problem of insufficient accommodation was compounded by the existence of a vast, amorphous, mobile population of unknown quantity.[32] The ancient towns, with their close-packed centres had become over-built, every nook and cranny being filled up, and

being no longer agreeable to the rich, are abandoned by them for the pleasanter outskirts. The successors of these rich are occupying the larger houses at the rate of a family to each room, and a population, for which the houses were not intended and quite unfit, has been created whose surroundings are truly degrading to the adults and ruinous to the children.[33]

The local Medical Officer of Health's Report on Cardiff for 1858,[34] for example, gives a list of 222 houses containing 2,920 people; one house of 5,500 cubic feet, a moderately sized house, contained 26 persons, and the average for one whole street was 21, the lowest number being 9. No. 7 Herbert Street, consisting of 6 rooms, contained 15 adults and 14 children. The houses in the crowded quarters were leasehold and, 'no great confidence having been felt in the permanence of the wonderful prosperity of the place', they were small and poorly built. Rents were high and increasing, and any increase in the amount of work available brought in a flood of people in their thousands. Just to illustrate what was happening under such circumstances we can take another house in Herbert Street for which the tenant paid rent of 12*s*. per week. He retained the parlour and the back bedroom for his own family of three. He let the back kitchen to a young couple with one child for 1*s*. 9*d*., the front kitchen to another couple plus a child for 2*s*. 6*d*., the half of another room to a couple with a child for 2*s*., the front bedroom to a pair for 2*s*. 6*d*. and he had three beds in the garret which he let to chance-comers for 4*d*. per night. Whole streets had beds in every kitchen, and yet everything that good administration could do was being done, but the only effect of frequent and systematic inspections followed by prosecutions which a sympathetic bench always allowed was that the homeless persons involved were chased into Roath and Canton which consequently became more crowded than the borough itself.[35]

In Merthyr the Police Inspector, who was also inspector of nuisances under the 1858 Act, reported to the Local Board that if the regulations regarding common lodgings were carried out 'half the registered houses would have to be closed'. The letting of single rooms to families was common and the inspector (and the Board) was obliged to tolerate this quite illegal situation on purely pragmatic grounds. The position was similar in Aberdare: 14, 15 and 14 persons respectively lived in three small cottages of three rooms each. The fundamental cause, as everyone knew, was what the local Medical Officer of Health called 'a paroxysm of trade which increased the demand for houses beyond the abilities of house owners and builders to satisfy', and consequently to send up the

Old Cardiff housing, Mason's Arms Court, off Frederick Street.
(*Cardiff City Library*)

rents.[36] Newport and Swansea, thriving cosmopolitan port-towns like Cardiff, had the same problems of overcrowding accentuated by their main commercial activity, and there is no point in multiplying examples.

Overcrowding was a main preoccupation with the by now aroused local authorities because it was always associated with the squalid run-down areas of towns, because overcrowded houses increased the possibilities of contagion, and because the sheer weight of numbers made essential improvements of their environments and the supply of basic sanitation difficult if not impossible. Overcrowded areas were feared also as men fear the unknown; inspectors of nuisances were often policemen because in many places they were the only men to whom the benighted inhabitants of these pitiful places would show any deference and obedience. And finally, because their populations were mobile they were thought to be, and in many cases were, the abodes of criminals or, as Dr Hunter and Dr Simon called them, 'the dangerous classes'. This 'pauperization' of once-respectable properties into places unfit for human habitation was not only a primary cause of disease and a major constituent in the events leading to the prevalence of endemic fevers among the poor and the epicycles of epidemics, they were also normally pestilential. The decent separation of the sexes was impossible under such circumstances and the corruption of the young was an unavoidable concomitant of such overcrowding. It is not the argument of this paper that such were the universal conditions in Welsh towns, or that such were environments in which the urban Welsh as a whole lived their lives. The argument here (to which I shall revert) is that sanitary conditions such as I have described, and the existence of areas of pestilential housing in all the growing centres of population, large and small, constituted a kind of reality which exerted a profound influence on the people as a whole.

The most detailed and scientific of the inquiries carried out in the 1860s was that on 'The Food of the Labouring Poor' by the physician and assistant to Dr Simon at the Medical Office of the Privy Council, Dr Edward Smith, and this, supplemented by inquiries by other inspectors into the environmental causes of mortality, provides the first objective assessment of the nutrition and general living conditions of the people during these central decades of the century.[37] Dr Edward Smith's brief had been to tour the towns of Lancashire to study the effects of the Cotton Famine on the health of the factory operatives, and it was in connection with this work and on the basis of the scientific evidence he there collected that he devised 'a minimum quantitative standard of subsistence'.[38] In the section entitled 'The economic and nutritive value of food' in his *Report on the Nourishment of the Diseased Operatives*[39] he gave the retail price of all articles of food in common use and their chemical composition in terms of carbon and nitrogen, that is to say, of energy-giving and tissue-building foods. It has often been pointed out how closely Dr Smith's analysis of the foods and his recommended diets accord with those of modern nutritionists.[40] Most of the trades he looked at were located in London and the midland and northern manufacturing towns but he devoted a section to one class of poor persons who were to be found universally in England and Wales, namely, needlewomen — a heterogeneous class consisting of persons who embraced the occupation when all other means of living failed, who were not in good health or were — as one so often sees in census returns — advanced in life and on the edge of pauperization. Judging by detailed demographic studies of many communities, both rural and urban, their numbers were significant, they were often widows and hence among the most deprived in the community. The Welsh *cofiannau* give numerous examples of the struggles of these unfortunate women to rear and to educate their children while avoiding the even worse rigours of the workhouse.

As part of his investigation of 1863 into the food of 'the poorer labouring classes', Dr Smith pursued his inquiries in parts of Anglesey, near Beaumaris, and between Denbigh and Conwy and between Dolgellau and Machynlleth, and in south Wales, beginning at Aberystwyth and moving to Lampeter and thence to Newcastle Emlyn, Milford Haven, Carmarthen and Swansea.[41] In this way, he was able to find examples of the diets of agricultural labourers in parts of the country where the railways had not penetrated and in places where industry had not yet disturbed the customary ways of rural life as well as in the hinterlands of important market and manufacturing towns. Dr Smith was obviously very taken by the Welsh labourers and their wives who, he remarked, 'although evidently of mixed race, were generally a sturdy and muscular people, enjoying robust health, and many [of the north Walians] remarkable for their chocolate-coloured hair,

large heads, tall and well-built bodies, as well as for their general
intelligence'.[42] In most respects he found the labourers of south
Wales and their families inferior in respect of their accommodation,
furniture, comfort and health, and intelligence. He tried to account
for the evident differences in the work opportunities available to
wives and children. In the beautiful part of north Wales tourism had
greatly increased the value of all kinds of produce, wages as well as
rents had gone up, and there was alternative labour for sons and
daughters in the expanding towns of the north and the south,
especially where the railway made communications easy and cheap.
The wages of labourers and skilled men, according to Thomas Gee
of Denbigh's accounts, had gone up by 75 per cent since 1850 (much
to that gentleman's annoyance), and this was roughly comparable to
the commodity rise over the same period.[43] But wages with food in
south Wales remained at the old rates of 4s. 6d., 5s. and 6s. per week,
even though food prices had increased at nearly the same rate as in
north Wales. Hence the heavy migration from the country to the
towns as industrial workers or to England as farm-servants,
sometimes to return years later with enough put by to buy a cottage
and a cow, marry and maintain themselves on their little holdings
supplemented by labour on the local farms.

'The most rigid economy', he observed, 'is a marked character
among the peasantry of Wales', and from the examples he gave such
rigid economy was the basis for their exemplary respectability.
Their houses were exceedingly poor, consisting simply of mud or
rough stone walls with bare ground and a thatched roof, a small
window and a badly fitting door. But he noted the ubiquitous
dresser, highly polished and often with a wonderful supply of
pottery and glass displayed upon it. Clearly the labourers he
described would appear to be similar to those labourers whom Dr
David Jenkins discusses as the occupiers of 'lle buwch' or 'lle dwy
fuwch' in south Cardiganshire.[44] The principal items in the diet of
the labourers were bread made of wheaten flour but often mixed
with barley in south Wales, and oatmeal, usually in the form of *sucan*
or *budran* or *uwd*.[45] The large quantities of barley consumed were an
indicator, thought Dr Smith, not of taste and preference but of
poverty. He noted that it was often obtainable by labourers from
their employers at wholesale prices. He calculated that the
consumption of bread stuffs was very large, averaging out over the
samples taken at 14 lb. per adult per week. Few vegetables appeared

to have been eaten, even potatoes being regarded not as a principal food but as an additional form of nutrient. Butter consumption was very small — 3 oz. per adult weekly in south Wales — and the only milk was buttermilk in south Wales and that infrequently, and cheese in moderate quantities — only on a Saturday in one instance. Meat was an exceptional food in most places: many labourers had never tasted butchers' meat. Most labourers and their families ate only hung beef and hung mutton, that is, the sides of animals slaughtered in winter, salted and hung for consumption during the summer. According to Dr Smith's colleague Dr Hunter, this often had the texture and colour of mahogany. Like bacon, it was used to make a thin form of *cawl*. In south Wales pigs were reared strictly for sale.

The conclusions Dr Smith came to can be summarized briefly. The average adult Welsh agricultural labourer had a higher intake of calories (carbonaceous foods) and of proteins (nitrogenous foods) than the agricultural labourer in England. Both were considerably above the minimum subsistence level.[46] But the variations in levels of nourishment from place to place were substantial. The labourers of north Wales, especially if they lived in, were better fed on more nutritional food than those in south Wales. The latter were inferior in all respects to all the labourers examined by him in England and Wales. They were inferior in health, in income, in kinds of foods and in the quantity consumed. The south Walians ate more cheese which, with bread, was the staff of life — but they were remarkable for the small quantities of meat and of fats they consumed. He noted everywhere in south Wales a deficiency of food — 'not more than sufficient to maintain health' — and, from the typical diets he printed, a sameness and monotony. It was the *families* of labourers rather than the labourers themselves who suffered most privation. As the eisteddfodic poem 'The Labourer' put it:

> The first meals of day, do I receive
> At 'Master's board'; but ah! to eat and feel
> That hunger is 'at home' in every breast,
> Makes my heart sick with more than hunger's pains
> And I lose all desire to eat
> For sorrow's fulness so chokes up all want.[47]

To say the least the diets everywhere were of doubtful sufficiency for health, particularly when other facts of life are taken into account as, for example, the economic life cycle of the family, the quality of housing, heating and clothing, the hours and nature of work, the location of the home and its distance from the workplace. Food, though the most fundamental staff of existence, cannot be considered in isolation from other factors in the social environment, and man is more than a machine for turning food into energy. Dr Simon commenting on this report, summed up in these words:

> That cases are innumerable in which defective diet is the cause or the aggravation of disease can be affirmed by any one who is conversant with poor law medical practice . . . Yet in this point of view there is . . . a very important sanitary context to be added. It must be remembered that privation of food is very reluctantly borne, and that, as a rule, great poorness of diet will only come when other privations have preceded it. Long before insufficiency of diet is a matter of hygienic concern . . . the household will have been utterly destitute of material comfort: clothing and fuel will have been scantier than food — against inclemencies of weather there will have been no adequate protection . . . There must be much direct causation of ill-health, and the associated causes of disease must be greatly strengthened by privation.[48]

Those are sombre words but it should be remembered that they refer in effect not only or merely to the labouring class: they apply with equal force to the bulk of the farming population, for in Wales the difference between the living standards of the tenant farmer and the farm labourer was marginal only.[49] As Dr Hunter reported a year later:

> The farmer in Wales as well as the labourer, must be taken to mean a person generally badly lodged, and insufficiently fed and clothed . . . The evil effects of poverty upon the health is rather increased by the frugal habits of the Welsh farmers . . . In Cardiganshire district a medical practitioner described the children as 'pining for want of food as soon as weaned', and thought that if the climate were cold the whole race would perish.[50]

I have enlarged on these aspects of the lives of the rural poor because it is often forgotten that the physical state of these people was such as to make them peculiarly susceptible to epidemics of fevers, such as typhoid, which were associated with poverty and poor living conditions. It was remarked by the Registrar-General in

Office Row, Nant-y-glo. Reproduced by permission from J.B. Lowe, *Welsh Industrial Workers' Housing 1775–1875* (Cardiff, National Museum of Wales, 1977). Photo: Jeremy Lowe

1861, for instance, that the epidemic of the previous year had been particularly severe in Wales and as appalling in its results in the coastal parts of Wales as in the industrial.[51] But these were the people who migrated in their thousands to the industrial regions of the south and the north, and it seems to be completely fallacious, on the basis of evidence such as this, to ignore the possibility, indeed the probability, that they took their diseases with them, or at least an inescapable proneness to exactly the same poverty diseases as afflicted the poor inhabitants of the towns. It was these migrants, physically strong as youths and perhaps with the bloom of the country on their cheeks, who fell an easy and early prey to excessive labour in cruelly dangerous conditions, the diseases of the noisome courts and undrained, unwatered industrial towns and villages, and whose lungs, already infested perhaps with the dreaded consumption, were soon poisoned by the foul air of collieries, mines, quarries and foundries. Within this context of health and earnings, of housing and food, of the certainty and regularity of income being more important than the amount of earnings, it is not the differences between agricultural labourers and industrial labourers and their families that are socially significant and important but the convergence between these different ways of life and the existence in town and country alike of a community of want. Disease and sickness in environments conducive to both were factors in one way and another in the creation of — or, should we say, in the re-creation of — a people. Right at the end of this period, in 1872, another Local Government Board inspector, who was very familiar with Wales, wrote:

> From this proclivity to epidemic maladies, from the similarity of labourers, which tend to promote frequent changes of residences, from the similarities of race, of language, and of habits, from the unfavourable climatic influences necessarily sequent upon residence in valleys, in such near neighbourhood to lofty ranges of hills, from all these causes combined there exists an evident unity in the region surveyed.[52]

This extraordinary, interesting proposition with its explicit definition of community in terms not only of language and culture, but also of work experience, of life-styles and of common suffering, leads me to my final problem. It is this. How did the people whose environments I have tried to describe apprehend and comprehend their situation? How did they understand the existence of disease and ill health, and how did they respond to its existence? First, let me remind you of whom we are thinking. It is not the gentry, not the professional men and their families, people of wealth and standing and dignity, but rather the common people, farmers and men and women and children, skilled and unskilled, engaged in manufacturing, in mining and quarrying — the working classes and those below them in social gradation and in terms of living standards, the residue of society, the people for whom there was no accounting. The distinction between the upper and middle classes on the one hand and the working classes and the deprived on the other is important for one very simple but powerful reason, namely, that the diseases which afflicted society with increasing force as population multiplied and small towns became large, and little villages huge agglomerations of men and women, were a threat to all people irrespective of class, wealth or dignity. Asiatic cholera is the classic instance of such a disease and the awfulness of its presence in a place and the terror in the thought of its fatal approach precipitated community action, or acted as a kind of moral catalyst whether the morality was secular and utilitarian or religious and evangelical.[53] Nothing did more to aid the sanitarian movement in its early stages and intermittently thereafter than the response of local and central government to the threat of an epidemic, but it is nevertheless true that even cholera might be quickly forgotten and its effects be measured not in lives but in money. The crucial difference was that the middle classes, unlike the lower classes, were selectively mobile: they could escape from the quarters of towns where disease thrived to new suburbs where disease and disease-bearing people could be held at bay. Harold Carter in several studies has shown how this was happening in this period in a number of contrasted Welsh towns.[54] In the old industrializing towns as in the swelling mining and manufacturing districts, fever and the fear that it engendered were the engine of change, the universal propellant in the process of social segregation. Cholera came only infrequently, three or four times in the century in epidemic proportions, but the other killer diseases, the so-called zymotic diseases, those fatal fevers and debilitating illnesses, were endemic wherever there was environmental pollution, bad housing and malnutrition. And working slowly and silently in the lungs and very bones of people was consumption — 'y darfodedigaeth'. All these diseases afflicted particularly the working classes and the deprived and were most common in poor working-class districts of towns from which there was no escape, or in the miserable cottages that passed for farmhouses in the countryside. Indeed, some diseases were recognized as 'poverty diseases' and were understood to be the products of excessive labour, malnutrition and bad housing.

> Llawer gwaith y gwelsom ddynion wedi bod yn gweithio yn galed am chwe' awr o amser, a hynny mewn lleoedd na byddont yn cael agos ddigon o awyr pur, nes y byddai'r chwys i'w weld yn rhedeg yn afonydd ar hyd eu hwynebau, ac wedi y cyfan ni byddai y ciniaw a gaent ond bara ac ymenyn, gyda the, a hwnnw yn oer ddigon aml. Pa fodd y disgwylir i greaduriaid sydd yn byw ar hyd yr amser yn y dull yma ddal i weithio yn galed heb i'r corff gael ei niweidio i raddau helaeth?[55]

> (Frequently we saw men who had been working hard for six hours at a time, and that in places where there was insufficient air, until the sweat poured down their faces in rivers, after all that having for dinner only bread and butter and tea, and that often enough cold. How can creatures who live like that continue to work hard without the body being seriously harmed?)

A consciousness of the fact that a predisposition to these killing and debilitating diseases, as well as the unavoidable risk to life and limb by violent accidents at work, was the universal and inescapable experience of the labouring classes came to be an important element in their awareness of themselves as a class. In this sense mortality rates and the social geography of certain diseases can be regarded as among the most important indicators of the essential differences between social classes. Many are the articles in magazines from the late 1850s onwards noting, and attempting to account for, the widening gulf between masters and men, between capital and labour, between the middle and the working classes. Indeed, according to *Geiriadur Prifysgol Cymru*, this is the time when 'dosbarth gweithiol' comes to be used with these special denotative meanings and these social connotations. According to a writer in 1869, the helplessness of the worker in the face of illness and its terrible consequences for his innocent family was a factor in the widening of the gulf between master and man. It was a cause of disharmony, it gave rise to belief that the worker was being exploited and debased, that the masters were taking advantage of the power of the state in order to enrich themselves and to depress those who were dependent upon them.[56]

It is interesting to note how much of the criticism of housing and living conditions generally reflects the views of the sanitary reformers and the medical officers of the central government.[57] Propaganda was the essence of the Sanitary Movement. Pamphlets, papers and the official reports of sanitary inspectors and Medical Officers of Health (local and central) were published and widely circulated from the beginning. Nor should we underestimate the efforts of Hugh Owen, Assistant Secretary of the Local Government Board who at the time was deeply involved in trying to persuade the National Eisteddfod — not very successfully in the event — to form a Social Sciences Section in which matters and issues relating to the well-being of the nation, including public health, social economy and other sociological topics should have a place alongside poetry and music.[58] While it is true, as Hywel Teifi Edwards, the historian of the restored Eisteddfod argues, that to have adopted the plans of Hugh Owen would have completely revolutionized the nature of the eisteddfod as an institution, it is worth noting that the eisteddfod was in any event in a state of rapid change, and that local eisteddfodau were, in effect, already moving towards an enhanced role for the institution in the culture of the localities and of the common people in general. It is difficult to avoid the conclusion that the attempt to create an informed public opinion on questions of health and social welfare among such an ill-used class of people would have been a work of the greatest significance and not without relevance for the Eisteddfod. As it was, public opinion was created rather haphazardly by means of the magazines and local eisteddfodau, but there is no doubt of its effectiveness by the middle 1860s. 'Dylai y dosbarth gweithiol', wrote one of the editors of *Y Beirniad* in 1863, 'deimlo yn ddiolchgar i'r awdurdodau am eu bod wedi teimlo y fath ddyddordeb yn eu hachos, fel ag i ymyraeth a'r mater hwn.'[59] ('The working class should be thankful to the authorities for being sufficiently interested in their cause as to interfere in this matter [i.e. housing].')

All this indicates to what an extent the enlightened opinions of the new social scientists and the advanced opinions of social reformers were being absorbed into the existing working-class culture with its characteristically high moral tone and teleological drive — its tendency, that is, never to lose sight of the ends for which man is created and society sustained. Owen Jones of Maentwrog argued that the quarryman's house should contain not only a living room and parlour on the ground floor but also a library:

> Llyfrgell lle y mae dyn yn cael fantais o weithio allan y galluoedd mawrion hyny y mae efe wedi ei fendithio a hwynt ragor un creadur arall yn y greadigaeth. Dyma y fan lle y mae efe yn dyfod i ymgydnabyddu a Newton, Miltwn, ac Owen, Glan Geirionydd, Caledfryn ac Emrys a llu ereill a yrasant fyddinoedd anwybodaeth i gilio.[60]

> (A library where a man may realize the great powers with which, more so than any other creature, he has been blessed. Here is the place where he becomes familiar with Newton, Milton, and Owen, Glan Geirionydd, Caledfryn and Emrys and a multitude of others who drove back the hosts of ignorance.)

Much of this will be immediately recognized as Victorian self-help and as being typical of Welsh working-class autodidactism and of the Nonconformity which nourished it.[61]

But only government, that is to say, local government backed by the legislative and financial power of central government, could provide the sanitary infrastructure on which community cleanliness and personal health and the cultural values extolled by Owen Jones could ultimately be based. The working class could do much for itself, and its leaders believed that it ought to do so, but it could be effective in the realm of public health only as a political class, or at least only after it had learned how to organize itself in pressure groups or as part of a political movement, both locally and nationally.

This was far more easily said than done, and what Thomas Gee and many other middle-class politicians took to be the apathy of the working classes was in reality the workers' own realistic assessment and understanding of their own situation. As I have already argued, the literature they were producing on industrial relations and on topics related to public health is evidence of a direct response both to deteriorating living conditions and to that work of education and enlightenment which the General Board of Health, and later the Local Government Board, saw to be essential if the health of the people was to be saved. Sir John Simon — that giant among Victorian civil servants — recognized that it was not merely the degradation of excessive labour, endemic sickness, and poverty that threatened the existence of particular communities and put at risk the social order of the community at large, but rather these physical privations 'complicated with the caducity and helplessness of ignorance'.[62] The numerous articles in magazines to which I have alluded, the extensive reporting and discussion of evidence published in Blue Books and in the annual reports of local Medical Officers of Health which appeared regularly in the newspapers — Welsh, English and bilingual — which were circulating widely in the industrial valleys, were not mediated down to them from on high but were in effect the working men's own independent attempts to understand the nature of their world. This infiltration of new knowledge and inculcation of new attitudes was necessarily a slow process for it had to contend with a universe of age-old superstitions and practices which were even more deeply entrenched in the customs and folk-ways of communities than organized religion itself. Indeed, they existed side by side, and when, as was sometimes the case, ministers of religion were also practitioners of unorthodox forms of medication, their role in the communities they served would be akin to that of medicine-men in primitive societies.[63] More normally ministers of religion were in the vanguard of the attack on superstition and credulity. For example, Revd Evan Davies ('Eta Delta') stressed the need to disentangle the essentially simple, easily learned and straightforward remedies of herbalism from the web of astrological and esoteric rubbish which, he said, had had the effect of depriving the lower classes of this excellent traditional knowledge.[64] Hence the large numbers of herbals that were available, either translations of old classics from the English or original compilations such as those of Revd Rhys Price of Cwmllynfell, and at a lower level the ever-popular almanacs.[65] The satirist 'Brutus' (Revd David Owen), editor of *Yr Haul*, was likewise as ferocious in his attacks on quack medicine as on pulpit quackery.[66] Hence, a great work of education was being carried forward, and I believe that this contributed as much to, if it was not indeed the essential structure of, working-class consciousness — as essential, for example, as the reconstruction of trade unionism.

Indeed, both these movements — the public health movement at this basic level of comprehension and the revived trade unionism of the middle decades of the century — have much to teach us about the nature of society in Wales at that time. A study of the correspondence relating to public health in Wales between 1848 and 1872, for example, or of Poor Law administration during this period makes it abundantly clear that co-operation with the middle class was not only theoretically justified but also in practice unavoidable.[67] The local government franchise, after all, was not universal, and the qualifications for election to a board of health were the possession of real or personal property. These qualifications were not abolished until 1882. A survey in 1886 of representation on local boards found that in the urban sanitary districts investigated 30.8 per cent of board members were shopkeepers, 17.5 per cent manufacturers, 11.8 per cent gentlemen, 8.6 per cent merchants, 7.7 per cent farmers, 7.6 per cent builders, 3.2 per cent lawyers, and 2.2 per cent estate agents (others 10.6 per cent).[68] It was upon sympathetic co-operation with individuals among these groups that any improvement in the physical conditions of the lower classes depended. For example, what pressure could the working classes bring to bear in Llanelli (Carmarthenshire) where the major landowners and the entrenched and corrupt *ancien régime* of shopkeepers opposed the raising of a rate for the cleansing of the place? Or in Bridgend where a Local Board of Health was formed in 1849 and thereafter systematically opposed any reforms?[69] The lower-class inhabitants of industrial towns could not rely on ironmasters and industrialists and manufacturers either, for generally they were loath in most places to interfere, as they saw it, with the market forces within which they operated and which therefore were sacrosanct. The Tredegar Iron Company held a stranglehold on developments in their region because they owned the Water Company, and the Merthyr Tydfil ironmasters in effect held up the supply of water to that benighted place for nearly ten years.[70]

Hence it was that only places with enlightened middle-class leadership could achieve substantial reforms quickly. Cardiff was in many ways a model of the reforming spirit, as was Swansea and, to a lesser extent, Newport. Wrexham's very conservative, if not reactionary, corporation rushed into taking out private Acts in the expectation that they could thus be more selective and therefore potentially cheaper than the more comprehensive general Acts.[71] Almost in every place, urban and rural, there was political conflict, but in this the working classes could take little part until they could be organized for those particular ends. Until the sweeping away of conflicting authorities and jurisdictions and the coming of greater democracy they were dependent upon the co-operation of enlightened members of the middle and professional classes — including ministers of religion — for the adoption and the efficient operating of the public health legislation of the period.

So we end with something of a paradox. On the one hand the deterioration of public health in the first half of the century led to an enhanced class consciousness in those most affected by it. But it led likewise to the growth not of class conflict such as had threatened the stability of the country in the 1830s but rather to class co-operation. One can virtually pin-point the years in which this was the most significant and far-reaching social movement of the time, and those years are, depending on local circumstances, usually to be found in the late 1850s and 1860s, between the passing of the first Health Act and the Local Government Act of 1871. During that time working class and middle class came to share the same moral universe, to sustain the same religious and cultural institutions, to accept the same market economy and to operate the same industrial organization where it most massively mattered, that is, in the shape of a sliding scale in the south Wales coal industry. That the Maesteg petition praying to be brought under the Public Health Act should have been grubby and dirty need not therefore surprise us. It had passed through all the hands that mattered.

3

Language and Community
in Nineteenth-century Wales

My theme is the difficult and puzzling one of the relationship of language to social change in nineteenth-century Wales. It is, of course, a very familiar one and for some people, particularly for those who are most sensitive to religious and cultural changes generally, it is a contemporary theme. It has always been felt that somehow these relationships, subtle and tenuous and ever-changing as they are, lie at the very heart of our civilization. This familiarity and contemporaneity, indeed much of the language that we necessarily use in setting out the terms of the problem, are what make the theme such a difficult one for the historian. It is easy to mistake the language of the present for that of the past and to fall into the trap of believing that the problem is the same for us as for past generations. Such anachronism is common, particularly among those for whom language has become a political issue and a motive for political action. But equally it is the existence of the language now that makes its persistence through time, and particularly through the crises of the past century or so, a question of the highest relevance and importance. What I propose to do is to attempt to study the language in relation to the major cultural forces with which it was constantly interacting. It is to the social aspects of language, or language as institutionalized and language as an institutionalizing agent, that I want to direct my attention. It was Vyrnwy Morgan who said in one of his books, 'All history is difficult but Welsh history particularly so.' Perhaps what follows will be a demonstration of that.

The problem that I want to keep in the forefront is relatively simple to state. It is this. How did it happen that the Welsh language survived when so many social forces appeared over the generations to be antipathetic to it? For example, there was the relative unimportance of the Welsh people within both the British and European contexts. Numerically, they were never more than two millions, and politically they can scarcely be said to have existed. There were serious doubts about their nationhood. They possessed none of the institutions of statehood and it did not appear, except briefly at the end of the century, that they aspired to possess them. Then there was the relative insignificance and inferiority of the Welsh language within the British and European cultural world. As the *Eclectic Review* put it, 'the retention of the language obstructs the progress of the inhabitants of the Principality in all the higher developments of civilisation.'[1] Nor did the language possess a socially acceptable prestige-value, more especially the prestige embodied in an indigenous Welsh-speaking aristocratic and gentry class. Furthermore, in an age which was increasingly 'fact-conscious' there was evidence enough of relative decline. The movements of the language frontier were observed and the growth of *Cymru ddi-Gymraeg* ('non-Welsh-speaking Wales') at the expense of *Cymru Gymraeg* ('Welsh-speaking Wales') noted. Finally, there was the virtually unanimous opinion of the Welsh élite — the educational, religious, commercial and political leaders of Victorian Wales — that the disappearance of the language was inevitable and a good thing. Why then did it not die? To look for possible answers we need to examine the relations of the language to the economic, religious and political life of the times and, in particular, we need to look into the new kinds of social relations which were being engendered by the concurrence of changes in these fundamental areas of human experience.

The first and possibly the most fundamental of the forces that we have to consider in its relation to language is that of economics. There are two factors which we must distinguish, namely, the demographic ones and the creation of surplus capital. Both grew enormously in the course of the century and both, as a consequence, profoundly affected what was happening to the language. In demographic change, there are two related aspects which are of importance in this, as in all other, respects. First, there is the aggregate growth in the crude numbers of the population — that is to say, of the numbers of people who, after taking into account migrations to places outside Wales, remained within the country. In the course of the century the population nearly quadrupled, growing from just under 600,000 in 1801 to just over two millions in 1901. This growth was not evenly spread throughout the century, but on the contrary varied greatly from decade to decade and from year to year. Thus, the rate of population growth was higher in the first half of the century than in the second half, but highest in the first decade of the present century. The differences are quite significant: the rate decade by decade runs like this: 15 per cent, 18 per cent, 14 per cent, 17 per cent, 11 per cent; then in the second half 11 per cent, 10 per cent, 11 per cent, 13 per cent, 14 per cent, and in the decade 1901–11 20 per cent.[2]

Obviously, this growth and its uneven occurrence over time affected the language. One simple but very important fact is that there were more people who could speak Welsh in 1901 than in 1801. J.E. Southall estimated that there was probably a total of about 1,060,000 Welsh-speakers in Wales and England, or something in the region of 54 per cent of the population within Wales, in 1891.[3] He and other commentators pointed out that even with the massive immigration of non-Welsh-speakers the proportion was still 50 per cent in 1901 and 44 per cent in 1911. It is important to stress these apparently simple facts and not to lose sight of the point that until well into the present century a large — though declining — population was Welsh-speaking. Later we shall have to ask more qualitative questions about levels of literacy and the state of the language, but it is sufficient at this point to stress that this was an undoubted consequence of population increase within the country and that the highest sustained rate of growth had taken place in the first rather than in the second half of the century.

More important than this absolute growth in numbers was the redistribution of population that was constantly taking place. The population of Wales was a highly mobile one and the movement was from rural to industrial areas and was, therefore, a largely internal migration of Welsh-speaking Welshmen. It was as if, to all intents and purposes, the unpopulated, unexploited parts of the country where mineral wealth had been discovered were being colonized by the Welsh people themselves. This was apparently so even though the strategy of that colonization, its character and its speed, seemed to be entirely beyond the control of the Welsh people. In the case of migrants from regions which had long since been anglicized in speech it was a migration of people who could readily reabsorb Welsh culture and be reincorporated into Welsh-language communities.

While, therefore, it was true that linguistically Wales was becoming a divided country and that the boundaries between 'Cymru Gymraeg' and 'Cymru ddi-Gymraeg' were constantly changing and zones of effective bilingualism or zones of linguistic neutrality were being set up, it is still necessary to emphasize that not until the beginning of the twentieth century had these movements fundamentally altered the linguistic balance nor had it become evident to contemporaries that, although its demise would probably be slow, the death of the language was now inevitable.

Clearly, in all this the nature of the industrializing process was crucial. In the first stages of industrialization migration from outside Wales was negligible and, throughout the coal era until the last two decades before the First World War, migration was still predominantly from Welsh Wales. It is necessary to emphasize the continuing Welshness of the new urban regions, those concentrations of people that had grown up in the hitherto unpopulated moorland on the coal measures and in the expanding industrial towns of the south-west and north-west. Even at the height of the invasion from England at the beginning of this century, there is evidence to show that the preference shown by these migrants for coastal towns rather than upland valleys helped to preserve relatively undiluted the essential Welsh-language basis of the new culture.

Certainly, there was plenty of evidence of change, but we can understand what this was only when we observe it in the context of a kind of *pura Wallia* which unselfconsciously survived.

The second economic factor is the creation of surplus wealth in quantities sufficient to maintain the necessary cultural overheads. Language — that is to say, the people who speak a language — creates its own characteristic institutions. This is particularly the case in bilingual or multilingual situations where there is inequality between the languages and in which the majority language lacks prestige or feels itself to be deprived or is regarded as culturally inferior. These institutions — the 'cultural overheads' — have to be financed and they can be paid for only out of the surplus wealth being produced by the community. These institutions in Wales fell into several groups. First, there were the eisteddfodau. These — strange as it might sound when we think of the colossal sums required to run the National Eisteddfod today — were largely self-financing and required but very little capital and that little required was spread, even in small localities, over so wide a contributory area

e scarcely detectable. Even that essential concomitant of the
lfod, the publishing of transactions and adjudications, could
ie for virtually nothing in newspapers and magazines. The
financial aspects of the eisteddfod in general merit separate study:
here it is sufficient to point out that they were devised in such a way
as to avoid capital outlay and to recover costs immediately. The
second of these overheads was the building where the eisteddfod
was held — halls, pubs, meeting places (other than religious ones).
In the nineteenth century these could be financed only by co-
operative means, friendly societies, temperance movements, clubs
and so on, or by local capitalists or individual firms, such as
ironmasters and coalowners, or by democratic local government
initiative (after 1886 and 1894) and working-class initiative. Finally,
and most typically attached to the language, were the means of
communication — the 'media' — which meant the printing press for
the publication of newspapers, magazines, pamphlets, books and
advertising. Now, it is probably impossible to cost the capital outlay
invested in these cultural overheads, but it is clear that in terms
relative to the amount of wealth being created by industry it was
trivial. Amenity buildings were extremely rare both in old and new
towns, especially the latter; and the press in Wales, with some
notable exceptions, was characterized by the fragility and insecurity
of its financial base. Whatever happened to the profits of industry,
very little of it was ploughed back into the institutions in which the
language could hope to thrive. But if this investment was trivial in
relation to productivity, it was enormous in relation to earnings.
That is to say, the institutionalizing of language under the
conditions of a maturing capitalism depended upon the surplus
increment in the earning capacity of the common people, and not on
the surplus profits of capitalists. Hence the importance (often
ignored in discussions like this one) of numbers of people. Lacking
state finance, having few capitalists or landed proprietors who were
prepared to be munificent in their patronage of the indigenous
culture, the language had to depend upon the individually minute
contributions of large numbers of ordinary people.

There is one other economic force which we must mention,
namely, improved physical communications — railways, roads and
better, more reliable and faster transport all round. This
enormously eased the movement of people and made possible the
rapid distribution of ideas. Obviously, these improved forms of

transport could have deleterious effects likewise: if it speeded up the internal movement of people it also facilitated immigration into and migration out of Wales. But there is no denying the impact of the railways and the means these placed at the disposal of the main cultural organizations for the rapid dissemination of ideas and thus for the growth of a sense of cultural unity. Macadam, Brunel, David Davies — the sense of achievement and of national cultural maturity which is present in Victorian Wales depended as much on these men, perhaps, as on the bards; as we shall see and as contemporaries recognized, even the powers of religious enterprise depended in large measure upon the effectiveness of the business entrepreneur and the engineer. But capital is essentially unattached to any culture and is not essentially based in any particular language. From the beginning, economic change had adverse effects upon the Welsh language and culture, in particular by associating the idea of progress with the English language. Economics tended to reinforce the prestige value of English and to lower the esteem of Welsh among the classes most sensitive to the possibilities of social change and mobility.

The second of the major forces is that of religion. That there has always been a close relation between the Welsh language and organized religion in Wales has been commonplace since the Protestant Reformation. After all, this is the essence of the Protestant Reformation, the substitution of a formal ecclesiastical language by a vernacular. The relationship is not a simple one, however, and always there have appeared to be elements of equivocation and ambiguity. For example, in theology there have always been quite fundamental differences of view. Many theologians have believed that the relationship between the language and religion is providentially ordered. Such a belief can be the basis of both a conservative and a liberal point of view, and go along with quite contrary ideas as to the social and political implications or the consequences of such a belief. For example, Charles Edwards, the seventeenth-century divine and historian, author of *Y Ffydd Ddi-ffuant* (1667), which has been one of the most influential books in the formation of Welsh culture, quite unequivocally believed that the union of Wales with England under Henry VIII was an act of God designed to make it possible for the true religion to be given to the people in their own language. The prerequisite, in other words, for the reception of an official form of

Protestantism (though not of unofficial forms) was the loss of independence or what vestiges of it remained at that time. Or, put in another way, Charles Edwards appeared to accept that political absorption by an alien people was the prerequisite to the reception of the written essentials of Christianity in the Welsh language. Some of our contemporary theologians as unequivocally reject that view and argue that it is the mind of God that since religion and language are indissolubly linked, political independence becomes a prerequisite for the survival of either or both.[4]

There are also those who believe that the Welshness of the revelation vouchsafed to the people of Wales is unique, and by definition different in important respects from that revealed in other languages to other peoples. Hence the belief that the Welsh language already possessed the core and kernel of Protestantism in the history of the Church in Wales — that the religious revolution was by definition conservative since it harked back to the purity of the Celtic Church. From this there follows the religious obligation to preserve the language, for, *mutatis mutandis*, to preserve the language is to preserve the uniqueness of the revelation. This is contested by others who hold that the medium of communication should not determine the message, that it is the substance of the revelation which must be proclaimed whatever the language and that the true faith is not diluted when it is anglicized.

It is not my purpose to develop these arguments either one way or the other. It suffices to point out that such questions could arise only in a bilingual society or in a society experiencing linguistic change. Hence, to mark the emergence of such questions into public debate is to mark a point of transition or of change in the religious sensibilities of the people concerned. Language in this sense is an indicator of religious ideology and of the value systems generated by religious organizations.

Looking at the nineteenth century as a whole there is no doubt that, whatever may have been generally assumed by religious leaders about the uniqueness of the Christian revelation in the Welsh language, they were unanimous in believing that there were special features belonging to the religious organizations which had been developed in Wales over the generations. For example, it was confidently held that Wales was the most religious part of Great Britain. And judged by the external standards of religiosity — numbers of places of worship and of attendants at places of worship

— this was certainly true. Probably this state had been reached as early as the mid 1830s, and it was confirmed by the mid-century census and by unofficial counts at various subsequent dates. It was also recognized as a unique feature and of immense significance that the appeal of religion in Wales by mid century was universal and its success not delimited, determined or otherwise circumscribed by class considerations. The working classes of Wales, observed Edward Miall, were a cheering exception to the religious apathy (at best) and antipathy (at worst) of their English fellows. Welsh commentators, such as Dr Thomas Rees of Beaufort and Swansea, went even further and claimed that nine-tenths of the working population were formally or informally attached to religious organizations. Factually, there is no doubt that Rees and the others were exaggerating: as we shall see there was a strong class element in the chapels as well as in the Established Church, apathy was constantly complained of and infidelity was by no means unknown. But it is the belief that is interesting and significant, the quality of myth which it generated, and which was typified as early as 1859, for example, by the question 'A ellid dychwelyd holl drigolion Cymru at Grefydd?' ('Can all the inhabitants of Wales be brought back to Religion?') as if this had been the norm at some point in the past. Welsh religious leaders emphasized yet another organizational difference, namely, the fact that, unlike in England, religion was equally successful in town and country. Here again there was a fatal lack of precision in their thinking, for they failed to recognize the fact that though the differences in Wales were less pronounced than in England, the town/country disjunction was present in Wales as well and that already it boded ill for the future. Finally, they took immense pride in the fact that the purity of the Protestant faith was nowhere more secure than in Wales. All in all, there would have seemed justification enough for the astonished and heartfelt delight of the eloquent commentators of 1850, 'O Gymru, pa le y mae dy debyg wlad dan y nef? A pha genedl dan haul a chymaint o ôl crefydd arni, ag sydd ar genedl y Cymry' — adding in true prophetic fashion, 'Nac anghofia doniau Duw.'[5] ('O Wales, where is thy like under heaven? What nation under the sun possesses more of the marks of religion than the Welsh? ... Forget not the gifts of God.') Notice that this has nothing to do with denominationalism. In this context the jealous denominational competition so characteristic of Victorian Wales was not a sign of weakness but an indication of

Engraving of Assembly of Welsh Calvinistic Methodists at Bala, June 1820.

vitality, an essential element in the development and maintenance of popular forms of religious organization.

We return to our central problem of the relation of language to religious experience when we examine the arguments used to explain this achievement. First of all, there was the historical argument. This was an argument of great persuasiveness and potency and one which, we might add, is still an essential element in the Welsh consciousness, however much contemporary historians might decry it. It was the equivalent of the 'Whig interpretation of history' and very similar in the well-nigh universality of its acceptance and its readiness to find in the past only what happens to be of importance in the present. It was first elaborated in the sixteenth century and had received its classical expression in Charles Edwards's *Y Ffydd Ddi-ffuant*. The core of the argument was that the justification of the union of the two countries and the guarantee of its permanence was the production of the Scriptures in Welsh. To this was added a further dimension, the essence of which was the failure of the Established Church to fulfil its proper evangelical missionizing function. In explanation of this, critics from within the Church itself, like Erasmus Saunders, tended to stress the malign effects of bureaucratic deficiencies, such as pluralities and absenteeism stemming from poverty,[6] while critics from within the Methodist movement concentrated on the Church's spiritual, doctrinal failures, its lack of vision, of zeal, of warmth and of a hunger for souls (this became the orthodox Methodist view very quickly and has remained an essential ingredient of Methodist historiography). What both had in common was the accusation that the Church neglected the language of the people and, counterwise, that the success of Methodism was primarily due to its unquestioning acceptance of the need to preach and to teach in the Welsh language; ironically and tragically for the Anglicans this was the statutory law of the Church. Gruffydd Jones and some of his predecessors had realized that only by using the language of the people could the people be saved. There are elements in this total argument from history — for example, the claim that the Church was sunk in apathy, indifference and worldliness, that it was 'anglicized', or that the Methodists were self-consciously 'Welsh' in attitude — which historians would no longer accept. It was not an age, as depicted by William Williams Pantycelyn, shrouded in night and heavy sleep, but rather an age of gestation and slow change in which forces which would secure the future of the language were at work precisely at the time when its rejection seemed most imminent and inevitable.[7]

In addition to this historical argument there was associated with it what we might call a sociological argument. In this also language played a critical part. It concerned the nature of the ministry and its role in bringing about those typically Welsh features in organized religion to which we have already alluded. It was pointed out, firstly, that the method of recruitment to the ministry ensured that it was in large measure socially identified with the chapel membership. The method of recruitment was the same in all the denominations though, of course, there were fundamental differences in the methods of ordaining to the ministry which reflected differences concerning the nature of authority in the different churches. The important element in the recruitment was the emergence of spiritually and intellectually superior men out of, or rather from within, the individual congregations. In all denominations, therefore, the congregations established norms of spirituality and intellect, and in Dissenting congregations these norms were absolute and beyond interference by any other sovereign body, while the modified presbyterianism of the Calvinistic Methodists was a way of formalizing and of enforcing the opinion of the churches at large. Within Nonconformity these norms changed with time and from place to place and from congregation to congregation. For example, formal learning was not held to be a *sine qua non* in the early decades of the century but became a primary *desideratum* in the second half of the century. In the silver age of religious growth it was the congregations which established the norms.

Secondly, it was emphasized that the Welsh ministry was not a settled ministry but, on the contrary, a very mobile or peripatetic one. It was pointed out that this was a priceless blessing alike to the churches, to the country at large and to the ministers themselves. Dr Thomas Rees,[8] for example, or Dr Abel J Parry, Rhyl,[9] the one a scholar and the other a preacher of peculiar power, both emphasized that they would have remained buried in their home villages or lost in the anonymity of towns had the system of perambulating ministers not been in operation. As it was, the system helped to maintain agreed standards of excellence within the denominations by ensuring that the most gifted should be universally known and acknowledged, and, of course, that these leaders should be suitably rewarded in terms of prestige and social class.

Thirdly, it was a missionizing ministry. It was this which justified and stimulated the mobility. Economics come into it as well. Many Independent chapels, for instance, for whom the settled ministry was important, just could not afford to maintain a minister. It was not until towards the middle of the century that the 'missioner', as distinct from the minister, came into his own in Wales and it is interesting to note that these missioners, including those employed by the Calvinistic Methodists, were felt to be most needed in the poorer parts of the country rather than in the rich towns — in South Pembroke and Radnorshire rather than in Nantyglo or Bethesda — in 'English Wales' rather than in 'Welsh Wales'.

Fourthly, it was necessarily a Welsh-language ministry. This was so despite the fact that the education which almost all of them received, once the idea of an educated ministry had become commonplace, was in English. But even then — from the mid century onwards — a minister could carry out his duties properly only with the Welsh language. It was only later that individuals would go to great trouble to acquire the English language as a *spoken* language.

Finally, it was therefore, for all these reasons, a ministry which mediated between the native population and the dominant and dominating culture over the border. As Christmas Evans explained in about 1837, the Welsh ministry undertook the obligation of making available the richest and most health-giving of English theological thought to their congregations.

> Ni adawsent hwy . . . neb llyfrau duwinyddol yng nghuddfeydd yr iaeth Saesneg heb ddwyn eu mêr a'u brasder i bwlpudau Cymru, gyda'u golygiadau cynenid ac athrylythgar eu hunain. Fel hyn fe gyhoeddwyd â thafodau Cymreig bethau mawrion Duw. Dygwyd allan bethau newydd a hen fel teisenau bob wythnos ar y bwrdd aur ger bron yr Arglwydd i borthi eglwysi Cymru.[10]

> (They allowed no works of theology to lie hidden in the caves of the English language without bringing the marrow and fat to the pulpits of Wales, adding their own original and exalted observations. In this way the great things of God were given utterance in the Welsh tongue. Each week new things and old were brought like sweetmeats and placed on the golden table before the Lord to feed the churches of Wales.)

In addition to the spoken word, there was the written word. The vast efflorescence of publishing in the Welsh language which had originated at the end of the seventeenth and beginning of the eighteenth century (before the Methodist revival) was so closely associated with religion as to be, and to remain, virtually a function of religion. This was the case even where, as for instance in historical scholarship, the subject of discourse did not formally come within the ambit of religion. It may be a mistaken idea, but it is not far from the truth, that the printing press became an extension of the pulpit, and the ministry came to have educative functions which in other societies would have been regarded as secular.

Clearly then, language was of cardinal importance and in the context of subsequent history one can see that what these early Victorian commentators were claiming was that they had succeeded in bringing to completion what government had attempted at the time of the Reformation but what their chosen instrument for this purpose, the Established Church, had conspicuously failed to do. They saw that the failure of the Church had been consistently a failure to use the language of the people. This view certainly ignores the enormous contribution of churchmen as writers, scholars, thinkers, patrons and saints to the development of Welsh-language culture. It probably exaggerates the extent to which the Church at the level of the parish church had become anglicized. But the fact remains that a cardinal plan in the strategy of revival and renewal which was being worked out and applied in the Church of England from the mid 1840s onwards was the rehabilitation of its Welsh-language heritage.[11]

But the testing times came when the impact of economic change began to alter the language composition of the country in an unmistakable manner. This, as we have seen, occurred massively in the last decade of the century though, of course, the process had begun earlier. It is arguable that so powerful was the alliance of language with religion that it was able to contain the challenge of English culture up to and even beyond the First World War, and that it was not prosperity but depression which ultimately broke the organic connection. That it was able to do so becomes clear when we examine some of the relations of language to politics.

Earlier we noted that there were elements of ambiguity or of equivocation in the relation of language to religion and we can understand that this was probably inevitable among a people who were constantly being reminded by circumstances of the linguistic diversity in their culture. We get glimpses of this in, for example, the increasing admiration of ministers for English culture. At first, as the quotation from Christmas Evans showed and as we know to have been the case with the leading figures of Methodism, this was confined to theology and works of piety, all of which (to the satisfaction of the leaders) were made available in Welsh. But a generation later Revd John Williams, Brynsiencyn, was claiming 'that it was necessary to advise the present generation of Welsh preachers to read Welsh books. They read English books galore, but many of them ignore their own vernacular.'[12] Notice too the enormous efforts which young men, aspirants to the ministry, put into learning English. Dr Abel Parry thought it required at least six months in an English school to learn the language, and what was so painfully acquired was likely to be used on all possible occasions with pride.[13] For these, English became an additional code, an indicator of social class, which is why they enjoyed using English when writing privately to each other and why they multiplied the social and public occasions in which its use might seem to be prescribed. We note also that the colleges and academies and eventually the University were all, with the exception of Michael D. Jones's academy at Llanuwchllyn, entirely and exclusively English institutions. Kilsby Jones points out that the venerable Dr Phillips used the Welsh Not (or its equivalent) in his school at Neuadd-lwyd, the resultant fund being used to provide the good doctor with his weekly ration of tobacco. Some of the colleges were aggressively English in tone and culture. Pontypool Academy under Dr Thomas Thomas, for example, was certainly so and we know that the great Dr Lewis Edwards thought of the new college at Bala as preparing young men linguistically for the inevitable flood-tide of English culture.[14]

This attitude to the two languages — the acceptance of the prestige-giving English language and the superiority of its cultural possibilities to those of Welsh even though the latter was still the language of primary communication — must be taken as one symptom among others of a very profound change taking place within organized religion. We might mention the new conscious-ness of architectural style in chapel building which now entered its mahogany phase: new chapels were described as neo-Gothic, or Classic with Ionian pediments, and so on, or in the Byzantine style, while the old original chapels were regarded as crude and vulgar.

Un o arwyddion daionus ein cyfnod . . . Boddlonwyd yn rhy hir ar yr
hen gapelau cyffredin, diaddurn, ysguboriaid eu dullwedd, fel pe
buasai raid i harddwch sancteiddrwydd oddimewn gymryd un
gydymaeth anharddwch ymddangosiad oddiallan.[15]

(One of the good signs of the time . . . For too long have we been
satisfied with the old, ordinary, undecorated, barn-like chapels, as if
it were necessary that the beauty of holiness internally should be
related externally to ugliness.)

It was said that ministers tended to ape the manners of English
ministers in style of dress and mode of living. No less an acute
observer than Professor Sir John Rhŷs in 1905 thought that even as
English sacerdotalism was interpenetrating the Established
Church, so 'in outward appearance the religious leaders among the
Nonconformist bodies assimilate themselves now more and more to
the clergy of the Church of England and the white tie has invaded
distant dingles where no such vision was formerly seen'. More
serious than that and much earlier in time was the readiness of
ministers who knew little English — like Dr John Thomas in
Bwlchnewydd, his first chapel in 1842, who used to switch to
English for the sake of the one monoglot English schoolmaster
whom he (of all people) had been instrumental in appointing. Here
we might remark that criticism of Anglican clergy in Welsh parishes
for providing occasional services for the sake of gentry families
came strange from the lips of such as John Thomas. More revealing
of the true situation and symptomatic of the social changes was the
movement to build chapels for the English resident in Welsh towns.
David Rees, Capel Als, Llanelli, was doing this virtually in
anticipation of an English invasion (which scarcely ever
materialized on the scale imagined by him) and even encouraged
Welsh-speaking members of the various Independent chapels to
migrate to the new English centres in order to help out. Thomas
Rees, Beaufort and Swansea, who certainly mastered the English
language sufficiently to write the kind of inflated prose that was so
typical of the worst Victorian pietistic style, had an almost
pathological urge to provide English chapels in Welsh towns. Nor
were the Calvinistic Methodists behind hand in this suicidal
enterprise. 'It would be wilful blindness on the part of the Welsh
Calvinistic Methodists if they refused to acknowledge the fact that
the Welsh were adopting the English language,' said the

Cymdeithasfa (Methodist Association) meeting at Wrexham in 1871. But this movement had started much earlier, in the 1850s. 'The jealousy with which the English language was once regarded, as a means of setting forth the truths of the gospel, has passed away,' declared the *Welsh Calvinistic Methodist Record* in 1852, and it advocated a diversion of capital from Welsh Wales to English Wales, from building Welsh chapels to building English chapels.[16]

Nothing is more symptomatic of this ambiguity and of the cultural shift that it signifies than the readiness to think of language in functional terms only and by implication to create a hierarchy of values with consequential language attachments. It was common by the middle of the century to accept that while English was the language of science, business and commerce, philosophy and the arts, Welsh was the language of religion. One can understand the psychology and, indeed, some of the reasons why such judgements should have become general. For one thing, they were empirical judgements, certainly so far as business and commerce, government and administration, law and philosophy were concerned. For another, the Welsh were becoming conditioned by then to the idea that Welsh was an inferior language. This had not been the case during the lifetime of, say, Revd Thomas Price ('Carnhuanawc'), who believed in 1834 that it was highly probable that English would go the way of Latin 'and be known only in musty parchments and old records, and that the ancient language of this island will again be the universal language of its inhabitants'.[17] There were also the contemporary anthropological notions which equated language with race: primitive peoples have primitive languages; compared with English, Welsh is a primitive language, *ergo* . . . Sir John Rhŷs was one of those who rejected such notions: skulls, he said, are stronger than consonants and race lurks when language slinks away. Arthur James Johnes was one of those who deduced racial characteristics from language. But above all the Welsh were accustomed to being distinguished as a religious people, predisposed to awe and wonder. 'They are mystics. They dwell in the realms of imagination' — and what mystic has ever understood the second law of thermodynamics?

So it is not to be wondered at that this notion of the restricted value of Welsh should have become so general. What is strange is that the religious leaders themselves, like Dr Lewis Edwards, should have agreed and, indeed, assisted in propagating it. For the implications of such a notion were very serious. Firstly, religion was being degraded in comparison with other mental and social activities and, secondly, religion was being defined in exclusive terms. Both of these were destructive of religion itself and made possible a total secularization of culture. For the reformers of the sixteenth century and the fathers of Methodism, religion was all-inclusive and theology the queen of the sciences. And one can see how this philosophy led to the pernicious education system by which Welsh was excluded from all schools — National, British, industrial, private, school-board. In 1852 only one industrial school in south Wales used Welsh as a normal medium of instruction and that was Sir Benjamin Hall's Abercarn Colliery School. Twenty years later the social scientist, Ravenstein, failed to find a single Welsh school in Glamorgan.[18]

The obverse of this coin, of course, was the image of what English was good for. Briefly, the advantages of the English language were what Lord Powis at the 1850 Rhuddlan Eisteddfod referred to as 'the highest objects of ambition', and since he was supported in this delphic remark by Sir Watkin Williams Wynn, Mr Mostyn and other gentlemen of rank and station he was probably referring to material well-being.[19] This, in fact, is what English was good for and it is ironic that at almost precisely the time when Matthew Arnold was extolling the virtues of Celtic literature to the philistines of his own country, the philistines of Wales should have been sacrificing that selfsame language, as one bard put it, 'on the altar of utilitarianism' and material welfare.

> Os ydych am barhau i fwyta bara tywyll a gorwedd ar wely gwellt, gwaeddwch chwi eich gorau, 'Oes y byd i'r iaith Gymraeg': ond os ydych chwi yn chwennych bwyta bara gwyn a chig eidon rhost, mae yn rhaid i chwi ddysgu Saesneg.[20]

> (If you wish to continue to eat black bread and to lie on straw beds, carry on shouting 'Long life to the Welsh language'. But if you wish to eat white bread and roast beef you must learn English.)

Thus David Davies of Llandinam, the exemplar of the self-made man. More of an image-maker, perhaps, was the Unitarian minister turned banker, Lewis Lloyd, the father of Lord Overstone. As *Y Geninen* put it,

Nis gwyddom am gymaint ag un Cymro uniaith a gasglodd gyfoeth
heb wybod Saesneg . . . Er fod Cymru yn un o rannau cyfoethocaf
Prydain Fawr, a'i thrysorau cuddiedig dan ei drwyn a'i draed, eto,
trwy ei anwybodaeth, ni wnaeth ddim ohonynt hyd nes i'r Saes
llygad-graf, profiadol ac anturiaethus brynu llawer maes ar gyfer y
trysor cuddiedig.[21]

(We do not know of a single instance of a monoglot Welshman who
has gathered wealth without knowing English . . . Even though Wales
is one of the richest regions in Great Britain, and her riches hidden
under his [i.e. the Welshman's] nose and feet, yet by his ignorance, he
made nothing of them until the keen-eyed, experienced and
enterprising Englishman came and bought the fields for the sake of
their hidden treasure.)

That is the authentic voice of Welsh philistinism and it goes on to
deplore the fact that there is no Welsh Samuel Smiles to guide the
footsteps of incipient child entrepreneurs into the rich paths of self-
help.

Ond y mae ein llyfrgelloedd Cymraeg yn ddiffygiol iawn mewn
llyfrau fel rhai Dr Smiles, ac eraill, a ddangosent i'r ieuanc yr hyn
sydd bosib mewn bywyd drwy benderfyniad, addysg, diwylliant,
gonestrwydd, sobrwydd, darbodaeth, a dyfalbarhad. Y mae llawer
Cymro, wedi dyfod i gyffyrddiad â llenyddiaeth y Saeson, wedi
dymuno mewn ing — 'O, na chawn i fyned yn ôl i ailgychwyn fy
mywyd eto; mi fynwn wneuthur rhywbeth iawn ohono.'[22]

(But our Welsh libraries are very deficient in books such as those of
Dr Smiles and others, which show to the young what is possible
through determination, education, culture, honesty, sobriety,
prudence and perseverence. Many a Welshman, after coming to
know this English literature, has agonizingly sighed, 'O that I might
not return to begin my life over again: I would be sure to make
something of it.')

It is difficult to imagine the stresses that such doctrines placed upon
the intelligent Welshman who was being taught at the same time to
think of his language as his most precious possession. Or how was he
to react when repeatedly told in his own language that his lack of
cleanliness, his readiness to tolerate dirty houses, the lack of pride in
manners and appearance of his women and, above all, his lack of

common honesty was attributable to his ignorance of the English language?

But having said that such was the general attitude we have immediately to qualify and to turn to quite contrary attitudes which were as widely held and could often coexist in the same person. For if it was universally recognized that English was essential for a number of prudential and utilitarian reasons, it was also for moral reasons a language to be feared and kept if possible on the other side of Offa's Dyke (or at any rate wherever the language boundary happened to run).

> [The English] . . . reveal more infidelity and beastliness in a week than many a part of Wales ever experienced; drunkenness, lewdness and all other curses of the English will flood our dear country unless we are prepared to withstand the attack and turn back the flood by raising the banner in the name of our God.[23]

English was the language of infidelity and atheism, of secularism, of the higher criticism, of extreme liberality in theology. Dr Thomas Charles Edwards, surveying the religious scene in 1892, saw scepticism and agnosticism spreading through Wales — in the villages, quarry towns, coal regions and even among the peasantry. 'Y mae y fath lyfrau anffyddiol a Robert Ingersoll yn cael eu darllen, nid gan ysgolheigion ond gan bobl gyffredin.'[24] ('Such infidel books as Robert Ingersoll's are being read, not by scholars, but by the common people.') He believed that it was not impossible that Wales could become irreligious yet again. 'Wedi ei dyrchafu hyd y nef, hi a dynir i lawr hyd uffern.'[25] ('Having been raised to heaven she will be dragged down to hell.') English was certainly the language of Tractarianism, of High Churchmanship, Anglo-Catholicism and sacerdotalism. English corrupted the 'natural' and pure political views of Welshmen. It was the language of socialism, of co-operation, of trade unions and of all political ideologies antipathetic to the official Liberalism of virtually all Nonconformist establishments. What must have been meant by this was that such ideas originated in and were mediated to Wales by the English language: for it is clear that these ideas, or moderate forms of them, were not long in taking on a Welsh dress. It was also the language of the quite opposite tendency to the levelling ideals of socialism, namely, the language of ostentation in dress and style of living, and

the English railway was the corrupter-in-chief. 'Ni fedr yr
agerbeiriant fwy o Gymraeg na thywysog cyntaf Cymru, yr hwn a
anwyd yng Nghastell Caernarfon.'[26] ('The steam-engine knows no
more Welsh than the first prince of Wales, who was born in
Caernarfon Castle.')

The Welsh language was a defence against these evils. There
seem to have been two reasons for this. First, the very simple reason
that the ideas did not exist in the Welsh language, and second, the
fact that the Welsh-language media were such as to lend themselves
to control from above. The first raises interesting problems in socio-
linguistics and it is probably to the second that one should look for
an explanation. The virtual monopoly of power in the cultural
sphere which was exercised by organized religion involved, in effect,
the exercise of a kind of censorship. It was not always thus: there
had been a time in the first decade of Chartism, for example, when
newspapers such as *Utgorn Cymru* managed to exist — albeit briefly
— outside the magic circle of denominational indulgence or
acquiescence. As late as 1849 Thomas Stephens, chemist and
littérateur of Merthyr Tydfil, was expressing satisfaction on seeing
the cause of 'Cambrian literature' being divorced from the tavern
and entering into alliance with the chapel, and one of the major
principles demanded was a return to the psychology and general
attitude (if not precisely in the same terms) of the Calvinistic
Methodists in the period of political revolution in the first three or
four decades of the century. 'It is not, gentlemen, in my estimation',
said the winner of the prize for the best *cywydd* of the 1828
Gwyneddigion Eisteddfod in Denbigh, 'the least valuable feature in
the advantages of the Welsh language, that it has been the means of
preserving the Welsh peasantry . . . from the pestilent contam-
inations of such writers as *Paine, Hone, Carlile*, and I will even add
Cobbett . . . Wales has ever remained in a state of peaceable
subordination.'[27] Control of the Welsh press, even though only a
partial control, ensured the perpetuation of that philosophy.
Thomas Gee had to be very careful what went into the
Gwyddoniadur, and John Jones, Talsarn, was deeply perturbed
when it became known that a Welsh version of *Chambers Penny
Encyclopaedia* — under the title *Addysg Chambers i'r Bobl* (1849) —
was being prepared for publication.[28] It is clear that John Jones was
familiar with volume I, in which he would have read the article on
'*Iaith*' (Language), and found that it was based on the philological

CHAMBERS'S INFORMATION FOR THE PEOPLE,

(In the Welsh Language.)

ADDYSG CHAMBERS I'R BOBL,

YN NGWAHANOL GANGHENAU

GWYBODAETH GYFFREDINOL;

YN

ADDURNEDIG A THROS SAITH GANT O DDARLUNIAU EGLURHAOL.

WEDI EI GYFIEITHU GAN

EBEN VARDD; CALEDFRYN; PARCH. OWEN JONES; Y PARCH. D. HUGHES, B.A;
GWEIRYDD AP RHYS; CLWYDFARDD; CREUDDYNFAB, AC ERAILL.

CYF. I.

CAERNARFON:

ARGRAFFWYD A CHYHOEDDWYD GAN H. HUMPHREYS, CASTLE SQUARE,

Lithograph, Copperplate, and Letter-press Printer by Steam, Binder, and Machine Ruler.

Title page of the 1849 translation into Welsh of the *Chambers Penny Encyclopaedia.*

theories of Horne Tooke, the radical of the previous generation, whose name was anathema to Welsh Nonconformist leaders. They may also have known that one of the Chambers brothers (probably Robert) was very likely the author of the controversial and rather scandalous *Vestiges of the Natural History of Creation* (1844). Note also the dismay with which John Elias regarded the inclusion of articles on politics in *Cronicl yr Oes* (established 1835 as *Y Newyddiadur Hanesyddol*), edited by Revd Roger Edwards who was a founder of *Y Traethodydd* (with Lewis Edwards).[29] This is why Welsh effectively failed to become a language of political discussion in the widest sense, why its vocabulary remained restricted, and why English therefore became the language for what it scorned or feared to express. This explains the kind of schizophrenic phobia of so many Welsh leaders: 'Learn English, my boy, to get on; but learn English and risk being damned and, what is more, risk bringing about the dissolution of the society we have created,' might nicely sum up the attitude.

I have only hinted at the complexity of this situation and these cultural developments, but it is clear to me that it is this that gives to Welsh politics in the last century its unique character. When one considers the social impact of the changes in the economic bases of civilization with which I started, the marvel is that Wales in fact remained the quietest, best governed, most law-abiding part of the United Kingdom. When one thinks of the appalling living conditions — of the food and housing in the rural districts from which people tried to escape in their hundreds of thousands, of the impact of the new industry on the old towns, of the creation of frontier settlements, 'condensations of people' in the iron and coal districts, of how sewers overflowed and water supplies gave out, of how housing deteriorated and disease raged among the poor, of the vacuity and hopelessness of the poverty of the unfortunate in society, of the harshness of social controls disguised as social services — do we not wonder? After the late 1830s and the final outbreak of violent forms of protest the people who were the victims of these changes suffered virtually without demonstrable revolt. They developed no mature trade unions, and almost the only politics they knew were those which could be discussed in the language of morals and middle-class values.

Why? It is not that the working classes were not aware of their situation and critical of it. The magazines are filled with articles on

'Cyflwr y Gweithiwr' ('The Condition of the Worker') and suchlike. But the analysis is in terms of the vocabulary made familiar to them in religious discourse and handed down to them by the ministerial class. 'Boddlonrwydd yng ngwyneb caledi yr amseroedd: rhaid i bawb ymfoddloni i'r gwahanol sefyllfaoedd ac ymdawelu tan alluog law Rhagluniaeth'. ('Resignation in the face of hardship: all must accept their diverse stations and be silent under the powerful hand of Providence'.) That is *Yr Haul*, the Church of England monthly, in 1851, but it was the commonly accepted philosophy.

> Y mae gwahanol raddau cymdeithas wedi eu trefnu gan yr Hwn sydd a'i Frenhiniaeth yn llywodraethu ar bob peth. Nid yw y gweithiwr yn weithiwr o ddamwain ac nid yw y cyfoethog yn gyfoethog o ddamwain . . . Na, cofied y gweithiwr, er ei les ei hun mai nid da rhyfela yn erbyn cyfreithiau gosodedig cymdeithas.[30]

> (The various gradations of society have been arranged by Him whose Sovereignty governs all things. The worker is not a worker by chance, nor is the wealthy wealthy by accident . . . No, let the worker be reminded, for his own benefit, that it is not fitting to rebel against the fixed laws of society.)

That was written by a worker and is taken from an eisteddfodic essay in 1852 in Merthyr. It shows to what an extent the working classes had been socialized in accordance with the norms of the middle classes. Hence, the relative weakness of class attitudes as reflected in institutions of a militant kind.

Yet it is clear that it was these selfsame people that for their own reasons and of their own volition clung to a language which seemed to give them no hope for the future beyond a compensatory heaven beyond earth, and a doctrine of self-improvement and competition which effectively condemned them to perpetual injustice. Why should they have reacted thus? The explanation, I believe, must be sought in the deep consciousness of the people themselves and we might consider some of the more obvious expressions of this. Firstly, let us not forget that the Welsh language was their language, the language of the common people, more than it was the language of savants and the literati. For the latter it worked in only well-defined social networks: for the former it worked through all networks — work, religion, politics, friendship. If there had been or was in the process of taking place, a betrayal, it was a betrayal of the clerisy, not of the common people, and if there was a crisis of conscience concerning the language it was a crisis only for the former.

Secondly, it was the language of the common people in the sense that it was incorporated into their own institutions. The chapels had originated as their institutions: it was they who had provided the élite, and for nearly a century there had been harmonious understanding and an implicit realization that they — the common people — could exert some kind of control. After all, this was why they were Nonconformists and not Anglicans.

Thirdly, the language had become a way of expressing social difference: in particular, it marked them off from the English aristocracy and the anglicizing middle classes. Closely associated with this was the function which language had for them of expressing national differences: it was a symbol and more than a symbol, for only in this language was the heroic past encapsulated, and only this language could bind the present in an organic continuum with the past. This led on, finally, to the function of language as establishing class differences, or, put in another way, of stimulating the growth of class-consciousness.[31] The Welsh language was a precious and singular possession of the masses of workers at a time when the dehumanizing and brutalizing forces of industrialism were alienating them from nature and from society. All this is to say that the language survived at the levels where it was most important that it should survive. It heightened the consciousness of the people, gave them self-confidence and pride in themselves precisely at the time when all else seemed to conspire to reduce them to the level of slaves.

This is why language is so crucial in politics. In my thesis language becomes the touchstone of both politics and religion, the certain indicator of profound spiritual change. Consider what happened when, by 1898 in south Wales and by 1900–3 in Gwynedd, it had become crystal-clear to all that the workers were an exploited class, that the basic inequalities in society were widening year by year. One effect was a marked movement away from religion, especially from the chapels. Large numbers of men became disillusioned with a religion which failed to speak out clearly on social issues of real relevance to ordinary men and which could organize only on political issues, such as disestablishment, which had become meaningless. Some turned to the new-fangled

Labour Churches. Others tried to reform the chapels by liberalizing their teaching in socialist directions, as did R.J. Campbell and Gomer Harris and the *English* branches of the Calvinistic Methodists. In essence this was an attempt to reuse the language for their own felt social needs. Maybe 1904–5 was the last attempt by ordinary Welshmen to make of religion what it had once been — popular, nonclerical, unlearned, unsophisticated, enthusiastic, organic in the community, and Welsh in language. The Revival failed in these objects, the first sign of failure, perhaps, being Evan Roberts's instinctive feeling that to try to give the Revival an English dress or to take it outside Wales would be to betray the newly gathered faithful.

Inevitably, the next movement would be in the direction of socialism, and by the years just before the war, from 1911 onwards, socialism and the new miners' union were becoming the new religion. The language of socialism was English. Of the first 130 Fabian Tracts,[32] for example, only two were translated into Welsh, and only three of the pamphlets of the Social Democratic Federation were available in the Welsh language.[33] To abandon Welsh became not only a valuational but also a symbolic gesture of rejection and of affirmation — the rejection of the political philosophy and the sham combination of Lib-Labism and the affirmation of new solidarities and new idealisms based upon a secular and anti-religious philosophy. Fifty years earlier the new unions of the coalfield had issued their pamphlets, transacted their business and organized themselves politically in Welsh. *The Miners' Next Step* was written in English and never translated. What some thinkers had consistently feared had come about: the language and the religion which had grown together would decline together.

I have tried to show that the causes lie deep in the consciousness of the nation and can be seen powerfully at work in the experience of only a few generations. Institutionally, these years saw the decline into a kind of impotence and irrelevance of organizations which for generations had contained and shaped the highest and noblest aspirations of the people as a whole, and which had provided explanations of existence in terms of a distinctive theology and history that had been sufficient for the times. Now, with the popular withdrawal from them, counter institutions, expressive of alternative cultures, came rapidly to the fore. Not necessarily antagonistic at first, and often existing institutionally side by side in the same industrial villages and towns, even as complementary beliefs and attitudes in the same individuals, it was the new that proved to be the most adaptable and which came finally to express the new-found confidence of a genuine proletariat.

4

Margam, Pen-hydd and Brombil[1]

It is not only observers coming in from outside who tend, for whatever reason, to have partial and distorted views about the places they report upon. Observers from inside can often be unaware of, or oblivious to, the true nature of the societies of which they are a part. This is because societies are rarely as simple and homogeneous as they might appear to be; under examination apparent uniformities often dissolve. This is particularly the case when ancient societies begin to experience some of the consequences which seem inevitably to follow the transformation of their economies. It is not always easy to detect the moment when such societies become aware of change, for change is rarely so sudden as not to allow of a transition stage from one to the other, and usually some communities within the larger whole seem to be more attuned to change than others, more sensitive and responsive to the imperious prerogatives of new social forces. This was the experience of large parts of south Wales during the early and mature stages of industrialization. In some parts of the coalfield, industrialization took place within the bounds of existing historical societies rather than on uninhabited mountain slopes and moorland like some vast *tabula rasa* receiving the imprint of the new. Margam, in Glamorgan, was one such ancient place. Here, the old confronted the new, and traditional forms of rural community observed the growth of new urban structures being promoted by industry. For the social historian the interest lies in understanding the ways in which the different communities — the old and the emerging — adjusted to each other, and how and what, in their different ways, they contributed to the new society which they were thus jointly creating.

Anyone writing about Margam must begin by paying his respects and expressing his indebtedness to many fine historians upon whose work his own must rest. These range from the magnificent Walter de Gray Birch whose history of the abbey was published in 1897, to the lowly but invaluable essayist whose history of Taibach was printed in the *Gemau Margam*, the transactions of an eisteddfod held in Taibach in 1872. Since then there have been numerous studies in various collections of essays and in the *Transactions of the Aberafan and Margam Historical Society*, in *Morgannwg* and elsewhere, as well as in those most interesting and valuable books on different parts of the locality by A. Leslie Evans and Neville Granville.[2] Reading these works, including some earlier ones like F. Evans's *Tir Iarll* (which occupied a prominent place in my father's bookcase), and J. O'Brien's *Old Afan and Margam,* has always been for me a kind of self-discovery, an investigation into the external circumstances of my own early life, for I had the good fortune to be brought up in Pyle, to have gone to secondary school in Bridgend, to have lived for some years in Aberafan, and to have worked as a railwayman in Cwmafan. It follows that my earliest recollections, going back to the early 1920s, are all of this area, and the tops of Embroch and Dinas, Mynydd-bach, Margam and Baidan were at one time as familiar to me as Mynydd-du or the uplands of Cardigan have subsequently become. I would not deny that my deepest sensibilities, and any feeling I have for the past, were shaped and nurtured by this wonderfully rich and resonant part of the county of Glamorgan.

The great estate of Margam has had a single history, its necklace of circumambient parishes sharing an experience of time in common with each other. The economic, social and cultural changes which took place over a period of two centuries or so, and which transformed the country as a whole, were experienced here as by one community, and here their working out can be studied microscopically. This is my subject, and it explains the title of this paper. Margam is the estate as a whole, the total community which experienced those changes. Pen-hydd stands for the farms of which the estate mainly consisted, and the Brombil represents the industrial activities which became increasingly important to the estate as time went on. But these three names have cultural dimensions also. Margam stands for the *ancien régime*, the old aristocratic values and social relations by which indeed it was defined. Pen-hydd stands for a related but dissimilar way of life, for different values and ways of thought. This was so especially in the realm of religion: its language was different and its organization developed silently but powerfully outside the park gates and beyond its encircling walls, creating a culture which was implicitly antagonistic to that of the estate. Finally, the Brombil represents the modernizing forces of capitalism and of the urbanization which was its most characteristic product. So I have three places to write about, all of them radically different from each other and yet none of them explicable except in terms of their relations to the others.

First, the Margam estate, both the place and the idea. So far as the place is concerned consider first its size. This was measured in three kinds of ways in the nineteenth century. First of all, there was its extent, measured in acres. The estate as a whole covered nearly 34,000 acres, including the whole of the parish of Margam (18,725 acres). It was thus very substantial even in a county where there were more great landlords than elsewhere in Wales.[3] It is the case that there were larger estates in Wales. Wynnstay (88,000 acres), Penrhyn (44,000), Vaynol (34,000), Trawscoed (44,000) and Tredegar (38,000) are examples. But Margam was different from all these and from the majority of all other large estates in that its lands were entirely within the county of Glamorgan, whereas all the others were scattered over more than one county. Moreover — and confining our attention to Margam itself — there was here a physical, topographical coherence which none of the others I have mentioned possessed to the same degree. You could walk or ride, as agents and preachers were often required to do in the performance of their duties, from Margam village to Baglan, through to Cwmafan and Pont-rhyd-y-fen and, following old ridge-roads and traversing the steep-sided valleys, go all the way to Llangynwyd, and from thence, travel down through Llangewydd and Laleston, Tythegston and Newcastle, to Pyle and Kenfig, and so on to Newton Downs without ever leaving the estate. And if you still had the energy you could take another walk and find Margam properties in nine other parishes extending deep into the Vale as far as St Brides, Llandough, St Mary Church and St Hilary.[4]

You would certainly be impressed on such a perambulation by the variety of landscapes you would pass through. The estate encompassed high moorland intersected by steep, wooded valleys. Between the mountains and the sea there were sandy downs giving way to rich, rolling, arable lands, and on the slopes of the hills abundant pastures and plantations of wood. The oak and beech which grew on the hills behind the castle were famed far and wide for the quality of the timber and the beauty of their appearance.[5] Well might preachers compare them to the cedars of Lebanon; no doubt they were as precious to Mr Talbot as the latter were to Solomon.

But size was not everything: income was as important a measure as extent, and every rood, rod and perch on this vast estate was put to good use. In 1872 the estate was valued at about £44,000 per annum, but that very considerable sum included the profits of industry. What lay under the soil was coming to be a more important source of income than what lay on the surface. Industrial leases in 1872 brought in more than one half of the total income, and to that sum has to be added way-leaves, urban rents and so on.

Nor was that the sum total of the income flowing into the estate. C.R.M. Talbot was an astute businessman with huge investments in industry. He was the chairman of the South Wales Railway and became a director of the Great Western Railway by which it was absorbed in 1863. If he was not the progenitor of the docks in Port Talbot, it was his readiness to invest heavily in them and to see to the progress of the Bill through Parliament that ensured their future and, of course, a steady income for himself.[6] Not that these industrial and business interests were sustained at the expense of the estate. On the contrary, it was his huge personal wealth which protected the estate against, and made it less vulnerable to, the vagaries of agricultural depressions, and which ensured for the farming community an expanding local market for their produce. When Talbot died in 1890 he devised to his daughter, Emily, the whole of his personal fortune of £2.5 million, but it is doubtful if the estate was in as good order as when he had inherited it sixty years earlier, and his daughter was faced with heavy expenditure and a less contented tenantry.[7]

There was yet another way by which an estate could be measured and compared with others, namely, by the numbers of tenants it had. All Margam farms were occupied by copyholders and tenants, many of whom were tenants at will. The reasons for this had a lot to do with the requirements of estate management, but it had as much to do with politics. There being no freeholders on his estate Talbot could exactly calculate the numbers of voters and their allegiance. It

(*Above*) Margam Castle *c.* 1841 and (*below*) a room in the castle, *c.* 1880.
(*National Library of Wales*)

was on such hard electoral facts that Talbot's political influence was founded. Taken together with the corresponding influence he possessed in the parliamentary boroughs of Kenfig (which was a pocket borough) and Aberafan, it can be appreciated that his estate was more than an economic source of income.[8]

The growth of industry, as we shall see, enhanced the power and prestige which he possessed. Talbot appreciated and anticipated the economic changes which would inevitably transform the estate. He was an advocate of industrialization: indeed, he more than anyone else could have retarded its progress by refusing colliery and mining leases or demanding harsh conditions. He could refuse to let railways run over his lands, as, indeed, was the case in Gower. No one who has walked up the Ffrwdwyllt valley, or along Cwm Pelena and looked across the valley to Ton-mawr can doubt that the cost of the engineering feats involved in transporting coal from these inaccessible places to the coast must have been horrific, and that a sympathetic landlord was probably a *sine qua non.* [9]

The industrial wealth flowing into the estate did not affect the status of its owner as a leading county magnate. It is a great mistake to believe that it ever did. Late in the nineteenth century the richest men in Britain were still mainly landowners, and far from being out of step with his millionaire contemporaries Talbot was their archetypal representative. What Phineas Finn's fellow club members sneer at in their post-prandial discussion in Trollope's novel is not the accumulation of wealth, but the deplorable fact that peers of the realm act like tradesmen in their pursuit of it. As Trollope has one of his disgruntled politicians say, 'The Earl of Tydfil and Lord Merthyr are in partnership working their own mines . . . with a regular deed of partnership, just like two cheesemongers.'[10] Talbot's commercial and industrial enterprise was the reverse of these satirical portraits. They made wealth in order to buy land and with it high status, whereas Talbot used his existing wealth and high status to exploit his estate in fresh directions in order to enhance his influence. In any case, Talbot was at the top of county society, and it was scarcely conceivable that it should be otherwise. In 1848 he succeeded the second Marquess of Bute as Lord Lieutenant and *Custos Rotulorum,* and evidently brought to that influential office a more liberal spirit than that which had animated his predecessor.[11]

Of less formal dignity but of far greater practical importance was the fact that he was a Member of Parliament continuously from 1830 to his death in 1890. In this period of nearly sixty years there were seventeen successive Parliaments, and he was usually returned as the senior county member. This looks as if it were automatic, and indeed, there were only two contested elections during the whole of that period. But that would be too simple an explanation. Talbot was a Liberal, and there would seem to have been only two matters of principle on which a majority of his constituents would have disagreed with him. Those were protection and the ballot. On all other central issues of economic policy and social policy and especially ecclesiastical policy, he and his constituents were in agreement. The contest in 1857 is important. This was the election when he and Henry Hussey Vivian ran in harness for the county, and when all five members returned were Liberals, thus establishing a new pattern of representation which was to survive even the radical reform acts which were to follow.[12] It was to survive also the huge party tensions generated by Gladstone's Home Rule policy. Talbot voted against Home Rule, but never became Liberal Unionist, which is as much to say that he was honest both to his own convictions and to those of his constituents.[13]

There are many other aspects of the personality and activities of C.R.M. Talbot as estate owner, industrialist and politician which are important, and some of them will emerge in what remains of this paper, but enough has been said here to illustrate the central importance of the estate in the development of the whole area.

I turn now to the second part of my paper, to Pen-hydd. 'Why Pen-hydd?' you may very well ask. First, because it was, and until recently remained, a typical hill-farm on the estate, and therefore well worth a visit. It is easy to find your way if you follow the directions of 'Matthews Ewenni' (Revd Edward Matthews), who was very familiar with the place. In his biography of Siencyn Pen-hydd he tells us how to get there:

> As one goes from Neath to Maesteg, a little beyond Pontrhydyfen, one climbs a hill along a twisting, harsh, inaccessible track, to the top of a mountain peak, uncultivated and wild. From there can be seen a number of lesser hills and valleys which together have the appearance of the head and horns of a stag: which is why, in all probability, our ancestors named the house, Pen-hydd, 'the stag's head'.[14]

There were three farms on Pen-hydd when Talbot entered into his inheritance.[15] Pen-hydd Genol (it sometimes appears as Pen-hydd Fawr) was a farm of 352 acres, and when Talbot inherited it it was worth £37. 1*s*. 8*d*. a year. There were only a few farms of that size on the Margam side of the estate: four in the range 300–50 acres, and another four of between 350 and 500 acres. There were only two farms of more than 600 acres, namely Havod, 616 acres in the Dyffryn Valley, and Tonmawr, 609 acres contiguous to the Great Park. But these, like Pen-hydd, were also upland holdings valued at £98 and £106 respectively. Of the total of 100 or so farms in the parish itself the great majority were less than 100 acres, most of those being less than 50 acres.[16] Margam, despite its great topographical variety, was an estate of small farms, and everywhere the land was carved into an intricate pattern of smallholdings, even the low-lying extents of Kenfig and the rich arable land around Pyle and the slopes of Baiden and Mynyddbach. The 1,000 acres of Margam Moors, for example, were divided into sixty-three separate holdings averaging about 15 acres in a range from 78 to 1 acre and an average value of just over £1 an acre.[17] In addition there were numerous cottages, houses and gardens, sometimes isolated on the verges of the cultivated lands, more often clustered together as if for comfort. These were the abodes of labourers, skilled and unskilled, without whom the estate could never have survived. Even quite moderately sized farms, like Newlands near Pyle, employed five persons even though it was only 99 acres. In fact, farms of only a score or so acres would normally require additional labour.

More striking in some of these mountain valley communities was the mix of agricultural and industrial labourers. As we shall see, some of the valleys were already industrialized to the extent that the collieries located in them gave employment to some of the inhabitants. Yet the propinquity of numerous small farms in these mountain parts, some scarcely farms but rather smallholdings, with the presence of craftsmen in traditional agricultural trades, suggests a very different kind of society both from the high valleys and pasture-land, and from the heavy industrial, urbanized communities near the harbour and in view of the sea. It is obvious from the 1851 census enumerators' returns that many of these little holdings were occupied by families who were mainly colliers: the head of the household might describe himself as a farmer but his sons as likely as not would be colliers. We can surely infer that the men who dwelt in those little farms with the lovely names — Hafodisha, Ton Owen, Hendre Forgan, Pentre Tippa, Pant-y-scawen, Rhyd-y-bombren, Nant-y-neuadd, Twmpath-y-gwccw, and so on — lived differently, created for themselves different communities, compared with the families who lived in Constant or Cotton Row in Taibach.[18]

What did these persons have in common? You will recall that they were all, either directly or indirectly, and whatever the size of their holding, tenants of the estate, the majority of them yearly tenants. This applied to the houses of the craftsmen and the labourers, many of whom were subtenants of the farmers and as such probably worse off than if they had been obligated directly to the estate. There were no freeholders anywhere in the parish. Matthews Ewenni records that a certain Ieuan Tyclai, a contemporary of Siencyn Pen-hydd, held that there were three wonders of the world. The first, that there was an endless, seemingly measureless immensity of land in existence: second, that somehow every perch of it was owned by someone, but not a square inch had come into his possession. The third wonder was that he was nevertheless a happy and contented man, probably more so than the men who owned much.[19] This home-spun philosophy by the end of the nineteenth century would end in a different conclusion indeed!

In the mean time, being property-less, holding farms of more or less the same size, having no freeholders as neighbours nor gentry farms of any kind near them except that of the agent of the estate, who lived in Baglan Hall and held farms in the Brombil,[20] and all bound to the owner of the estate by conditions laid down in identical agreements, the farmers constituted a very special kind of community. The obligations they owed to the estate were precisely defined as to the economic ones, such as the prompt payment of rent, dues and tithes, and the maintenance of the buildings and the repair of hedges and fences, whatever the depredations of game, as also the payment of poor rates and other taxes. But custom and tradition were important factors also, as was the deference which they all owed to the head. Whether such obligations were felt to be oppressive is difficult to tell, though it is significant, I think, that very few Margam tenants gave evidence before the Welsh Land Commission in 1893. But, at any rate, there was never any shortage of tenants despite the possibilities of alternative occupations.

Nevertheless, it would be a mistake not to recognize the harshness of farming life on the estate. Underneath Matthews Ewenni's comic characterizations, his charming and vivid descriptions of these communities in his many writings, lay a world of unremitting labour for men, women and children. The boys and young men who went to work in the collieries and tinworks and copperworks down on the plain were already disciplined to hard labour, accustomed to obey and without very high expectations as to the rewards of their labour. Dragging a breast-plough on the barren slopes of the hills was, one might say without cynicism, a good preparation for dragging a coal tram underground. The wages of an outdoor farm labourer at the end of the century were about 15*s*. to 18*s*. (or 75p to 90p) per week, 'upon which', as the local MOH put it, 'with frugality, he and his family, if not too numerous, can manage to live'.[21] Since the diet of farmers as well as labourers was very simple, consisting for the most part of bread and butter or bread and cheese, and since bacon appears to have been the staple meat, usually as a broth with vegetables, and fresh meat or poultry was eaten only on occasional Sundays, we may presume that those wages represented the least that a family of that size might be able to survive on. It was said that the local cheese, made from skim milk, was sometimes so hard as to require a hatchet to cut it.[22] Nor should we be deceived into believing that the thatched, whitewashed cottages we see in old photographs were either comfortable or healthy to live in. According to expert evidence, many of the farm buildings and labourers' cottages were old and dilapidated. Some were one- or two-roomed with space for sleeping accommodation under the thatch, with no window or door on the far side, and thus badly ventilated, cold in winter, too warm in summer, and lacking any but the most primitive facilities.[23] There was little overcrowding, except in the smallest of the cottages where as many as eight might live in two rooms, for rising birth-rates coincided with industrialization and the works were only a step from the farms.

What these farming communities were aware of were the benefits of co-operation. Indeed, before the coming of the tractor and mechanization many of the seasonal tasks in the agricultural year, like the succession of harvests and shearing, could only be done by co-operative methods. It was on such occasions that tradition and custom were at their strongest and work was intermixed with play. Matthews Ewenni's life of Siencyn Pen-hydd is a marvellously rich portrayal of the ways in which community was expressed by means of recreation. Bando was a sport in which the parish, as a parish, excelled, but there were also football and other, sometimes unsavoury, forms of recreation which Matthews does not mention. All such recreations tended to be bibulous occasions, and it was no doubt easy for people who were overworked and whose living conditions were not of a high standard to drink more than was good for them.[24] It is also relevant to point out that both the *cymorthau* or work-group system with its associated recreations and the popular games and sports belonged to the communities organizing them rather than the estate as such. The only regular contact between the body of tenants and other dependants and the estate was the annual ploughing match. The aim of this institution was to improve the agricultural labourer by 'bringing the labourer nearer the farmer, the farmer nearer the agent, and the agent nearer the landlord'.[25] How effective this great chain of rural being was is impossible to tell because we have only the agent's opinion. Probably it assisted significantly in the maintenance of some form of community on the estate, but one wonders how effective it was compared with self-generated, traditional, inwardly controlled institutions created by the communities themselves. One must always bear in mind that these were almost grotesquely different from the world of rank, riches and privilege. To the latter the mountain communities must have seemed crampingly restricted in all aspects of existence; their almost total economic state of dependence, their rustic and low status, and the bucolic, if not comic, naïvety and narrowness of their cultural pursuits and interests, and their strange religious ways outside the walls of the abbey and church. Where could two such different worlds meet except in the formal, deferential observances of a ploughing match?

This brings me to the other, symbolic connotation carried by the name Pen-hydd. Jenkin Thomas (1746–1807), to give Siencyn his baptismal name, was, according to his biographer, as well known in Glamorgan as the sun, the stars and the planets. In what constellation, one wonders, did that leave Christopher Rice Mansel Talbot room to move? Siencyn was 'Apostol Pen-hydd', the Apostle of Pen-hydd, one of those exhorters and preachers among the early Methodists in these parts, whose work reminds one irresistibly of the old friars who had likewise dwelt among this mountain people, taught them and ministered to their spiritual needs. Nor is the resemblance entirely fanciful. Pen-hydd had been one of the thirteen granges on which the economy of the Cistercian

(*Above*) Pen-hydd Farmhouse, the birthplace of Siencyn Penhydd.
(*Below*) Cwmafon Valley.

abbey had been based in medieval times.[26] Six of these granges were in the parish of Margam[27] and four of them, including Pen-hydd, were provided with chapels where the lay brothers worshipped, and the tracks and narrow lanes along which the monks made their laborious ways from grange to grange and chapel to chapel still traverse these heaped-up mountains. Like the stalls and pens and living quarters the chapel of Pen-hydd has long since disappeared.[28] Only the tracks remain — roads are social as well as geographical facts — to show how the granges and farmsteads constituted a religious community. For the whole of this region is redolent of its Christian past. Here lies Bodvoc 'dan ei grwys', and not far away is Crug-y-Diwlith which, according to some antiquarians, had religious associations.[29] It is striking, also, how tenaciously these mountain people clung to the old religious customs and superstitions. *Plygain*, with its lighted candles, prayers and chanted carols, was kept even in chapels as committed to Protestant Nonconformity as Capel y Rock, Cwmafan, and Carmel, Aberafan.[30] Hence, the early Methodists and their successors were working within a very old and still powerful tradition of Christian worship. When 'hen Gapel Gyfylchi' was taken over by the Methodists to serve the scattered farms in the valley, names had changed and words had come to mean different things, but social needs and the means to supply them remained the same.[31]

In the conditions prevailing in this parish in the eighteenth century and for most of the nineteenth, it may be that a perambulating ministry was still the only one possible. For the greatest challenge facing the Anglican Church in the diocese of Llandaff, as in all other mountainous dioceses, was not only the poverty but also the almost unmanageable size of the mountain parishes. Margam, which covered, as I have already noted, 18,725 acres, belonged geographically to the Blaenau, and it was flanked to the north by Llangynwyd (15,460), whose three so-called hamlets were larger than most of the parishes of the Vale. The other neighbouring parishes, though smaller, were also hill parishes inhabited, like Margam, by relatively isolated farming and collier communities. It is important to stress this relative difference in the size of the parishes in this part of Glamorgan. The mountain parishes (the Blaenau) averaged 15,000 acres, the parishes of the Vale only 2,000 acres.

No wonder that the pastoral care available to their inhabitants was deemed to be inadequate once a new kind of spirituality had entered into the lives of some of its children. What was the position? Briefly, at the beginning of the nineteenth century there was the parish church of St Mary's, Margam, with seats for about 500 persons, and maybe that was adequate, so far as numbers go, for a population of about 1,800.[32] But with the sudden increase in population and the creation of large settlements of people in places distant from it, the parish church seemed suddenly to be marginalized, and the need for another became a priority. There were, of course, the churches of the neighbouring parishes — St Mary's Aberafan, Michaelstone-super-Avon, Baglan, Pyle with Kenfig, to mention only those within the estate boundaries or within fairly easy distance — and no doubt Margam parishioners attended these churches, though for the great festivals of the Anglican calendar their own parish church would be where they would be expected to attend. Not that Methodists made much of distance: they would happily walk ten miles or more to receive the monthly sacrament ('bore pen mis') at the hands of an evangelical clergyman.[33] A chapel of ease, Groeswen or Holy Cross, was opened in 1827 to serve the district between Aberafan and Margam. Talbot gave the land, and the church, which was built by subscription and grants from the Church Building Commissioners and the Incorporated Church Building Society, could seat about 500 and was bilingual.[34] The historian of Taibach, writing in 1873, remarks that the communicants were not numerous. The endowments of this additional church, like that of the beautiful mother church, were small, and the income of the perpetual curate, who had charge of both, could not have been more than adequate, probably less than £100.[35] By the middle of the century the Church was entering a period of increasing efficiency. Aberafan with Baglan was disunited, St Mary's restored and the ancient church at Baglan replaced with the new, splendid St Catherine's, erected at the entire cost of the widow of Griffith Llewellyn of Baglan Hall. In Michaelstone-super-Avon, where population growth had likewise been very great, the old church was taken down and a new one built on land given by the Earl of Jersey and the Company of Copper Miners.[36]

But the parish church was no longer, if it had ever been, the powerhouse of spirituality in the parish. The spiritual drive and creativity which characterized the nineteenth century had its origin in the small communities of the hills. The religion of the mountains was of the congregational type, and was dependent upon small farmers and craftsmen rather than aristocrats and rich people for its support. It was dispersed rather than centralized, scattered rather than focused in one place. The farmhouse was its meeting-place, and the hearth its altar.

Yet to believe that religion of this kind was an anarchic, undisciplined, primitive thing would be a great error. The denomination (as the Calvinistic Methodists became in 1811) to which the preachers like Siencyn Pen-hydd belonged, maintained a strict orthodoxy in belief and an unremitting discipline in matters of organization. Not since the high noon of Catholicism, when the abbey had ruled over the parish, had the sanctions of excommunication and social ostracism been so strictly applied. We must think of the parish of Margam, therefore, as constituting in terms of organized religion an intricate nexus of believers with meeting-places set up in farmhouses, barns and cottages, in course of time settling upon one barn in Dyffryn Isaf Farm as the most convenient for the whole community. It was to this barn that the Revd Mr Jones of Llangan, Peter Williams, the Revd Thomas Charles of Bala, William Williams Pantycelyn, Ebenezer Richard of Tregaron along with many other lesser men came to preach the Gospel and, as the historian of Capel Carmel, Aberafan, puts it, it mattered not that the place was crude in appearance, undecorated and as plain as the farmers' own cottages, for it was the home of 'the spirit, the Life and the Truth' ('yr Ysbryd, y Bywyd a'r Gwirionedd').

There is no need to trace the histories of the various denominations as they developed in the course of the century, for that has been admirably done by Leslie Evans in his history of Taibach, and in the various chapel histories.[37] But there are two aspects of this growth that strike me as being important in the development of the district. First, the urban townships of the parish owed their religious institutions to the pre-industrial valley communities. The town was evangelized by the country, not the other way round. This was true of all denominations with settled ministries in Taibach, Aberafan and Port Talbot. The only exceptions were the Wesleyan Methodist and the Primitive Methodist denominations, both of which were urban, rather than rural, churches. Secondly the social roles fulfilled by these institutions multiplied as time went on, coming to include some which were distinctly secular in character. Indeed, the advance of secularism in this sense can be taken as a measure of the degree of urbanization at any particular time.

I turn finally to the third of the places in my title, namely, Y Brombil. Brombil stands for that other social force, industry which, working within and through the ancient society of the estate, completely transformed it and created something new. Brombil stands for the world of venture capital, of engineering and chemistry, of steam power, of furnaces and manufacturing, of concentrations of people, distillations of workmen, of skills and wage labour. These developments you could see, look across at from the Brombil, and you could also gaze over the channel along which plied the ships which linked all this activity to a world undreamed of hitherto in the valleys of Brombil, Crug-wyllt or Cwm Maelog. There is no need to labour the point that industrialization did not begin in, nor was it confined to, the Brombil. All these southward-looking valleys from the high hills were being bored into, pitted along their river-banks, from early in the eighteenth century. Cwmafan, Oakwood and Pont-rhyd-y-fen, Cwm Dyffryn in the Ffrwd-wyllt leading up to Bryn (or Bryn-troed-cam) and Cwm Farteg, and on the east Cwm Cynffig and Bryn-du, Aber-baiden and Cefn Cribwr — these, as well as the slopes of the mountains running down into the Llynfi valley, had all had their industrial possibilities investigated from an early period. 'Eiriol mae pawb am arian' (longing are all for money), commented the author of *Hanes Taibach*, quoting an old poet, when he notes the coming of the first entrepreneurs to the district in the middle of the century and the grant of the first mining lease in 1757. There is no need for me to trace the subsequent developments: the first copper smelting in 1774 and the manufacture of copper sheeting not long afterwards; the spread of tramroads from the hills and the rapid industrialization of Cwmafan with iron, then tinplate and finally copper by 1838; the building of the docks between 1834 and 1837; or to speak about that remarkable pair, John Reynolds and Robert Smith, who gave a new turn to developments, until finally Vivian of Swansea, the world's largest copper smelter, brought his capital and skill to bear.[38] Instead, I shall consider some of the consequences of those processes.

Population change is the most sensitive index of industrialization, and the decennial censuses show clearly how the coming of industry to the region concentrated the people in a few places and thus changed the balance of communities which had survived for so many generations. Margam parish showed a steady growth of about a fifth each decade from the 1830s until the middle decades when it settled down to about half that rate. Pyle scarcely changed at all until the 1840s and 1850s — which is as much as to say that it was losing population — after which it grew by about the same rate as Margam for twenty years or so. It was in Cwmafan that the really startling change came. There, in Lower Michaelstone, between 1831 and 1841 population grew from 793 to 2,132, a rate of 168 per cent. The same happened in the parish and borough of Aberafan, the rate and timing being almost identical. Hence, the time of change came towards the end of the first half of the nineteenth century, and continued its by then inexorable course.[39]

What this means is that up to the middle of the century, and maybe a bit beyond that time, Margam and the adjacent parishes remained fundamentally what they had been for many centuries. Change had come slowly in the eighteenth century, slowly enough to be absorbed and to be comprehended rather than as something catastrophic or revolutionary, the social implications of which could not but be detrimental to their best interests. As I have observed, the pockets of industry, the mining for coal in the valleys and even those activities taking place on the banks of the river and near the old borough, were intermixed with farming or other traditional occupations. We have all wondered, I am sure, at the kind of pre-lapsarian innocence of those woodcuts and water colours of iron-smelting enfolded among trees with figures of men and pack-horses making their leisurely way along pleasant-looking tracks. The collieries in the Brombil were relatively small, that is, relatively to what they were to become when copper-smelting really took off and iron and tinplate manufacture increased demand for coal. In the early 1840s the Brombil colliery employed 95 men and boys, and the Taibach Copper Works employed 188 persons (including 16 females).[40] Those men and women and children who had forsaken the land for these newfangled and not altogether respectable ways of earning a living still belonged to the old society. The colliers lived cheek by jowl with the agricultural labourers and indeed the occupations of many were probably mixed. The industrial and the agricultural workers shared the same universe. Their preoccupations were the same, they ate the same food, dressed alike, lived in similar cottages even when their cottages were strung together in rows. They had the same amusements, the same recreations, they possessed the same customs, venerated the same heroes and they worshipped together.

After the middle of the century change became rapid, and the old universe passed into forgetfulness or nostalgia, or was rejected as anachronistic for a modern people in a developing society. From now on the pace of industrialization speeded up. Vivian's Copper Works in Taibach, the related complex of yellow metal manufacture and the making of copper implements, chemical works and the devil's mix of by-products from the spelter, increased the demand for coal even further, and new pits were opened, including the ill-fated Morfa Pit which was producing 150,000 tons a year by the mid 1860s and which had also taken the lives of seventy-seven men and boys in a succession of explosions between 1849 and 1870. Of course, not only Morfa blew up from time to time: twelve were killed in Bryndu in 1858 and another six in Kenfig Hill colliery.[41]

For the pace of change had speeded up: this was a different world. Mark how, as early as the 1870s, the area's historian finds it difficult to discover how things had been arranged in those pre-industrial times. Or note how Matthews Ewenni underlines the quaintness of dress, of speech, of behaviour, of the characters from the past whom he describes. And note also how popular his book was: four editions, each larger than the previous one, in the twelve years between 1855 and 1867, which was precisely the period of greatest change. Much of the attractiveness of *Siencyn Penhydd* to Matthews Ewenni's contemporaries must have been that he was depicting a time which had passed, or was rapidly passing away. The Cwmafan and Pont-rhyd-y-fen which he described were now urban communities, Aberafan was a proud and growing town, and Taibach had already obliterated some of the old houses and farmsteads that its name denoted. All possessed the characteristics of urbanity.[42]

This urbanity was typical of the townscapes now rapidly developing on the south Wales coalfield. Its most obvious feature was the close association of housing with workplaces. In Taibach and Cwmafan, as in the Swansea Valley or along the mouth of the River Neath, the houses of the workpeople lay adjacent to, sometimes intermixed with, the furnaces and mills, the tramways and railroads.[43] This was true also of the old borough, but with this difference, that the ancient nucleus remained substantially unchanged while intensive housing developed around it as the outskirts of the borough and the fringes of the harbour became industrialized.

Crucial to the urbanization of the area as a whole — the southern fringes of Margam, the marshes around the river mouth where sheep and deer were fattened, and the Afan Valley — were first, the influence of landlords, and second, the existence of the old borough. Talbot, while encouraging industrialization in principle, also inhibited its spread by ensuring that it did not interfere with the amenities of his park and the beauty of his surroundings. Copper-smelting laid waste the slopes of Ynys-y-gwas and Y Foel to an extent comparable to the denuding of the Lower Swansea Valley of its vegetation. Aberafan, however decayed it may have been at the beginning of the century, grew in consciousness as it expanded in size, its image of itself as a town became more pronounced, and its liberties, such as they were, established a tradition of urbanity at the very heart of this new industrialization. But this did not come about without conflict. Indeed, the most decisive social conflict in the district took place when the movement for the incorporation of the borough of Aberafan began in 1854. It was opposed by a majority of the old burgesses — the urban *ancien régime* — and advocated by the new middle class which industry was in the process of creating. The middle classes, or as they preferred to think of themselves, the representatives 'of property and respectability and intelligence', believed that the old system of government worked against the best interests of the town and district for the reason that the burgesses were mainly labourers and others in low conditions of life, unable to read and write, liable to choose as officers men like themselves quite unfit for the duties of local government. Under the Municipal Corporations Act this state of affairs would cease and the borough be administered by the educated, the politically aware, the socially improving middle classes. When, five years later, the borough was incorporated, local administration was placed on a rational and more orderly democratic basis better equipped to understand and to deal with the huge problems of a mature urbanization.[44] But fused into the spirit of sanitary improvement and municipal reform was class-consciousness, and paradoxically, the movement which destroyed the old regime of a non-political body of largely irresponsible burgesses laid down the conditions for the creation of a modern working class which would itself, in due course, achieve power in local affairs. Aberafan could now modernize itself and with it the whole of the district. That Aberafan and Taibach were very different places from Merthyr Tydfil and the other towns in the mining and manufacturing districts of the northern rim of the coalfield was due to this crucial and momentous change.

As in Hafod (Swansea), the Vivians put up new and excellent housing for their workmen. They owned 282 houses in Taibach in the 1860s.[45] Taibach, like Aberafan and Cwmafan, had its market, its shopping streets and offices for the new professional men, such as lawyers and the numerous agents that industry required. Such middle-class families put up housing appropriate to their perceived status, and these detached and semi-detached dwellings, as was the case in all the south Wales coastal towns, were to the west of the works with their noxious fumes and unpleasant vapours. Pen-y-cae and the road to Baglan was a world away from Inkerman Row and the Barracks, yet it is noticeable also that the carefully planned housing in the centre of Taibach, like Y Waun, Cwmafan, set standards which were tolerably high in those central decades of the century.[46]

One must note also the appearance of public buildings, like the Victoria Institute (1887) and the Workmen's Hall in Taibach built by public subscription on land given by Talbot for the numerous friendly societies of the town. Above all, there were those towering chapels and, at the beginning of the twentieth century, the wonderful St Theodore's Church standing four-square in the adjacent parkland. It is a mistake to imagine that when these religious buildings were put up in such profusion they were intended to cater simply and solely for the religious and cultural needs of particular congregations. It was urban pride as well as religious conviction that set them down so proudly among the long rows of houses, and the social roles they fulfilled added to the pride in urbanity which was so characteristic of mid-Victorian towns. Vivian's school, likewise, imported into the district standards of excellence for which the Hafod Schools were renowned throughout Britain.

But there were also to be seen, as essential and apparently inescapable consequences of industrial urbanism, the stigmata of suffering. As the towns grew in size so also did disease and sickness intensify, and the new technologies took little account of the appalling toll in life and limb that the new industrial processes seemed to take for granted. Smelting ores and rolling metals were terrifyingly dangerous quite apart from the unhealthy conditions in which they were carried out. The copper workers and the colliers were doubly at risk, for the polluted atmosphere of their workplaces was not avoided when they returned to their homes after their long and arduous shifts. And if, as was generally the case in much of the new housing developments, the shelter provided was adequate, their sanitary conditions were as often as not deplorable. Inspectors sent down by the Medical Officer of the Privy Council reported in 1859 that 'every sanitary law is violated in every conceivable way', and that 'there were few parallels in England to the lamentable sanitary condition of the place'.[47] In Aberafan and Taibach, as in all towns of similar character, it was endemic disease and the regular visitation of epidemics which aroused public opinion and began the long processes of cleansing, supplying clean water, disposing of sewage and founding medical services. Cholera struck in Aberafan and Taibach in 1832, in 1849 when there were 120 deaths (the author of the *History of Taibach* says that he attended twenty-six funerals in one week), in 1855, and again in 1866, when seventeen died.[48] 'Every visitation of cholera in England has had its victims more or less in this borough', was the sad conclusion to be drawn from the statistics.[49]

I turn now to other, cultural aspects of this new urbanism. I have said little about the mass of the population beyond noting their numbers and their geographical distribution. Where did they come from? Clearly, a high proportion were locally born. In 1861 of 401 persons living in the eastern side of Margam only forty were from outside Glamorgan, and most of those came from other Welsh counties. The same was more or less the case in Taibach and Aberafan, the proportion of persons from England being somewhat higher.[50] But industry could not have expanded to such a degree without heavy in-migration. All the entrepreneurs, though less so in the coal industry, had to import labour. Vivian brought with him process workers, men with the skills they had learned in Hafod, and it was said that he tried to break a strike of colliers in the Morfa Colliery in 1870 by bringing numbers of Cornishmen and others from over the Bristol Channel. It was mostly these unfortunate men who died in the explosion which soon afterwards followed, victims, it was thought, of their own inexperience.[51] Twenty-five out of twenty-eight of Margam Castle's house-servants were recruited from England.[52] Yet all these communities were predominantly Welsh-speaking. In 1901, by which time the flow of English-speakers into the district had become a flood, 61.2 per cent of persons over three years of age were recorded as Welsh-speaking. The Revd R. Morgan, the author of the history of Taibach, speaks of 'the scores' of monoglot English and of the deep concern he and other cultural and moral improvers felt as a consequence of this.[53] Many, perhaps most, cultivated Welshmen in those central decades of the century had a deep antipathy towards these strangers in their midst, believing that they were morally inferior to the Welsh. Obviously this was a convenient and, to us today, an unpleasant prejudice, but whatever its justification it shaped attitudes which were of the essence of the dominant culture of the time. Richard Morgan's 'History' is very revealing in this respect. The full title of his work is 'Traethawd ar Taibach, yr hyn oedd, yr hyn yw, a'r hyn a ddylai fod' ('An Essay on Taibach, as it was, as it is, and as it ought to be'). It thus has a strong moral tone and purpose. This can be seen in the last section, 'Taibach as it ought to be'. He gives a high priority in the improvements he advocates to the foundation of English-language religious causes so as to provide English-speakers with the kind of religion that Welshmen had provided for themselves. That is, Welsh chapel-goers should build chapels for English people. And, of course, this came about, and a chapel was built (Bethany Presbyterian) to add to the Wesleyan and Primitive Methodist causes which already existed. I do not believe that there was a similar philanthropic movement in Cwmafan.

The other improvements he advocates are equally interesting and revealing. There ought to be a public reading room: better to read newspapers and magazines than waste time in pubs or hang around street corners. He thought there should be a restaurant or eating-place, a co-operative store, and the friendly societies should cease meeting in pubs. Such a radical change as this, of course, never came about: furnacemen, roller men, ballers, puddlers, colliers needed great quantities of liquids, and beer was a healthier drink than plain, unfiltered water; if it is true today that there is no such thing as pure water it was certainly the case in Aberafan in 1870. What was achieved, however, was a Workmen's Hall in Taibach, and this, in such a working-class community, was a clear mark of urbanity. This was in 1872, and it was in this Hall that the first of a new series of eisteddfodau was held in the year of its opening. This eisteddfod deserves to be remembered for the quality of its prize essays. I have quoted extensively from the 'History of Taibach': it is the work of a real historian who sought for and tested his sources. The other was an essay by Benjamin Griffiths (Index) entitled 'Cenedlyddiaeth' (Ethnography). As the author put it: 'Testyn eang iawn ydyw, yn gofyn am ymchwliad manwl, a thuag at hyny rhaid cael meddwl rhydd oddiwrth ragfarn a dallbleidiaeth' ('This is a very wide topic demanding careful research, for which is necessary a mind free of prejudice and partisanship'). The work was rewritten and published separately in 1882, with a syllabus in English: 'Er mwyn y cyfeillion yn mhlith y Saeson, attodir y crynodeb byr canlynol'.[54] (The following summary is added for the sake of our English friends.) *Gemau Margam* contained much more than this, and though the quality is extremely uneven the book itself is a landmark in the cultural development of the place and a sure sign of its urbanity. In due course a library was built: and who can measure the debt we who learned to read in it owe to those early pioneers?

We have come a long way from Siencyn Pen-hydd and Matthews Ewenni. It is only by the most diligent research that the faint outlines of the world they inhabited can be recovered. Few of the old farms survive. Pen-hydd Fawr, much added to, can still be found, but not its neighbours Pen-hydd Genol and Pen-hydd Isaf. Ton-mawr is a collection of houses unrelated to anything in particular, its collieries razed and its tips landscaped. Cwm-Gwynau, where my father worked briefly in the early 1920s, has long reverted to the quiet greenness of the tree-clad valley, and it is difficult now to reconstruct the shape of its industrialism or to imagine the sounds of trains and of men at work. Where have they gone, these places? They are as far away 'in the dark backward and abysm of time' as the old monks of the abbey now are, and just as difficult to recover. Yet, like the unchanging shapes and contours of the hills and valleys themselves, the main features of the communities which experienced such profound changes can be recovered, and something of the quality of the lives of the people retrieved to enrich the quality of our own.

5

1848 and 1868: 'Brad y Llyfrau Gleision' and Welsh Politics

Mae Cymru a'i thrigolion wedi dyfod rywfodd yn wrthrychau sylw cyffredinol. Daw Saeson fel gwybed dros Glawdd Offa, ar lun Golygyddon, Adroddwyr Papurau Newydd, Dirprwywyr Llywodraeth, a rhyw fwnws o'r fath: a gwelir y gweilch hyn, yn llawnder eu hurddas swyddogol, yn bwrrw golwg arnom, yn ffurfio eu barn am danom, ac yn cymryd arnynt ddeall pob peth am ein rhif, ein moesau, ein crefydd, a'n ffasiynau, ac yna heb wybod mwy am danom na'r twrch daear am yr haul, a ddychwelant gan wneyd eu storiau, a llunio y chwedlau mwyaf rhyfedd, digrif, a disail.

Y Diwygiwr, Mehefin 1847

(Wales and her inhabitants have somehow become the object of general interest. Englishmen, in the shape of Editors, Newspaper Correspondents, Government Commissioners and suchlike creatures, are crossing Offa's Dyke like flies; and these wily knaves, in the fullness of their official dignity, look us up and down, and take upon themselves to understand everything about our numbers, morals, religion, and fashions, and then, knowing no more about us than moles about the sun, they return whence they came concocting their stories and fashioning far-fetched, absurd and baseless fables about us.)

In the political history of the nineteenth century the 1860s were the decade of most momentous change in Wales. This was the decade which saw political demonstrations of an unprecedented kind: relatively peaceful, orderly and constitutional where before they had often been violent and disruptive; imbued with a deep religious tone, more often than not with ministers of religion conspicuously present, and using the language of morals and religion to define secular aims and temporal objectives. Such popular political movements were common to all parts of the country, rural as well as urban, as frequent in colliery, ironworks and quarry villages as in the deepest rural solitudes and farming communities. This was the decade when, for the first time, the representation of the country in Parliament seemed at last to reflect, or to be coming to reflect, the political opinions of the majority of the people. It was the decade when the grip of Anglican Toryism seemed to be slackening in Wales and Nonconformist Liberals felt themselves to be on the threshold of an inheritance which they had long claimed but hitherto always in vain. For many contemporaries it was the time of liberation.

Such profound changes as these in mentalities and structures were not brought about quickly. They were the end result of changes which had been twenty years or more in the making, and the elections of 1865 and 1868 marked the culmination of conscious efforts to bring about political change. In this the publication in 1847 of the Reports of the Education Commissioners of 1846 played a critical part, for these reports were profoundly political in both substance and intention, and therefore inevitably, as some foretold, in their consequences. The politicization of the people of Wales grew out of, and was nurtured by, the cultural gap between, on the one hand, what the Blue Books reported and, on the other, the reality as perceived by the communities themselves. Why this should be so, and why such consequences followed are the questions I shall seek to answer in this essay. I shall do so by examining, first, some salient features of the social context in which they were produced, secondly their political background, and thirdly the ways in which both social and political developments combined to bring about fundamental changes in the political culture of the country at large.

The thirty years or so between 1840 and 1870 were decades of tremendous social change. This was the period when Wales was transformed, when it passed the point of no return between being an undeveloped, backward country to becoming a region of highly specialized, wealth-creating industries and commercial enterprises. In 1840 its population was growing, as had been the case for maybe a century or so, at a high, though declining, rate of growth but consistent with the rate of growth of the three previous decades: 15.6 per cent between 1830 and 1840, 11.2 per cent between 1840 and 1850, 10.6 per cent between 1850 and 1860, and 8.8 percent in the last decade. Contemporaries were thoroughly aware of this growth: the evidences of their eyes and the constantly increasing pressure on available resources in land and food provided a general, if subjective, idea of what was happening. From the beginning of the 1840s, however, population figures were being collected in a more scientific manner and published more widely than ever before. Metropolitan and provincial statistical societies flourished and their journals published local studies, collected and put together by private individuals and sometimes public bodies, as well as analyses of the constantly increasing flow of population and other social statistics emanating from central government. It is unlikely that the publications of such societies circulated widely in Wales where there were few libraries outside the homes of the gentry likely to be interested in such matters: an exception was the Swansea Literary and Philosophical Society founded in 1835 which subscribed from the beginning to the *Transactions of the London Statistical Society*. It also carried out its own investigations: the *Fifth Annual Report of the Council of the Royal Institution of South Wales* contained such an inquiry into the population of the Municipal Borough of Swansea. The general reader depended for his information upon weekly English-language newspapers, most of which, as a matter of course, carried material reprinted from the London newspapers, and on the brief paragraphs and occasional articles which appeared irregularly in the Welsh-language monthly magazines. Population growth, nevertheless, was a major preoccupation of political thinkers, philosophers, theologians, churchmen and religious leaders of all kinds. What relation did it have to the increase in poverty in town and country which was so ominously reflected in the huge increase of pauperism and the frightening rise in the poor rates? What relation did it bear to the outbursts of disorder in the appalling industrial towns of the coalfields and in the depressed countryside? Indeed, this more than any other feature of the changing times engrossed their attention, for it was commonly believed that it was population growth that underlay most of the social problems which troubled the minds of men and caused their hearts to fail for fear.

About one all-important aspect of population growth contemporaries could not have exact and reliable knowledge until the publication of the 1851 Census, namely, the way that the population of the country was being redistributed between rural and urban

Mid-Victorian Wales

parts of the country. The distinction between urban and rural populations is of primary importance in understanding social developments in those decades, and this too was sensed if not properly understood by contemporaries. The 1851 Census showed that approximately 9,000,000 or 50 per cent of the total population of England and Wales was urban, and ten years later the 1861 Census remarked that 'the English nation' (i.e. meaning England and Wales) had 'assumed the character of a preponderating city population', and all the indications were that this process would continue inexorably. Even though Wales contained no cities and only a few large towns, it was clear by the central decades of the century that the same fundamental shift was taking place there also. In 1841 only Merthyr Tydfil (34,977) and Swansea (24,604) were large towns as defined by the new Census classification, but ten years later Newport had 19,323 and Cardiff 18,351 while Merthyr had grown to 46,378 and Swansea to 31,461. Other towns of lesser magnitude, like Bangor, Caernarfon and Pembroke, were likewise growing at varying rates depending on their individual economies, and by 1871 the towns of the coal valleys and quarrying areas had taken off into sustained growth.[1]

There thus occurred a fundamental shift in the balance of population between town and country. The counties where extractive and manufacturing industries were located grew far more rapidly than the rural counties, for it was there that 'the engine of change' which was empowering the transformation was located. In 1841 the industrial counties of Glamorgan and Monmouthshire contained between them nearly one-third of the total population of Wales (Glamorgan 16.36 per cent, Monmouthshire 12.84 per cent). By 1871 Glamorgan alone had nearly one-third of the total (28.16 per cent), Monmouthshire substantially more than a tenth (13.83 per cent). In 1871, that is to say, 42 out of every 100 lived in those two counties, and, the most portentous change of all, nearly a half of these were crowded into the industrial towns and valleys.

The other side of this coin, of course, was what was happening demographically to the counties which contained no industry, or not enough to upset their population balance or that of the movement of their inhabitants as a whole. Contemporaries knew enough about demographic trends to understand the social significance of the statistics revealed in the census and in the Annual Reports of the Registrar-General. Above all, they could see with their own eyes the seemingly endless trek of people from the country to the new manufacturing districts and the old-established towns and ports now so rapidly being transformed by industry. Yet the rural counties were not being emptied of people — the high birth-rate and a gradually declining death-rate ensured that this did not happen — but the structure of their populations was being fundamentally altered, and their societies were diverging more and more from those of the urban areas.[2]

There were other changes in the structure of the population being observed at this time and which the mid-century census revealed in all their complexity. It was a young population. In 1851 46 per cent of the total population of 1,188,914 were aged 19 years and under, 29.4 per cent were aged between 20 and 39, 16.2 per cent between 40 and 59, 7.4 per cent between 60 and 79, and less than 1 per cent over 80 years of age. By 1881 the relative youth of the population, especially with regard to the under 19 years and the 40 to 59 age-groups, was even more pronounced. Every other person was under 20 years of age, and every fourth person was under 9 years of age. Only about one in ten was over 60, and the over-70 group was relatively small indeed. There were differences in this respect between the industrial and the rural areas, and in the age structures of the sexes: the preponderating proportions of young people over the middle-aged and the old were more pronounced in industrial areas, for it was young people who moved from the impoverished countryside to places where there were modern economies to sustain them. Here also were large numbers of young unmarried males who had migrated to the iron towns from neighbouring counties or by stages from valley to valley. So many of these young bachelors were there that the normal numerical superiority of females over males in the population was in these places reversed, and contemporaries were no doubt correct when they attributed much of the disorder endemic in the iron towns to the undisciplined, rough and rowdy behaviour of these matrimonially unattached young men.[3]

The occupational structure of the population was also changing very rapidly during these decades. Aggregate numbers of people engaged in agriculture declined steadily from decade to decade, even in the deeply rural counties, while correspondingly, though at a much higher rate, numbers employed in the industrial and manufacturing towns and mining districts expanded enormously.

The so-called simplicities of the old, familiar farming and pastoral societies survived for the time being, but in the industrial areas and wherever railways penetrated there developed a great multitude of occupations. The census reports now contained scores of new classes of occupations: skilled artisans and mechanics as well as huge numbers of miners and colliers, ironworkers, smelters of copper and zinc, and a greatly expanding class of shopkeepers, tailors, shoemakers, male and female servants and other service occupations. In addition, there was a spectacular growth in the professional classes: agents and managers, clerks and book-keepers and brokers. What the census revealed was not simply a growth in the numbers and proportions of persons engaged in industry but a growth in the complexity of society unimagined by previous generations.

The appearance of these urban masses, these 'condensations of people' (as the geologist William Conybeare, Dean of Llandaff, called them)[4] in the new 'mining and manufacturing districts' of south Wales in what was, in effect if not yet in name, a conurbation stretched out along the northern borders of Glamorgan and Monmouthshire, could not easily be comprehended either by the people themselves or by observers from outside. There were now more kinds of urban society than there had been ever before. The old, familiar towns and boroughs still survived, though greatly changed in their appearance and social structures, while others, like Swansea, Neath, Aberafan and Cardiff in Glamorgan, Newport in Monmouthshire, and Caernarfon in Caernarfonshire developed into major ports and centres of extractive and metallurgical industries and of manufacturing. These were all towns, properly so called. They had defined boundaries, known systems of democratic government, a sense of institutions and of urban propriety and, in most cases, endowed and other types of schools which, however imperfectly, provided a fair proportion of the children with at least a modicum of education. All these characteristics of urbanity were lacking in the new mining and manufacturing areas, and it was these places, constantly growing, ever renewed with fresh incomers, where new social relations were being forged and whose communities could best be described in terms of class rather than by rank or degree, which were largely unknown and forgotten except during a riot or a strike, that were the most characteristic product of the industrial age. The complementarity of town and country, the meshing of the one into the other in the pursuit of their common needs, seemed now to be breaking down. 'Probl y dref, a phobl y wlad', as a carefully composed, sensitive article in *Y Traethodydd* for 1852 concluded, were not the same kind of people; their life-styles were diverging, their behaviour and moralities coming to have little in common. Even in their religious beliefs and customs there were new tensions. This was the world, fractured and uneasy with itself, that the people themselves were striving to understand. It was also the world which powers from outside now sought to investigate for their own purposes.

I turn now to the reports themselves. The key to a critical understanding of the reports of the commissioners is the oft-forgotten fact that, in essence, they were but the latest in a relatively long series of official papers designed to elicit information regarding the provision and quality of education for the working classes and the poor in England and Wales. These, so far as the central government was concerned, began with the Reports of Committee on the Education of the Lower Orders, under the chairmanship of Lord Brougham, in 1816–18. Intended as an investigation of the educational provision and needs of the metropolis, it was soon extended to cover the rest of England and Wales. It took evidence as to charitable endowments, and gave an account of all endowed schools in every parish in the land with a view to illustrating the extent of educational deprivation. Then in 1833, after the failure of a bill sponsored by Brougham in 1820 to create a state-aided system of elementary education, the Reform government of Lord Grey made a grant of £20,000 to the two main charitable educational societies, the National (Church of England) Society and the British and Foreign (Nonconformist) Society. The grants were made on fairly strict conditions and the annual reports they were required to publish added to the corpus of information available. More important were the inquiries and reports issued during the 1830s as Parliamentary Papers, such as the return of 1833 (the Kerry Returns) which enumerated all schools in every parish in England and Wales, and the series of inquiries into the education of the 'Poorer Classes' which appeared as Select Committee Reports in 1834, 1835, and 1837–8.[5] The Census of Education carried out, like the Religious Census, as part of the 1851 Census, was the most efficient and comprehensive of these attempts by government to collect factual information regarding the nation's schools.[6]

Historians have long argued about the reliability of such investigations, but it was government papers such as these and the annual
reports of the two great charitable societies which provided the bulk
of the evidence on which policy was based, and it was to these that
critics and supporters alike appealed in the ensuing debate.[7] In
addition to these official investigations private individuals and
pressure groups, such as the Central Society of Education, also
published reports on the state of educational provision in particular
places, and the London and provincial Statistical Societies devoted
much of their time to the collection and discussion of similar
statistics. Thus, the *Journal of the Royal Statistical Society* for 1841
contained a paper on the 'Statistics of the population in the parish of
Trevethin (Pontypool) and at the neighbouring works of Blaenavon
. . . chiefly employed in the iron trade, and inhabiting part of the
district recently disturbed', by G.S. Kenrick of the Varteg Iron
Works. George Smith Kendrick was one of the proprietors of the
Varteg Hill Iron Works in the parish of Trefethin in
Monmouthshire, and it was he who provided Tremenheere with the
information on which he based his estimates of the school-going
population of the iron districts. Kendrick's paper, it should be
noted, was the first investigation of its kind by a local resident to deal
specifically with a Welsh town. The same author contributed
another such paper on Merthyr Tydfil to the same journal in 1846.
Kendrick's social surveys, though less sophisticated than some of
the other papers published in that periodical, paid particular
attention to educational provision and religious instruction, and
tried to relate them, on the one hand, to the quality of housing and
general standards of living of the workmen and their families, and,
on the other, to the manners and habits of the people as he himself
had observed them. His conclusions, as we shall see, differed not a
whit from those at that time being carried out by the government's
Inspectors.[8]

A change of the utmost importance took place in 1839 when the
administration of the education grant, which was increased to
£30,000, was entrusted to a Committee of the Privy Council with
Dr James Kay (later Sir James Kay-Shuttleworth) as Secretary.[9]
Two Inspectors were appointed, Revd John Allen, vicar of Prees,
Shrewsbury, and chaplain of King's College, London, for the
National Society schools, and Seymour Tremenheere, a barrister
and Fellow of New College, Oxford, for the schools of the British

REPORTS

OF THE

COMMISSIONERS OF INQUIRY INTO THE STATE OF EDUCATION

IN

WALES,

APPOINTED BY THE COMMITTEE OF COUNCIL ON EDUCATION,

In Pursuance of Proceedings in the House of Commons, on the Motion of Mr. Williams, of March 10, 1846, for an Address to the Queen, praying Her Majesty to direct an Inquiry to be made into the State of Education in the Principality of Wales, and especially into the means afforded to the Labouring Classes of acquiring a Knowledge of the English Language.

IN THREE PARTS.

Part I.—CARMARTHEN, GLAMORGAN, and PEMBROKE.
Part II.—BRECKNOCK, CARDIGAN, RADNOR, and MONMOUTH.
Part III.—NORTH WALES.

The title page of the 'popular' edition of the 1848 'Blue Books'
('Llyfrau Gleision').

Society.[10] John Allen, who became archdeacon of Salop in 1847, came of a notable Pembrokeshire clerical family, though this was not noted at the time, and he was responsible for all the early reports on Pembrokeshire schools which, incidentally, he thought to be vastly more efficient than any others in west Wales.[11] Their reports were published annually with the Minutes of the Committee of Council which were presented as Official Papers to both Houses of Parliament. When Tremenheere resigned after a dispute with the British Society in 1842 to become a part-time Assistant Poor Law Commissioner and the first Factories Inspector, his place was taken by Joseph Fletcher, a barrister who was also a very distinguished statistician and Secretary of the Royal Statistical Society.[12] In addition to their normal reports the Inspectors were sometimes required to report on particular places at the request of the Committee, and for this reason some places were visited by more than one Inspector at more frequent intervals than the rest. South Wales, especially Monmouthshire, was one of these districts, along with Staffordshire and Durham, and this remained the case until the appointment in 1849 of Revd H. Longueville Jones as Inspector for the whole of Wales.[13] It is scarcely necessary to point out that the evidence collected by these Inspectors, though very full regarding available facilities for schooling, was in other respects, as Forster always emphasized, 'very imperfect'. It could scarcely be otherwise: their districts were huge, there was no systematic methodology to guide them, and they were moving into almost entirely foreign, if not alien, territories. Some of their reports read like voyages of discovery, journeys into unknown regions and communities among people as remote socially from the world of Oxford colleges and well-endowed rural livings as the kraals of darkest Africa. In this respect their reports resemble those of other social investigators of the time who were opening up darkest England and darkest Wales to the uncomprehending gaze of the governing classes, such as Mayhew and the anonymous *Morning Chronicle* correspondents in south Wales in 1850.[14] Above all, as we shall see, they shared certain preoccupations and their investigations were guided and determined by powerful philosophical and political preconceptions.

No new principle had been involved when Parliament made the grant of £20,000 for education in England and Wales in 1833; the Church had been given £1 million in 1818 and another half million in 1824 to aid in the enlarging of old churches and the building of additional ones in populous places. These funds were administered from the centre by the Church Building Commissioners and the Ecclesiastical Commission, and contemporaneously the Church Building Society had been founded to raise and disburse charitable funds for the same purposes.[15] What was new in 1833 was that now Parliament was preparing to grant money to assist in the provision of schools for the children of Dissenters from the Established Church, the British Society being the instrument by which its largess would be disbursed. Because the grants were made proportionately to money raised privately, a relatively small part of these funds was in fact awarded to Nonconformist communities, and the bulk of the funds went to the National schools of the Established Church whose supporters, though fewer, could command more ample resources than their rivals. Nevertheless, this was anathema to people of High Church tendencies who deplored this outrageous interference by the secular state in the affairs of the Church, and most churchmen (though there were significant exceptions) accepted as axiomatic that the education of the people was the prime responsibility of the Church, and that only the Established Church could be entrusted with it. Anything which encouraged the spread of Dissent would lead inevitably to religious and social anarchy. Nonconformists, especially the old Dissenting denominations, agreed that religion and education were organically connected, but they believed that the formal teaching of religion should be kept separate from secular education and be left to parents and Sunday schools. These were the Voluntaryists, but it was also the view of non-religious educational movements, such as Chartism, which was particularly strong in south Wales. Chartists were 'combining for the education of their own children' in the belief that the people's education was safe only in the people's hands.[16] In the event, the secretary of the Committee of Council was authorized to come to agreements with the Church and the Nonconformists regarding the role of religion in the schools. Thus, the Church was able to ensure that the men appointed as Inspectors of the National Schools should be acceptable to the bishops. These agreements exerted a profound and baleful influence on the way education thereafter developed.[17]

The Committee of Council — a board of five Privy Councillors charged with the consideration and supervision of grants — was established in April 1839 and the first two Inspectors received their instructions in the following January.[18] Between those two dates an event had taken place which was crucially to affect the way education was to develop in subsequent years not only in Wales but in England as well. That event was the Newport Rising of November 1839. This was the year when Chartism was at its strongest and most challenging. Some historians believe that one in five of the total of adult men and women in industrial Monmouthshire and Glamorgan were committed Chartists and that many more had signed the national petition which was presented in July 1839 calling upon Parliament to enact the six points of the Charter. Behind it, in south Wales especially, was a new kind of radicalism based on the idea of class and the conflict of interests between the owners of capital and the workers who created their wealth. This was Chartism, as Sir Thomas Phillips put it, 'in its worst manifestations — not as an adhesion to political dogmas, but as an indication of that class-antagonism which proclaims the rejection of our common Christianity, by denying the brotherhood of Christians'.[19] Already by the summer of 1839 Chartism was a mass movement in industrial south Wales and the region was seething with unrest. Lord John Russell, Liberal Home Secretary and a strong advocate of a secular school system, said in the debates on the Charter in early August that the Chartist demands were so revolutionary and complex that the laws of the land were inadequate to deal with the movement, and he moved for an increase in the armed forces to deal with the challenge it posed. He attributed the disorder to a fundamental lack of a proper system of education designed to instil the virtues of obedience in communities of people among whom normal deferential attitudes had not developed. 'We have', he said, 'particularly in the manufacturing districts and especially in certain parts very large masses of people who have grown up in a state of society which is lamentable, if not appalling to contemplate. It is not a society growing up under the hand of early instruction, with places of worship to attend, with their opinions of property moulded by seeing it devoted to social and charitable objects, and with a fair and gradual subordination of ranks: but it is . . . a society necessarily composed of the working classes with certain persons who employ them, with whom they have little connection, regard, or subordination, and unhappier neither receiving in schools nor in places of worship that religion and moral instruction that is necessary for knitting together the inhabitants and classes of a great country.'[20] The Newport Rising confirmed the worst fears of the government, and this was reflected in the reports which the Inspectors thereupon began to return to the Committee of Council.

The first of these reports was that of Seymour Tremenheere who was instructed to inquire into the state of elementary education in the mining districts of south Wales in December 1839, just a month or so after the march on Newport. His instructions were comprehensive: he was to examine all schools whatsoever (and not simply schools attached to the two societies), and he was to rely on the local gentry, magistrates, clergy and others for 'the means which you will possess of prosecuting your inquiries in person among the working classes themselves'. Tremenheere spent the next six weeks in 'the parishes which were the focus of the late insurrectionary movement', namely, in Merthyr Tydfil and the parishes adjacent to Bedwellty in Monmouthshire. His report is of the utmost interest not only because it was the first and most detailed survey of any part of Wales yet to appear, but also because it created an image of industrial south Wales which subsequent reports of the Inspectors invariably substantiated. The 1847 Reports stem from the 1840 Report; the root was the same and they were watered and fed by the same hands.[21]

The social conditions of the masses of people congregated together in and around the ironworks visited by Tremenheere and the extent of the educational destitution he found there horrified his political masters. There was no doubting his description of the utterly appalling conditions in which most people lived: other Inspectors confirmed them and, as we have seen, Kenrick's paper on Pontypool and district in the influential *Journal of the Royal Statistical Society* for 1841 provided testimony of a most impressive kind.[22] Indeed, later inspections served only to deepen the impression of almost unrelieved social deprivation. Other themes were struck in that first report which later investigations commonly elaborated. One was the fact, as Tremenheere and his colleagues saw it, that poverty was not a prime cause of this deplorable lack of schools and equipment. Tremenheere, a sympathetic environmentalist rather than a cold moralist, went out of his way to emphasize that, by and large, the workmen in the ironworks were extremely well paid for their labour however hard, dangerous and unhealthy that work might be. He laid out what he claimed were verifiable statistics as to weekly wages for skilled and unskilled work, and attempted a cost of living comparison designed to show that parents earned enough to pay for the education of their children. Yet he found to the contrary (though hardly, one imagines, to his surprise) that of a sample of 17,000 children between the ages of three and twelve years something like 70 per cent did not attend day school, and that the remainder who were at school were scarcely any the better for it, so bad was the little that was available. Irrespective of their earnings, whether the parents were relatively well off or poor, children were put to work at the age of seven or eight years — girls as well as boys. In short, there was an indisposition on the part of parents to look for education for their children and a wilful blindness to the benefits, both to the children and society, that education would bring.[23]

Closely allied to this theme was an indictment of the capitalist class for failing in their duties towards the multitudes of people who had been gathered together in such insalubrious places by their instrumentality. This was a common complaint at the time. Leaders of the church building programme, in which the government was heavily involved financially, constantly drew attention to the culpable neglect of industrialists, or indeed, of landed proprietors, in failing to provide additional places of worship in their localities.[24] Governments were, perhaps, too sanguine that individuals and firms who neglected their religious duties should be readily forthcoming in respect to their secular ones. Sir Thomas Phillips, author of *Wales: The Language, Social Condition, Moral Character, and Religious Opinions of the People, considered in their relation to Education* (1849), barrister and colliery proprietor who was knighted for his part in defending Newport against the Chartists, was one of a very few of the gentry resident on the coalfield to respond to the Committee of Council's appeal for philanthropic support for the cause of education.[25] In a memorial to the Committee he declared that though the presence of armed soldiers was sufficient to overawe the disaffected portion of the population 'the only agency by which the ignorant and disaffected . . . can be taught their duty to God and man is to be sought for in providing for them the means of sound moral and religious training'. Yet he had failed to find support for the building of a school for 200 or 250 children at a cost of £600.[26] Agreeing, the Committee put the argument even more starkly, appealing to prudential considerations and the profit motive as well as morality:

> It cannot be in the interests of wealthy proprietors that the labourers (by whose misguided turbulence their security and peace have been disturbed) should continue the prey of low moral habits, to a large extent without religion, in gross ignorance and consequently the easy victims of the disaffected and of the emissaries of disorganizing doctrines. Nor can it be in the interests of proprietors, who have so much wealth at stake, that the children of this population should grow up ignorant, irreligious, corrupted and misled. Insecurity of life and insecurity of property are inseparable [and] industry will thrive in proportion to the security of the capital invested and as the labourers are skilful, intelligent, steady and industrious.[27]

Prudence had its moral aspects, of course, and it was emphasized that property had duties as well as rights and it was an evil to neglect the well-being of dependent people. This was particularly the case because, as the Revd Henry Moseley put it in reporting on Cwmafan in 1846, the relation between the workman and the capitalist in a free market is not one of equality, for the former is under a necessity to seek work and the choice of place of work seldom altogether in his power. The employer, therefore, must 'take care that, in accepting his services, he does not place him in circumstances morally or physically injurious to himself or his family'.[28]

Such moral arguments were uppermost in the minds of most of that first generation of Inspectors, and all, including those who were not ordained clerics, such as the sensitive, far-seeing and deeply sympathetic Joseph Fletcher, one of the ablest of that new generation of social investigators, were imbued with the pervasive Evangelicalism of the times. The majority of the first Inspectors were ordained clergymen who had been vetted by their spiritual superiors: but the prudential and the moral combined powerfully in the minds of most critics.[29] As the Revd W.H. Bellairs put it in his 1845 Report on the Western District, 'It is to be hoped that a higher principle than that of fear, will induce those who are able, to forward the work of education in this district (i.e. in Merthyr Tydfil). But at any rate it may be borne in mind, that an ill-educated, undisciplined population, such as exists among the mines of south Wales, is one that may be found very dangerous in the neighbourhood in which it dwells, and that a band of efficient schoolmasters is kept up at a much less expense than a body of police or soldiery'.[30] Or as Connop Thirlwall, Bishop of St David's, observed in 1846 in the House of Lords with respect to his diocese, 'If the means of education had been more extensively employed some years before' the burden of maintaining soldiers and police in the wake of the Rebecca Riots would not have arisen.[31]

Not that social conditions and their lamentable educational consequences were to be found only in Wales. On the contrary, they were the common experience of almost all mining and manu-facturing regions in England as well, and the language used to describe them in the reports of the Inspectors was very similar. Such regions were Staffordshire and the Black Country generally, parts of Durham and the northern counties and, of course, the great towns and cities of England. Fletcher was of the opinion that the mining and manufacturing districts 'were peculiarly unfavourable to the prosperity and even the existence of day schools', that is to say, in the very spots where they were most needed. This was because such places lacked resident patrons and managers such as existed — or were supposed to exist — in rural districts. They were 'purely places in which to work and make money', not places to be at rest in to enjoy it, and he added that they could scarcely be blamed for abandoning 'its smoke, its dirt, its bustle, its deformation of the face of nature, and the independent rudeness of its millions'.[32] According to Moseley, children were in a state of greater neglect in Staffordshire than in any other labouring population. Schools in his district seemed to be 'graduated according to the moral and intellectual debasement of the people: an ignorant and a debased population and a bad school go together'. In one place of 12,000 inhabitants only 150 children were at school. Here the law relating to the employment of children was notoriously evaded by employers who were just emerging from the condition of labourers, and were often as hard, coarse, brutal and ignorant in their manners as the class out of which they were emerging. Despite high wages men and their families lived 'in most squalid and miserably dirty and worst furnished abodes, their children . . . worse clad and more neglected, their wives more slatternly and poverty stricken, and about each of them fewer appliances of comfort, and fewer sources of happiness . . . than I have observed in respect to any other labouring population'. In a striking and memorable, if romantic, image Moseley wrote that 'the country, no less in its moral than in its physical aspects, seems to be scorched up: and as I have stood at night on some of the commanding eminences, and seen it extending beneath my feet like one vast multitudinous city, lighted up by unearthly fires, and sending up from all parts great volumes of smoke, and other earthly sounds, I have been unable to separate in my mind this prospect from the impression I have received of the condition of the people who inhabit it.'[33] But such pity, if pity it was, did not alter the fundamental fact that the people were largely responsible for their own poverty by their habits of improvidence and gross carnality. Doubling their wages would not necessarily lead to an increase of their social happiness but rather to their deeper degradation.[34]

There was, however, one theme which was unique to Wales, and that was the existence of the Welsh language. All the Inspectors from Tremenheere onwards regarded the Welsh language as the greatest single obstacle to the creation of a satisfactory system of schooling such as would bring about the reformation of manners in the country. Tremenheere in 1840 noted that English grammar was taught in only 17 of the 47 day schools in the district and that very few magazines and newspapers in the English language were sold by the so-called booksellers, market stall-holders and hawkers. There was no demand, he wrote (apparently with no sense of the ridiculous), for London newspapers among the working class. Not that provision in the Welsh language was much better. The bulk of reading material available in Welsh was religious, and the few Welsh periodicals circulating in the district were likewise religious and 'the information they contained on passing events, or on science and literature of the day, scanty and incomplete'.[35] He remarked that the people were 'chiefly indebted for such progress as they are making in the English language' to the Sunday schools where they picked up a superficial reading knowledge only. The Inspectors, wherever they might be in England as in Wales, were acutely aware of the central importance of language. It is obvious that they found it difficult to communicate with people whose accents made them wellnigh unintelligible in conversation. 'Discordant utterance of articulate sound' was how a Factory Inspector described the speech of northern children,[36] and the Committee of Council Inspectors constantly refer to what apparently sounded to them like mere noise when in fact children may have been reciting verses or reading prose with good levels of understanding. Thus, one Inspector reporting on the North Midlands District in 1847, made the point that schoolmasters from the south of England 'do not succeed well in the north';[37] the spoken language was coming to be what it had never been in previous centuries, an indicator of class, and already there is apparent a north/south English linguistic divide. Remarking on this snobbish attitude to the normal, 'uncultivated' accents of provincial peoples Dr Lewis Edwards concluded that Professor Wilson and Dr Chalmers of Edinburgh would be classed as bunglers, and Lords Brougham and Campbell be judged unfit to teach in an English school.[38]

Against that background and nursing such prejudices the feelings of the Inspectors when they came to Wales were unmistakable. Unsympathetic as some of these gentlemen were to the ways of life of the working-class communities they visited, some of them were appalled to be confronted with an entirely foreign language. One of the Inspectors thought it a somewhat comic situation to come across a monoglot Englishman teaching monoglot Welsh children. As Inspector Mitchell reported: '. . . one of the most amusingly ridiculous, though rather provoking days I passed, where two-thirds of the children knew no word of English and the master had not troubled himself by any vain endeavours to learn Welsh'.[39] The Inspector's sympathies seemed to be on the side of the master. Revd H.W. Bellairs, reporting on Monmouthshire in 1847, made exactly the same points as his colleague. The Welsh language was 'a difficulty', a hindrance to communication, a bar to religious as well as secular knowledge. The bulk of the children know only Welsh, and 'throughout the county there is also a strong Welsh accent, influenced, doubtless, by its contact with Wales, which renders the work of instruction more difficult than it otherwise might be'. Also, the schoolmasters are strangers from 'a distance, unaccustomed to the habits of the people, liable therefore unintentionally to offend, and against whom there is a prejudice; this prejudice is so strong, that I question much if under ordinary circumstances it is to be overcome . . . There are, I suspect, but few Englishmen with sufficient tact or sympathy to find their way into a Welshman's heart, so as to induce confidence and affection.'[40]

Some of the Inspectors were not entirely unsympathetic with regard to the language problem. Tremenheere's 1840 Report does not describe a hopelessly illiterate population, but rather a population struggling to achieve literacy in Welsh, and the list he gives of newspapers, magazines and books to be found in the houses of the work people and available for sale by resident and itinerant booksellers, though pitifully inadequate in the eyes of Oxford graduates, was evidence of a people venturing to educate itself. It was a wasted effort because of the indifferent quality of the reading material available, in particular its strong religious bias which could not, in his view, compensate for the lack of reading material of a utilitarian kind. Joseph Fletcher, who succeeded Tremenheere as Inspector of the British Society, took a somewhat more enlightened view of the problem and, possibly because of his more 'scientific', objective attitudes and his more extensive knowledge of rural Wales, was less pessimistic than his predecessor in respect of Welsh culture. Reporting in 1846, the year when the Commission of Inquiry was issued, Fletcher observed that the schools in remote localities were 'types of the best of those in which limited day-schooling of the Welsh has heretofore been conducted'. All the schools he had visited, in populous as in rural areas, were 'properly village schools' struggling to provide an education in English, 'the language of promotion' and therefore the language that the mass of the population were eager to learn. So powerful was this motive, he observed, that parents with a little English endeavoured to speak it to their children, even though this would inevitably over time lead to the extinction of the Welsh language. In places within reach of the border it was not unusual to employ monoglot Englishmen as teachers. It was this desire on the part of the common people to acquire English without any express intention of abandoning Welsh which justified the view that Wales was 'peculiarly deserving of their Lordships' liberal regard: for they [the Welsh people] have to encounter all the difficulties [of two languages] in addition to those of poverty, dispersion, and much indifference'. He advocated teaching through the medium of Welsh as the most practical and civilized way of enabling the children to acquire English.[41]

The Inspectors did not confine their investigations to industrial places; they visited every county and reported with equal fullness on schools in rural areas and the social conditions of the agricultural communities they served. Their results confirmed what the Church Building Commissioners and the Church Building Society already knew, that the crisis of religious and educational destitution was not merely or mainly an urban problem but was the condition characteristic of much, if not most, of rural England and Wales. As in industrial areas, so in agricultural communities, many landed proprietors seemed insensible to the appalling backwardness of their dependants. In rural Radnorshire, for example, where there was no language problem, no 'stranger could go through the district without being strongly moved to do all that might be within his power to draw attention to the existing condition of things'.[42] The situation in the whole of mid and west Wales, with the exception of English-speaking Pembrokeshire, was similarly melancholy. How could poorly endowed clergy with the care of huge mountain parishes, very often more than one such parish, be expected to act as successful schoolmasters as well? Some regions of mixed economies, such as the Midland District, which included parts of mid Wales, might suffer the worst of both worlds. Henry Moseley, reporting in 1845, stated that in a district having a population of not less than 100,000 people in the employ of twenty-five 'noble and opulent landowners and commercial companies, having also a return of net income from land and trade amounting to no less than £50,000 annually, the sum subscribed annually towards the maintenance of schools is less than £50'.[43] There were no resident gentry and none but poor clergy to fill the social gap between the upper and the lower classes. But at least there was nowhere in Wales the practical 'heathenism' that Moseley found in south Staffordshire or 'the dense, stolid, bucolic, Hampshire-pig ignorance' that Allen found in the south-east in 1845.[44] 'Results such as these', reported Fletcher, 'completely extinguish our belief in rural innocence.'[45]

The Minutes of Council with their voluminous appendices of reports and statistics were widely read by the political classes. Along with other Blue Books (or official government papers), such as the First and Second Reports of the Royal Commission on the Employment of Children of 1842 and 1843, the Reports on the Operation of the Mines Acts 1844–9, the 1844 Royal Commission of Inquiry for South Wales (the Rebecca Commission), and many more, they provided the stuff and substance of debate on most issues of social policy, including religion, in the country and in Parliament. The reports of the factories and mines inspectors were widely disseminated, copies being sent to all proprietors of collieries, magistrates and other interested parties, and they were invariably quoted and discussed in local and provincial newspapers and magazines. The commissioners appointed to inquire into the operation of the Mines Acts were, as part of their brief, instructed to inquire at the same time into the state of the population in the mining districts, and the report on south Wales, published in 1846, received wide publicity.[46] Its author was Tremenheere, now on the threshold of a distinguished career as a factory inspector, and its interest lies in the changes he was able to note in the area since his first and pioneering report to the Committee of Council in 1839. In 1839, it will be recalled, he had found 'a population of 58,000 persons, immersed in habits of sensuality and improvidence, earning very high wages, wasting nearly one week out of five in idleness and drunkenness; working their children in the mines and elsewhere at the earliest possible age: a very small proportion of the adults of either sex being able either to read or write, and neglecting the means of education for their children, except what was scantily and imperfectly given at Sunday schools. Accompanying this state of sensuality and ignorance was a very prevalent feeling of disaffection towards the State, and of suspicion, if not hostility, towards their employers.' Some things had not changed and might even be worse — drunkenness, for example, and housing and sanitary conditions as revealed in the Second Report of the Health of Towns Commissioners by Sir Henry de la Beche. In education there were improvements to report but the district was still very imperfectly supplied with schools despite the efforts of some of the ironmasters and the expansion of religious provision. Only good schools would 'aid materially in spreading the English language; the ignorance of which is one of the great causes of the backward state of the Welsh part of the population'.[47]

By 1846, therefore, there existed a substantial body of evidence regarding the educational state of Wales, something like an agreed analysis of its main features and causation, and an influential body of opinion regarding the most effective remedies. Thus when, in March 1846, William Williams, one of the MPs for Coventry since 1835, moved for 'an Inquiry to be made into the state of Education in the Principality of Wales, especially into the means afforded to the labouring classes of acquiring a knowledge of the English language'[48] it was inevitable that his request should be granted.

William Williams (1788–1865), a native of Llanpumsaint in Carmarthenshire, was an immensely successful London cloth merchant who had represented Coventry since 1835: he was known as 'Williams, Coventry' in his native county. In Parliament he was a prominent Radical and, as befitted a member for the most 'popular' constituency in England — three-quarters of the electorate was working-class and the Dissenting interest was very powerful — he was a consistent advocate of an extension of the suffrage, the ballot, and popular education, and a reliable exponent of Nonconformist aims and policies. He had voted with Peel on the Maynooth Grant, was a supporter of a national system of education as this was being currently developed in Ireland, and had voted for the increase in the education grant and the revised Instructions. When he spoke in the House of Commons he was addressing a ready, willing and informed audience, many of whom probably regarded such an inquiry as otiose so irrefragable did the facts appear to be: or, in the words of the Bishop of St David's, 'superfluous because there could be no doubt of the facts'. And in the forefront of their minds was the memory of the Chartist Rising of 1839 and the more recent Rebecca Riots. There was no one present at the debate to question the quality of the information given or to doubt the accuracy of the facts cited, and certainly no one either competent or sympathetic enough to question the attitudes of all the speakers to the Welsh language. Indeed, there was nothing new in what Williams had to say, and his argument was a distillation of facts, opinions and pleadings long made familiar in the government publications mentioned above. Williams added a few of his own: the Bishop of St David's *Charge* of 1842 was one. In this Connop Thirlwall, who greatly admired the Welsh language and who had learned to read it sufficiently well in the year of his consecration to begin taking Welsh services, wrote that the weakness of the Welsh language was that it gave the poor no access to books: 'They consequently remain destitute of that information which they might have derived with ease and pleasure from works written in their own language.'[49] Nevertheless, the bishop consistently advocated the teaching of both languages as the ideal solution.[50] But for the most part Williams's information was drawn from published sources and reflected the ideas and prejudices and the social ideals of a majority of his listeners. Education for such as him, especially when there was a powerful economic, utilitarian argument in its favour and the memory of recent disturbances to sharpen it up, was mainly a means of exerting a more effective control over the working classes. 'An educated people could be governed easier and much cheaper than an uneducated, ignorant people, besides the vast social and moral power it conferred in a

LORD JOHN RUSSELL AND THE PRIVY COUNCIL.

My Lords,—England and Wales are so destitute of the means of religious training that they are fast sinking into a state of Barbarism. It appears from this letter, which was sent me by the Rev. Chaplain of a prison, in Lancashire, that few can answer any religious questions beyond the first in OUR beautiful Catechism. " I asked a boy six years old (who had been very properly committed to gaol for looking over the stile at the Squire's game)," says the Rev. gentleman—"WHAT IS YOUR NAME? BILLY. WHAT DID YOUR GODMOTHERS PROMISE FOR YOU IN YOUR BAPTISM? I HAS'NT GOT NONE. WHO IS YOUR CLERGYMAN? DON NO. WHO IS THE BISHOP OF YOUR DIOCESE? DON NO. WHAT IS THE NAME OF THE SOVEREIGN OF THESE REALMS? DON NO." (Sensations of astonishment and horror here seize their Lordships, and their hair stands on end!) Now my lords, such being the proved condition of her Majesty's subjects, with regard to *religious education*, I propose the establishment of a Committee of Council to effect, *covertly* and *by degrees*, that which Parliament cannot accomplish by reason of pressure from without, as proved in the case of Sir J. Graham's bill.—(Shouts of Hear, Hear !—Bravo the Whigs !—Long life to Johnny !—Long live Church and State !)

Bendefigion, y mae Cymru a Lloegr mor amddifaid o foddion meithriniad crefyddol, fel y maent yn cyflym suddo i gyflwr o farbariaeth. Offeiriad parchedig, yn y llythyr hwn, a ddywed nad oes neb o'r Cymru na'r Saison a fedr ateb un cwestiwn crefyddol heblaw "BE DI DENW DI !!!" Efe a brofa hyn trwy hanes bachgen chwech mlwydd oed, yn y carchar am edrych dros y gamfa ar helwriaeth y scweier. Gofynais iddo—"BE DI DENW DI? BILI. BETH A ADDAWODD DY FAMAU BEDYDD DROSOT TI ? 'DOES GIN I 'RUN. PWY YDI PERSON Y PLWYF ACCW? DWN I DDIM. BETH Y GELWIR YR ARGLWYDD ESGOB? DWN I DDIM. BETH YDYW ENW EI MAWRHYDI GRASOL SYDD YN AWR YN LLYWYDDU Y DEYRNAS HON? DWN I DDIM." (Teimladau o syndod a dychryn yn disgyn ar yr Arglwyddi, nes mae eu gwallt bob un yn codi i'w syth sefyll !) Yn awr gan fod y mater fel hyn wedi ei brofi, mewn perthynas i'r diffyg o *addysg crefyddol*, yr wyf yn cynyg fod i *Gomiti* gael ei sefydlu i gyflawni y gorchwyl y methodd y Senedd a'i gwblhau o herwydd dylanwad y bobl ar yr aelodau, fel y gwelwyd yn amser ymgais clodwiw Syr James Graham i ddyrchafu ein Heglwys ar bwys y trethi i fwy o fuddioldeb i'r dosbarth llywodraethol.—(Llefau diddiwedd—Rhagorol ! —Da iawn Jonni ! Byw byth y bo'r Whigiaid !)

Cardiff: Printed by D. Evans, at the "Principality Office."

Cartoon by Hugh Hughes (1790–1863). (*National Library of Wales*) national point of view.' If the people had been educated the march on Newport and the Rebecca Riots would not have occurred, and 'the people would have redressed their grievances by constitutional means instead of violence' — an ironic comment indeed on the nature of those incidents and an indication of the speaker's blindness to the political aims of Chartism. Finally, he appealed to financial self-interest. Economies would have been made on two commissions of inquiry, the current expenditure of £140,000 on barracks at Newport, Brecon and Bristol saved, and schoolmasters at £50 per annum would have been cheaper and more effective than the fifty-seven policemen who were now a burden on the rates of south-west Wales. Very substantial money had been invested on education in Ireland and Scotland: 'If the Welsh had had the same advantages for education as the Scotch, they would, instead of appearing a distinct people, in no respect differ from the English: would it not therefore be wisdom and sound policy to send the English schoolmaster among them?'[51]

Responding, Sir James Graham, the Home Secretary, thoroughly agreed with all that Williams had said, though he did not think that a royal commission was appropriate, and in the event the inquiry, which was instituted by the Whig administration of Lord John Russell, was under the authority of the Committee of Council. But on the fundamental principles adumbrated by Williams the Home Secretary agreed, namely, that the education of the poor was very deficient in Wales, and that this was because 'the country laboured under a peculiar difficulty from the existence of an ancient language'. Defending what the government was already doing by legislation to improve the physical condition of the working classes, especially in Wales, they were now 'prepared to admit that their social, moral, and religious condition does require alteration'. 'I entertain no doubt whatsoever', he said, 'that their ignorance greatly interferes with their prosperity, and prevents them rising in the scale of society: and I regret to say that in some parts of the Principality the ignorance of the people not only lowers them intellectually, but depraves their moral qualities.'[52] This was language stronger even than Williams had used, but it precisely encapsulated the essence of Williams's case. Three years earlier Sir James Graham's Factory Education Bill, which would have taken a major step towards a national system of compulsory education, had been defeated by an unholy combination of Churchmen, Dissenters and Voluntaryists. 'In Ireland', he said, 'a system of national education had been set on foot: would to God that we could agree among ourselves as to the means of effectually extending it!' There is no reason to doubt the genuineness of this fervent prayer, and perhaps every reason to regret that a national system of education should have failed at a time when the need was so clearly recognized. But not everyone agreed with him, and prayers for the success of the opposing side were as fervent as his.

The only Welsh members to speak in the debate were Charles Watkin Williams Wynn of Glascoed, the distinguished politician, Conservative member for Montgomery county, and D.A. Saunders Davies of Pentre, Conservative member for Carmarthen county. Wynn declared that he knew nothing about south Wales because bad communications between the north and south prevented much social intercourse between the two parts of the country, but doubted that the educational state of north Wales was as neglected as Williams made out. This was generally the view of north Walians, some of whom evidently resented being tarred with the same brush as the turbulent south Walians. 'Yn amser y Siartiaid Cymru oedd dan y lach, ac nid mynyddoedd a godre Sir Fynwy. Yn amser Rebecca Cymru a geblid, er fod rhannau helaeth a phoblog o Gymru heb wybod dim am y fath symudiad, ond drwy glywed son.' (In the time of Chartism it was Wales that was under the lash, and not the mountains of the north of Monmouthshire. And in the time of Rebecca it was Wales that was libelled, even though large and populous parts of Wales knew nothing about the movement except by hearsay).[53] He made the important point, well understood by Church reformers (he had served on the original Commission of Inquiry into the Church of England in 1835), that the principal cause of the deficiency in Wales was the great extent of the parishes and that a great improvement would arise if they were divided — a matter which that same administration tackled with Peel's New Parishes Act passed in that session. Davies's contribution was less substantial, and confined to defending his own class against the charge of indifference: he knew landlords who were generous supporters of schools but he agreed that there was a great want of education. And so it was that the first government inquiry specifically concerned with Wales since the age of Cromwell was set up by a Whig government with Tory support, on the initiative of one of the leading Radical members of the House and without a voice from Wales to dispute the appalling aspersions and atrocious libels both of the proposer of the motion and of the grateful government minister. Inevitably the Commission would proceed not merely on the rather neutral instructions of the Committee of Council but also in accordance with the language of the Home Secretary.

The Commission was issued on 1 October 1846 and the Commissioners appointed by the Committee of Council were about their tasks by the end of the month.[54] R.R.W. Lingen (later Lord Lingen, 1809–1905), was a Fellow of Balliol and about to be called to the Bar. He became Assistant Secretary to the Committee of Council in 1849, and Secretary when Kay-Shuttleworth retired through ill health later in the year, eventually becoming Permanent Secretary to the Treasury. Jelinger C. Symons (1809–60), likewise a barrister, became an HMI on completing his part of the Inquiry, and he published extensively on social and educational topics. The third, H.R. Vaughan Johnson, had but recently graduated as an MA, and was called to the Bar in 1848. Thus, the Inquiry was entrusted to three very able young men, well-educated and well-connected. They were also extremely efficient and industrious. Lingen started his inquiry into the counties of Carmarthen, Glamorgan and Pembroke on 18 October and had completed it by 3 April. His report is dated 1 July 1847. Vaughan Johnson, who was responsible for the whole of north Wales, reported a year after his appointment. Symons wrote two reports, one on the counties of Brecknock, Cardigan and Radnor dated 3 March 1847, the other, on Monmouthshire, dated 1 September 1847. Assistants were employed to take evidence and to be responsible for reporting on parishes which could not be visited by the Commissioners in person. They also acted as translators, and seem to have been responsible for the collection of schedules which had been distributed to all chapel Sunday schools. The statistical tables, which are such a notable feature of the report, were put together with the assistance of the Council's own clerks and followed closely the pattern established by the Inspectorate. Altogether this Inquiry, from the point of view of the Council, was a most impressive piece of work, and it is astonishing that so much could have been accomplished in so short a time.

It is significant to note why it was thought important that Symons should report separately on Monmouthshire. There were two sets of reasons. First, the county, or more specifically the northern group of industrialized parishes, was thoroughly Welsh 'as regards the character, habits, and language of the larger part of its inhabitants', and the picture of the mining population would not have been complete 'without some statement of the conditions of that section of it which presents stronger features than any other branch of the same heterogeneous community'. But secondly, there was the political animosity aroused by the 1846 Minutes regarding the new arrangements for the training of teachers. 'The hostility evinced towards your Lordship's Minutes of Council of 1846, made known just previously to my arrival in Monmouthshire, in some measure, and in some cases, extended itself to my inquiry, and impeded its execution.'[55] This is a reference to the Resolutions passed by the two denominations in specially convened county meetings condemning the Minutes of 1846 as a threat to religious liberty and an attack on Nonconformity. Leading Dissenters in the county, including the Revd Thomas Thomas, Principal of the Baptist College at Pontypool, and the Revd Evan Jones (Ieuan Gwynedd), Independent minister of Tredegar, all of whom were convinced Voluntaryists,[56] eventually agreed to give evidence after being persuaded by Symons that 'an inquiry into facts, and a faithful representation of the statistics of the case' was as essential to their cause as to any other philosophical standpoint.[57] It is possible that in the course of his perambulations in the county, Symons may have heard of the lectures Thomas Thomas was giving in various locations, and he may even have seen the printed version, the title of which read, *A Course of Lectures on the Present Duties devolving on Christian Professors as Members of a Civil Community. Lecture the First. The Duty of Religious Men to study the time in which they live, and to apply their energies to the Right Conduct of Public Affairs.* It was published simultaneously in London, Newport, Pontypool, Abergavenny, Cardiff and Tredegar, and sold for twopence or eight shillings for a hundred. Perhaps Symons had every cause to be worried! Nothing illustrated better the essentially political nature of the Inquiry, and one can readily understand why it was bound to have political consequences.

The case of Monmouthshire also highlights the intense interest with which developments were followed in Wales. Indeed, it would be strange if they had not been so regarded. The denominational magazines, such as the Baptist *Seren Gomer*, and the Independent *Y*

Diwygiwr, which was edited by the Revd David Rees of Llanelli, the leading radical of his denomination, as well as the English-language weekly newspapers all carried reports of parliamentary proceedings, especially religious affairs, and were particularly vigilant with regard to education.[58] The Committee's instructions to the three Commissioners were translated and printed in these and other magazines.[59] In addition Hugh Owen, who had campaigned indefatigably on behalf of British Schools in Wales since 1843, and who founded the Cambrian Educational Society in 1846 in order to persuade his fellow Nonconformists to apply for the various grants which the 1846 Minutes now made available, published a letter in the Welsh magazines carefully explaining the purpose behind the Minutes and the way to apply for the grants. Hugh Owen, in effect the Council's most powerful advocate in Wales, insisted that he and the Cambrian Educational Society were completely impartial and independent of the government, and that his sole purpose was to persuade those who loved freedom of conscience and could see the need to provide their children with education to grasp the opportunity offered by the government: 'oedwch ond gronyn bach, a bydd wedi ei cholli — wedi ei cholli am oes' (delay for only a short time and the opportunity will be lost — lost for an age).[60] All the denominations were apprehensive respecting the effect the new Minutes would have on their schools. For the Anglicans, the Bishop of St David's led a deputation of three, the others being Bishop Short of St Asaph and Sir Thomas Phillips, to the Lord President to plead for Wales to be treated as a special case, in particular that Welsh-speaking Inspectors should be appointed for the Church schools, that grants should be given to the Welsh Committee of the National Society to enable them to set up teacher training institutions to serve north and south Wales, and to give an augmentation of one half rather than the one third laid down in the 1846 Minutes to properly certified teachers.[61] Kay-Shuttleworth received memoranda along the same lines from the inhabitants of Carmarthen and from the ministers and deacons of the Calvinistic Methodists meeting in Brecon, both of whom argued that because of its special circumstances, especially the language difficulty and the poverty of the country, the Minutes should be suitably adapted.[62]

This concern with the educational policies of government was characteristic of an age which was fundamentally religious. It was religion that provided the intellectual, spiritual and moral

framework for the lives of the vast majority of persons, and t
prevalence of superstition, or belief in magic and omens, and the
readiness of townsfolk as well as country people to resort to witches
and 'wise-men' ('dynion hysbys') coexisted, so far as ordinary
people were concerned, with the truths of revealed religion and the
high status invariably accorded to ministers of religion. Nor did the
existence of atheists, agnostics and so-called infidels here and there
do more than point up the fundamental acceptance of orthodox
religion. Long before the Religious Census provided them with the
kind of quantitative evidence they had hoped for, Welsh religious
leaders of all denominations (including Anglicans) claimed that
Wales was the most religious part of Great Britain. The
denominational periodicals contained, month by month, lists of
newly erected chapels and school-rooms, their seating capacities,
building costs and debts. Likewise, they always included detailed
accounts of ordinations, lists of ministers, obituaries, and the
proceedings of county, provincial and national associations. By the
mid 1840s denominational statistics already indicated that there was
ample provision in most of the counties, even in the industrial
counties where the need was greatest and the challenge to organized
religion, due to the constant flow of immigrants, most pronounced.
Indeed, as early as 1833 *Y Drysorfa* was calling for prudence and
restraint in the anarchic building activities of the time.[63] The
Census of Religious Worhsip of 1851 (published in 1853)
vindicated those claims. It showed that there were 4,006 separate
places of worship containing a total of 1,005,410 sittings for a
population of 1,188,914. Commenting on these figures and the
relative ratios of provision throughout England and Wales Horace
Mann, the civil servant responsible for taking the Census, remarked
that Wales was favourably circumstanced 'nearly all the Districts
having a surplus of provision . . . fortunately basking in an excess of
spiritual privileges'.[64] However backward and deprived Wales was
with respect to other aspects of its social reality — and no one denied
that this was true — in the provision of places of worship it was very
advanced. There was thus a widespread belief that the people had
achieved great things where it most mattered, without government
direction or assistance, indeed often, as in the quite recent past, in
the teeth of government and ruling-class opposition. This in turn
helped to raise their self-confidence while at the same time alerting
them to the other cultural possibilities of their achievement.

Not all these places of worship had Sunday schools attached to them and not all had separate schoolrooms or vestries, but the Education Census revealed that there were 2,771 Sunday schools with a total of 269,078 scholars of all ages.[65] These figures again showed that the provision of Sunday schools was more ample in Wales than in England and that the numbers of scholars were proportionately greater. North Wales, with 32.9 per cent of the population attending Sunday school, and south Wales with 22.4 per cent headed the list of provision by registration counties.[66] All the Inspectors were aware of the work of the Sunday schools — indeed, their attention had been particularly drawn to them in the original instructions — and they often marvelled at their efficiency, the enthusiasm with which they were conducted and their extraordinary popularity. These were community schools properly so called, centres of popular, self-directed education — 'gwerin-addysgiaeth' the magazines called it — which rose and fell in response to need and changing resources. Behind them were the denominations providing impetus and assisting in their continuity especially by publishing articles and reviews of new publications designed to help them and to furnish them with suitable reading material. The significant expansion of publishing books and periodicals specifically designed for the schools, such as *Yr Allor i Blentyn, neu wobr i ysgolhaig y Sabbath* (1846), which this entailed is one of the outstanding features of the age. No wonder that the founder of the Sunday schools in Wales, the great Thomas Charles of Bala, should be so venerated throughout the country as the greatest benefactor of the Welsh people, and no wonder that they should have been so proud of the structures that they had erected on his foundations. But this very satisfactory situation, as the Inspectors never ceased to point out, was balanced by deplorably large deficiencies in the provision of day schools. The Education Census put north and south Wales at the bottom of the list of county provision in England and Wales.[67] Likewise north and south Wales were at the bottom of the county list in the provision of literary, scientific and mechanics' institutes.[68]

It is not surprising, therefore, that there should have been everywhere in Wales an intense interest in what governments were about with respect to education, and what education should be about. Naturally enough, given the primacy of religion in the culture of the age, it was the relation of education to Christian belief that was given the priority. For example, the opening essay in the first number of *Y Traethodydd* in 1845 was on 'Rhagoriaeth Gwybodaeth' (The Excellence of Knowledge); knowledge about God and the destiny of man, knowledge of God's creation and the means available to the human mind to grasp its complexity so as to understand his own part in it.[69] What was education for if it were not to equip people to understand the importance of such questions? An article in *Seren Gomer* for 1847 argued that a general education ('Addysgiaeth Gyffredinol') was a prerequisite for such understanding, and that that was precisely what was lacking in the education of Welsh children.[70] The full title of the journal was *Seren Gomer; neu, Gyfrwng Gwybodaeth Gyffredinawl i'r Cymry (Star of Gomer; or, General Knowledge Medium for the Welsh People)*, and more than any other of its contemporaries it tried to make up for this deficiency by including a greater proportion of articles and other contributions on secular topics than was the case with the denominational magazines. The same was true of the non-denominational *Y Traethodydd*, which was patterned on the English quarterlies and designed to raise the level of discussion on current issues and, in particular, to avoid the bitter sectarian in-fighting which characterized most of what passed for theological debate. But as its editors (Dr Lewis Edwards and Dr Roger Edwards) soon discovered, this could not be done without cutting out theology altogether and that, in the climate of the age, was unthinkable and commercially out of the question.[71] That first number included the first of many articles by Dr John Phillips whose work for the British Society was so admired by the Inspectors. Nor is it really surprising that most of these studies should have been about content rather than about styles and techniques of teaching and the quality of the provision. The size of the current investment in religion relative to the level of incomes was enormous, and one can appreciate the proud satisfaction of the common people with the buildings and equipment they had provided out of their meagre resources, and that these were judged to be sufficient unto the time. Whether measured quantitatively, as by the Census, or judged by the extensive knowledge of the Scriptures which enabled whole congregations to follow and to understand deeply allusive and exegetical sermons and other discourses, and to read abstruse and controversial theological material in the periodicals, the success of the Sunday school movement seemed to them to be incontrovertible. The Welsh people had the key to success, and who can blame them for blowing their own trumpets? Connop Thirlwall, as one might expect, went to the heart of the problem when he questioned the value of such uncommon amounts of biblical learning and such a surprising familiarity with divinity if, as he evidently thought to be the case, it did not go hand in hand with a superior morality.[72] But judging by those same standards of private and public morality religious leaders believed that they were justified in claiming that the character of the people had been elevated by their means and especially by the Sunday schools. It was Bishop Ollivant of Llandaff who observed that 'had it not been for the exertions of dissenting bodies, our people must have been consigned to a practical heathenism'.[73] It was not the fault of the Sunday schools, so they argued, that drunkenness should be endemic, or that the bastardy rates — a sure indicator of morality for the Victorians — should, as was also the case in rural England, be very high. The agrarian and urban disturbances of the time alarmed and dismayed religious leaders as much as they did the governing classes, though they were less prone to fits of hysteria. Indeed, it is the tension between ideal and reality within the religious communities themselves that a reading of contemporary literature reveals. To this all the churches and Sunday schools were sensitive, as they were to the charge of hypocrisy and connivance with those age-old, but deplorable, courting customs, such as 'tumbling', or 'caru yn y gwely', said to be prevalent in certain rural communities. For all were agreed that their most important task was precisely to raise the general standards of behaviour of individuals and communities, not only to keep alive but ever to refine the sense of right and wrong in their own congregations and in the larger society outside. In fact, from the historian's point of view, what the developing situation regarding education revealed was the existence of conflicting moralities between, at one level, the different religious bodies and the communities of people among whom they were planted and of which they were organic parts and, at another more formal and institutionalized level, between those communities as a whole and the new government and Church-led morality represented by the Inspectorate and the Commissioners. It was this spirit that lay behind the intense distrust and suspicion of what was intended by the education clauses in Sir James Graham's Factory Bill in 1843. A

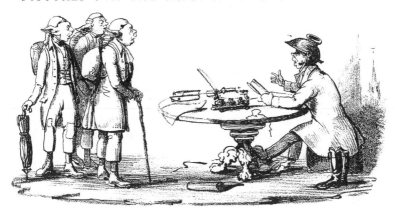

GATHERCOAL SCUTTLEWORTH'S FINAL CHARGE TO THE SPIES.

" The Whig Ministry are resolved to punish Wales for the dangerous example it gives, to the rest of the Empire, by its universal dissent from our Church! I now inform *you*, in confidence, that this is the real object of this espionage,—you are to help their lordships (of the Com. of Council) to make out a case against voluntary religion, by collecting such evidence of its connection with immorality, disloyalty, and barbarism, as will disgust the public mind of England, thereby preparing it to sanction the (despotic) scheme in contemplation for driving the Welsh back to the *true Church*. The use of the Welsh LANGUAGE being known to be favourable to the propagation of earnest personal religion, both the LANGUAGE and the NATIONALITY of the Welsh, as well as their religion, are to be destroyed! Your *professional*, with your personal *art*, will enable you to select such witnesses, and cull such evidence, as may secure our object without exciting suspicion. My lords have authorized me to assure you that you shall be made *gentlemen (!)* on your return."

GATHERCOAL SCUTTLEWORTH YN GOLLWNG YMAITH YR YSPIWYR.

" Y mae y Whigiaid yn penderfynu cosbi y Cymry am eu *hymneillduaeth*, yn yr hyn y rhoddant esiampl ddrygionus i'r deyrnas oll. Yr wyf fi am hyny yn dweyd wrthych chwi, *yn ddistaw*, mai gwir ddyben yr·yspiaeth hon yw, *profi cysylltiad crefydd wirfoddol â barbariaeth, anfoesoldeb, a gwrthryfelgarwch, fel y ffeiddier y fath grefydd gan y Saison,* (anwybodus) *ac fel y delont yn foddlon i gymerawwyo y moddion* (gormesol) *a ddyfeisir, gan arglwyddi y Cyngor, i yru y Cymry yn eu hol i'r* " WIR EGLWYS." Ceir fod yr IAITH Gymreig yn wasanaethgar i daeniad crefydd bersonol ; rhaid i chwi gasglu y fath dystiolaethau i'w herbyn, ac yn erbyn holl arferion cenedlaethol y bobl, fel y gellir dystrywio y rhai hyn GYDA'R GREFYDD. Cewch gan yr OFFEIRIADAU (gwrthodedig gan y bobl) y fath dystiolaethau ag sydd eisiau. Er mwyn cuddio ein dybenion ewch at *rai* o'r Ymneillduwyr, ond yn benaf at rai a enwir i chwi fel rhai *lled hanerog*. Rhoddwyd i mi awdurdod i addaw y gwneir chwi yn *foneddigion (!)* ar eich dychweliad."

Cardiff: Printed by D. Evans, at the "Principality Office."

Cartoon by Hugh Hughes. (*National Library of Wales*)

movement so creatively successful in the field of religious education was confident of its ability to teach the truths of revealed religion to its children in day as in Sunday schools and thus to raise the character and reputation of the nation without the interference or direction of the state and the state church. It was this spirit that was aroused by the Reports of the Education Commissioners.

The Reports were published in three folio volumes of more than 1,200 pages in the late autumn of 1847. A one-volume epitome of 546 pages was issued at the same time. This volume was later translated into Welsh and published early in 1848. The formal Reports contained full statistics in tabular form of the number of schools in each parish visited, distinguishing those parishes where English was the prevailing language, and those containing mining populations; the numbers of scholars, male and female, and the same expressed as proportions of the total populations; the numbers of persons under and over fifteen years of age attending Church and Dissenting Sunday schools. There were also statistics on the all-important matter of attendances, the state of repair of school buildings, and the educational records of teachers, trained and untrained, and many other quantifiable aspects of education. In many respects these statistics resembled, and were probably patterned on, the tables published with the HMI's reports to the Council. Some places carried out their own surveys, and these were included in the copious appendices to the Reports. For example, the Dissenters of Llanfair Caereinion and district came to the conclusion that the Instructions given to the Commissioners were deficient in important respects, and therefore they organized their own inquiries.[74] This takes up twenty pages in the north Wales volume and is, in some respects, a more sophisticated survey than that carried out by Johnson — though the Inspector pointed to some fairly obvious deficiencies. These collections of data, official and unofficial, constitute an invaluable historical source which has been used pretty exhaustively by local historians, though the Report itself still awaits the academic study it deserves. Contemporaries studied it carefully and few if any commentators could resist the conclusion that, so far as day or secular schooling was concerned, the Welsh people were indeed badly provided for. Neither could they, nor did they, resist the inevitable corollary that, however successful their provision for religious education, in practical secular knowledge they were appallingly deficient. Lingen's conclusion that 'the education received at a Sunday school is nothing like sufficient for the wants of the poor'[75] was universally accepted, as the evidence set out in the appendices so clearly demonstrated. Symons, an altogether cruder mind, was more dismissive, though even he was deeply impressed with the extensive benefit they were capable of if properly reformed. In particular, he disapproved of the practice of teaching children to read in Sunday schools, seeing this as 'a perversion of the object and spirit of the institution', which was to instil moral instruction and religious knowledge. In his view it was 'a fallacy to say that no secular instruction is given in Welsh Sunday-schools: this *is* secular instruction, and of the most profitless and least spiritual kind.'[76] He also observed what many Welsh advocates of popular education in Wales were increasingly coming to deplore that much of the Sunday-school teaching amounted to little more than 'doctrinal and sectarian discussion',[77] an opinion which was already becoming common, as we have seen, in some literary circles.

What few could accept was the opinion of all three Commissioners that the blame for this lay in the existence of the Welsh language and the prevalence of Nonconformity. In the minds of the Commissioners and of their political masters the two were connected, and it was in the connection that the evil resided. The language was the major isolating factor in the life of the ordinary people: it isolated the Welshman from all influences except those which arose within his class; he lived 'in an under-world of his own', as Lingen put it;[78] 'a disastrous barrier to all moral progress', as Symons expressed it.[79] According to Lingen it distorted the class system, by isolating the mass of the people from their natural leaders, and compelled the ordinary man to the life of a helot or labourer; 'they are never masters . . . never found at the top of the social scale', either in town or country, lacking the entrepreneurial spirit, initiating nothing new, no new enterprise or source of profit or means of social advance.[80]

All three Commissioners and virtually all of those who gave written or verbal evidence believed that literature in the Welsh language was wholly inadequate as a vehicle for modernizing the nation. The language was rich in theological and poetical works, but 'its resources in every other branch', reported Johnson (relying on an analysis of the 405 books circulating in north Wales), 'remain obsolete and meagre', adding that 'even of these the people are left in ignorance'. Of the 64 poetry books (the largest single category in his list), he observed that 62 of them dealt with religious subjects or topics of local interest. It included Pughe's translation of *Paradise Lost*, which 'bore a high reputation among a few Welsh scholars, but is as unintelligible as the original to the Welsh people'. Even the two books on astronomy and natural philosophy were translations from the English chosen on account of their religious character, and the five arithmetical books, the fourteen grammars and thirteen dictionaries 'were not found in use, where they are most needed, in the schools [but] they are confined to the libraries of those who have leisure and learning'. The same general criticism applied to the periodicals, virtually all of which were denominational, almost exclusively religious, bereft of general knowledge, and polemical in tone and purpose.[81]

The alleged inadequacy of the language as a medium of communication in 'modern' subjects was illustrated in a most timely and startling fashion when a translation of the Reports came to be made. It appeared early in 1848 under the title *Adroddiadau Dirprywyr Ymholiad i Gyflwr Addysg yn Nghymru, a Benodwyd gan Bwyllgor y Cynghor ar Addysg* and printed in London for HM Stationery Office. Lingen's Report was translated anonymously, but as the introduction is dated from Llanwrtyd, January 1848, it is probably the work of Revd James Rhys Jones (Kilsby), Independent minister, who knew Williams and was in fundamental agreement with his views regarding the Welsh language.[82] Part II was translated by Revd John Jones (Tegid), incumbent of Nevern, scholar and man of letters.[83] Part III was also probably the work of Kilsby. The interest of the work lies in the attitude of the translators to their work. All three emphasize the inadequacies of the Welsh language when translating the sophisticated prose of the Commissioners into the common language of ordinary people. Kilsby Jones quotes with approval Lingen's judgement that Welsh 'is a language of old-fashioned agriculture, of theology, and simple rustic life',[84] the language of an underclass living in a world of their own, cut off from all external influences. He often felt the truth of this observation as he tried to convey the ideas of the Commissioner in Welsh. 'Lingen', he says, 'writes like a scholar and a learned man, and it is easy for educated men to understand him: but it is not

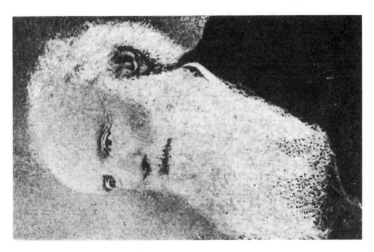

(*Left*) Revd John Jones ('Tegid'), and (*right*) Revd James Rhys Jones ('Kilsby'), translators of the Education Reports of 1848. (*National Library of Wales*)

always easy to make him intelligible to a class of readers who are
bereft of much knowledge apart from religion. So far as possible', he
goes on, 'a literal translation has been avoided: but sometimes this
has been unavoidable, because the monoglot Welshman does not
possess ideas corresponding to those used in the original.'[85] Tegid
included a glossary of his versions of some of the more difficult terms
encountered in the course of the work. Many of these words must
have been as unintelligible in Welsh as in their original English and
most of them have mercifully sunk into a deserved oblivion.[86]

The anonymous translator of Part III declared that he had striven
to produce a faithful version, correct as to language, and intelligible
to the reader. 'Ond sonir am lawer o bethau yn yr Adroddiad, nad
ydys yn arfer ymdrin a hwynt yn y Gymraeg; ac y mae ynddo
ymadroddion nas gellir eu cyfieithu, yn drwyadl. Am hyny, bu raid i
mi arfer rhai geiriau newyddion ansathredig, ac ymfoddloni,
weithiau, ar ddynesu at feddwl yr awdwr.'[87] (But the Report treats
of many things that we are not accustomed to discuss in Welsh; and
it contains expressions that cannot be fully translated. Therefore, I
was obliged to use new, uncommon (or obsolete) words, and to be
content, sometimes, to approximate to the meaning of the author.)
There follows a glossary of 102 such terms.

Of course, it is notorious that Kilsby Jones was wholly in
sympathy with his friend William Williams's contention that there
could be no modernization, no social progress in Wales until the
English language was universally used alongside Welsh, and that he
was deliberately exaggerating the difficulties in communication
between the two languages in order to enforce his point and justify
his attitude to the need for English teaching in all day schools. Prys
Morgan has recently shown how quickly new vocabularies of
technical terms in modern subjects were adopted in the first half of
the century,[88] and Elwyn Hughes has illustrated from a variety of
sources the contemporary urge to create a scientific vocabulary and
to develop a prose style appropriate for the dissemination of
scientific knowledge.[89] Nevertheless, the fact remains that there
was, and must have been, a serious linguistic barrier preventing the
kind of intellectual development desired by all educated persons. In
this context it is relevant to recall Lewis Edwards's animadversions
regarding the low valuation accorded scholarship in Wales ('syniad
isel y Cymry am ansawdd a gwerth dysgeidiaeth') and on the need
for language schools or academies which would concentrate on the

mastery of Greek and Latin as the essential keys to the understanding of English and other modern languages.[90] The value in particular of Lingen's report is that he directs attention, in a remarkably 'socio-linguistic' way, to the nature of the society of which Welsh was the language. 'Through no other medium than a common language can ideas become common. It is impossible to open formal sluice-gates for them from one language to another. Their circulation requires a net-work of pores too minute for analysis, too numerous for special provision. Without this net-work, the ideas come into an alien atmosphere in which they are lifeless. Direct education finds no place when indirect education is excluded by popular language, as it were by a wall of brass.' But this situation of isolation and exclusion was changing as migration brought English people into the land, and as the new post roads and railways multiplied the points of contact between the two cultures.[91] Symons, whose report on Monmouthshire, judging by the weight of quotation from it in the newspapers and periodicals, was read with particular interest because of the recent disturbances, added the idea that 'a spirit of sedition' was a characteristic of such socially and intellectually isolated communities, the Welsh language being the medium by which revolution could be plotted and concealed from the authorities, and the chapels — those self-developed forms of religious organization — providing the means and the inspiration.[92] This latter charge was not frequently expressed in such bald terms in the formal reports, but it was a constant refrain, implied when not direct, in much of the evidence printed in the appendices, the bulk of it given by churchmen, and corresponding exactly to the opinions expressed in the proceedings in Parliament which gave rise to the Inquiry in the first place.

Such issues as these were matters of debate and familiar to the readers of the more literary periodicals. There were many, like Kilsby Jones, who agreed with much of what the Commissioners had to say about the Welsh language, and there were others who had long since advocated English-language teaching and, of course, the debate has continued to our day. What few could accept was the wholesale condemnation of the morals of the Welsh people. In addition to being ill-educated, uncouth, ill-mannered and altogether socially degraded they were morally depraved and corrupt. It was this which added passion and hatred to the critical evaluations of the reports by Nonconformists and Anglicans alike.

Evan Jones (Ieuan Gwynedd), Independent minister of Tredegar,[93] Revd David Rees, Independent minister of Llanelli (Carms.) and editor of the radical periodical *Y Diwygiwr*,[94] Dr O.O. Roberts of Bangor,[95] and above all Lewis Edwards of Bala[96] and Henry Richard[97] were the most substantial among the Nonconformists. Revd Thomas Price (Carnhuanawc), incumbent of Llanfihangel Cwmdu, the famous historian and littérateur,[98] Dean Cotton of Bangor, the historian Jane Williams (Ysgafell) whose *Artegall, or Remarks on the Report* (London, 1848) was published anonymously, and Thomas Phillips, author of the most substantial book of all, *Wales: The Language, Social Condition, Moral Character, and the Religious Opinions of the People, considered in their relation to Education: with some account of the provision made for education in other parts of the Kingdom* (London, 1849) were the leading Anglican critics. But these were not the only ones to attack the Reports, and it is likely that most people would have learned about them in the magazines, all of which gave copious quotations, especially from the appendices of evidence, some of which were also available in the English version of the epitome and to a lesser extent in the Welsh version as well.

The Commissioners' instructions were basically those given to HM Inspectors though with detailed reference to the language of instruction in the schools, and an additional clause which read, 'You will also be enabled to form some estimate of the general state of intelligence and information of the poorer classes in Wales, and of the influence which an impoved education might be expected to produce, on the general condition of society, and its moral and religious progress'.[99] Connop Thirlwall, who was resident in his diocese at the time, regretted that the instructions contained this clause, believing such an investigation to have little to do with the purpose of the Inquiry. 'And where no authentic statistics could be obtained, I very much doubt whether either sweeping assertions on the morals of a district, or particular instances of moral turpitude, were of value sufficient to counterbalance the mischief of the irritation they were likely to produce.'[100] But the invitation having been made to pronounce on the morals of whole neighbourhoods and, by extension, of the Welsh people, the Commissioners, far from being forced into doing so (as the bishop went on to suggest), bent to their work with an almost unseemly readiness, with ears alert to the often lascivious and prurient gossip of their informants, noses to the odours of unventilated cupboard beds, and eyes for the grotesque and the absurd.

It is interesting to observe how the three Commissioners went about this task and how they defined the terms of the instruction. Symons, who 'shrank from offering [his] own conclusions were not [his] responses enlightened by the salient nature of the facts'[101] emphasized the all-encompassing poverty of the farming populations of his district, the farmers being poorer than cottagers in English agricultural counties, their housing hardly superior to Irish huts, and the dirty habits of the inhabitants of the little towns and villages. In the industrial side of his district he found less than usual attention to cleanliness and comfort, and in Brynmawr and the mining communities the familiar conditions of rapid urban growth prevailed.

As for serious crime, there are 'few districts in Europe where murders, burglaries, personal violence, rapes, forgeries, or any felonies on a large scale, are so rare'. But there were 'few countries where the standard of minor morals is lower'. There was much pilfering but no robbery. Petty thefts, lying, cozening, every species of chicanery, drunkenness (where the means exist) were scarcely regarded as sins. Above all was the want of chastity in the women which resulted from the practice of 'bundling' and much increased by night prayer meetings 'and the intercourse which ensues in returning home'. Symons's seven pages on morals consist of copious extracts quoted verbatim from evidence presented by his informants, the vast majority of whom were ministers of religion (25 out of 32), with connecting passages by himself underlining their salient features. His general conclusion was that the morals of the people are at a very low level, and that 'immorality prevails rather from the want of a sense of moral obligation than from a forgetfulness or violation of recognized duties'. Yet 'the jails are empty'.[102] This he attributed 'to the extreme shrewdness and caution of the people'. Some characteristics were to be admired, but the overall impression of his general conclusion as to the morals of the whole population of his district was very dark indeed, and such as to confirm, with a vast amount of detail, the preconceptions regarding the state of the country of those who had sent him forth on his journey of discovery.

Johnson, who reported on north Wales, went about his task in a somewhat different way. He took evidence from a wider spectrum of informed opinion than Symons, and very perceptively came to the conclusion that the levels of intelligence he found in most places corresponded with the educational means afforded the different sections of their population. Welsh people, because of their Sunday schools, were far more literate than English people of the same class or rank in society, and were often astonishingly competent within the narrow confines of their religious interests.[103] He worked methodically through the attainments of farmers, tradesmen, sailors and quarrymen and marked the different degrees of imperfection characteristic of them. These he relates to social facts which go a long way to explain rather than to condemn them. The main instruments of education, he observes, have been exclusively religious, and the chief promoters of religion and civilization have been the poorer classes themselves who are 'naturally unconscious of social defects to which they are habituated'.[104] He applies the same mode of thinking to the moral conditions of the different kinds of societies he found as he moved from place to place — farming communities, quarry villages, towns and ports, and the mining districts. He concluded that they differed in their moral characters, the mining and industrial towns and villages of the coal regions of Denbigh and Flint being the most depraved and he found this to worsen 'on approaching the English border'.[105] As in the rest of Wales there was an absence of heinous crime, and apart from the wool towns of mid Wales no sedition or disaffection 'within the memory of man'.[106] Only in Newtown and Llanllwchaearn and Llanidloes, where Chartism had briefly flourished, was there a tradition of extreme radicalism — Paine, Volney and Owen were still read in these places[107] — and the people of north Wales remained deeply conservative and distrustful of all things new. Only the unchastity of the women — 'the besetting vice of North Wales' — seriously impaired his view of a region which had attained surprising levels of good behaviour by its own volition. But this 'peculiar and barbarous' vice remained 'unchecked by any instrument of civilization' and 'had obtained so long as the peculiar vice of the principality, that its existence has almost ceased to be considered as an evil'. He quotes in full the long and detailed evidence of Revd J.W. Trevor.[108] The high illegitimacy rate in Anglesey 'is enough to prove the moral degradation of the common people'. 'The morals of the Welsh people are totally corrupt and abandoned in this respect' and not to be restrained by religion or conscience 'while the common people herd like beasts'. Fornication is not regarded as a vice, scarcely as a frailty, and he gives examples (in lascivious detail, it might be remarked) to prove that 'the minds of our common people are become thoroughly and universally depraved and brutalized'.[109] Trevor's conclusion that the present system of education in Wales was utterly powerless to meet this appalling evil can scarcely have encouraged the Lords of the Committee of Council on Education.

Lingen presented his material in a somewhat different way. His report seems to be more 'objective' than that of Symons, possibly because of his more critical 'sociological' bent. He seeks for explanations of the phenomena he encountered on his journeys through the southern counties in the differing social structures and in the constant flows of population from one to the other. The general review of the circumstances of the district with which his report opens is really a most perceptive analysis of an entirely novel state of social development and more profound even than that of Fletcher, the best equipped of the Inspectors to have visited those places. This is not to say that he is not as sensitive as the others to the moral factors at work, and he can be as censorious and as dismissive as they. His prejudices are their prejudices and those of the class they all belonged to, and he is as blissfully unaware as they of the racism implicit in some of his judgements. He finds, for example, a general disregard for cleanliness and decency to be more marked in Welsh than in anglicized districts.[110] He was fond of making nice distinctions. The population of Eglwysilan 'is ignorant and immoral, though not flagrantly so'.[111] But as a rule Lingen's observations on the morality of his district were kept to the appendices along with the reports of his assistants and the verbatim and written evidence of their informants.

It was some of these that gave greatest offence. Revd David Owen (Brutus), one-time Independent minister but now editor of the Church of England monthly *Yr Haul*, in the columns of which he satirized and lampooned his Nonconformist contemporaries, animadverted on the lying, cheating and unchastity of the common people as evidence of the general level of ignorance, and on religious revivals as occasions for and the cause of immorality. Religious enthusiasm heightened the sexual proclivities of young people. 'No educated man joins in them', he said, 'and something of the same results accompany common prayer meetings.'[112]

Many other such pieces of 'documentation', some even more offensive, were brought together by Lingen in an appendix of extraordinary power and impact.[113] Evidently Lingen had circulated a series of queries regarding the morality of the industrial part of his district to a number of men acquainted with the condition of the people in their particular areas. The queries *in toto* amount to a definition of 'morality' and throw a great deal of light on the nature of the inquiry itself, both the observers and the observed. The following are the specific questions: domestic accommodation; sobriety; providence and economy; religious feeling and observance; care for their children, and sense of parental responsibility; feelings towards their employers and superiors; capability of forming a judgement on the true interests of their class, and general intelligence; whether improving or retrograding, and in what respects, and whether likely to continue in the same direction; whether their moral condition is improved, or the reverse, by good times; extent to which English is understood; position, character and influence of females among them, and how far the duties of mothers and wives are adequately understood and fulfilled. Finally, they were invited to give an opinion on whether an improved system of education was required for that population, what means existed for procuring it, and the best manner of employing those means.

A total of seventeen informants responded with more of less detailed statements, and these were arranged in tabular form, presumably in order to facilitate comparisons of district with district. These were Llanelli and neighbourhood (R.J. Nevill and W. Chambers), Vale of Swansea (P.S.L. Grenfell), Vale and neighbourhood of Neath (J.T. Price and W. Jevons), Cwmafan and neighbourhood (Revd R. Morgan and Captain Lindsay), Vale of Llangynwyd (C. Bowring, Revd T.H. Jones, C.J. Hampton and H.A. Ford), Vales of Taff and Aberdare (Revd J. Campbell, Revd Williams, H. White, Evan Evans, T.W. Booker, and Revd John Griffith). This was a fair coverage of the Glamorgan and east Carmarthenshire side of the coalfield at a time when the smelting of iron and non-ferrous metals was the predominant industrial activity of the region and when the new coalfield settlements were rapidly developing a character of their own distinct from that of the older towns and villages and farming communities of the hills. It will be noticed that eleven of the respondents were industrialists as owners or agents, and that Merthyr Tydfil and Aberdare industrialists are conspicuous by their absence. White, the Dowlais surgeon, was well qualified to give answers at a higher state of objectivity, perhaps, than the three ministers of religion, one of whom had been in the district for only three weeks. Apart from the industrialists there were five ministers and one surgeon. Of the ministers of religion four were Anglican and one Nonconformist.

Clearly this was not a sociological survey in the modern sense of the term, and it would be anachronistic to treat it as if it were such. But for contemporaries the education Inquiry as a whole represented a high level of investigation, one which possessed an authority and dignity next to that of a royal commission. This is why it had been so generally welcomed and its conclusions eagerly awaited. Nor is it relevant to our historical inquiry that the Lingen queries themselves and the sequence in which they were placed should reflect less a scientific, positivistic theory of behaviour than a very conventional, moralistic one. Their quality is evident when they are compared with the less searching, more open-ended questionnaire circulated by Symons in connection with his Monmouthshire inquiry.[114] But all the observers and almost all their informants lived in the same moral world and it was because, in this fundamental respect, they therefore spoke the same language that the answers to the queries caused so much offence to the people they observed and whose moral world was so different from theirs.

Particular attention was given to the answers Revd John Griffith, vicar of Aberdare, gave to the queries.[115] Briefly, this is what he had to say. The houses of the people were all well built and comfortably furnished, 'some, indeed, for that class of person, extravagantly so'. There was little sobriety, especially at weekends and after the monthly settlement 'when the carousal is generally extended till Tuesday'. Nothing could be more improvident than the Welsh miners and colliers, most of whom were in debt to the truck shops. In religion they are very excitable and lacking mental discipline. 'Properly speaking, there is no religion whatever in my parish; at least I have not yet found it.' While fond of their children, they have no idea of parental responsibility, take their boys away from school as soon as possible, and rejoice to see these 'men in miniature' adopt the bad habits of their parents. Since they are totally uneducated and live only for the day, they regard labour simply as a means of financing their own sensuality. The parish is retrograding educationally, and morally their condition is worsening, for 'there is more improvidence, more drunkenness, and . . . more actual want of food in good times than in bad'. As for the position, character and influence of women:

> Nothing can be lower, I would say degrading, than the character in which the women stand relative to the men. The men and the women, married as well as single, live in the same house and sleep in the same room. The men do not hesitate to wash themselves naked before the women; on the other hand, the women do not hesitate to change their under-garments before the men. Promiscuous intercourse is most common, is thought of as nothing, and the women do not lose caste by it.

How different were the observations of T.W. Booker in the adjacent column![116] Unlike the newcomer Griffith, this ironmster had resided in the mining and manufacturing parts of Glamorgan for thirty years and observed the development of the coalfield at close quarters. His observations stand in stark contradiction to those of Griffith. Despite the baneful influence and tendency of the beer-shops, 'habits of sobriety are on the whole well cultivated', and providence and economy 'as well observed . . . as by that of any part of the United Kingdom'. The women were 'kindly, tenderly, and respectfully regarded', 'chaste but confiding, honest and industrious, exerting great influence, and understanding perfectly and fulfilling the duties of wife and mother'. On the face of it, it would be reasonable to suppose that Booker's very optimistic view of coalfield society, based on a lifetime's observation, was more reliable than Griffith's sweeping condemnation based, as it was, on scarcely a month's residence. Booker, whose Pentyrch and Melingriffith Tinplate Works with their associated villages were located on his Whitchurch estate near the town of Cardiff, was a paternalistic employer who believed that 'it is found practically that good and orderly workmen are not content with slovenly and defective domestic accommodation, and that it is not less the interests of the employer than of those employed that the means of comfortable domestic accommodation should be afforded'.[117] Griffith was a young, well-educated, upper-class Welshman from Cardiganshire whose career in the Church was being advanced by some of the most influential Glamorgan gentry families. Naturally enough, his social ideas and political views accorded with those of his class and patrons, and it is these that are reflected in his answers to the

Commissioner's queries. Not the least beneficial of the effects that were to follow the publication of his replies in Lingen's volume was the conversion of Griffith to Evangelical social doctrines, the defence and advancement of the working class, and to Welsh Nonconformist Liberalism, and alienation from the Tory establishment of the Vale and its ecclesiastical allies in the Llandaff diocesan hierarchy.

The furore sparked off by the publication of the Reports of the Commissioners has been often described:[118] indeed, this is one of those episodes in Welsh history which the social or collective memory has been at pains to keep alive. The numerous pamphlets, articles and other writings, including the drama which first popularized the opprobious title *Brad y Llyfrau Gleision* by which they have always been known, have been given their due meed of attention, indeed, in some respects, more attention than the Reports themselves. Some of these writings, among them those of Lewis Edwards, Ieuan Gwynedd and Henry Richard, rose to the occasion and achieved high levels of critical appraisal and literary merit. Others, no less vehement in their condemnation of the Reports and their authors and associates, merely used them as rich mines from which to dig missiles to hurl at their opponents. For a year or so the periodicals let scarcely a month go by without references to them, so much so that the polemic engendered by them threatened to displace the interdenominational bickering which characterized so many of them. Yet ironically, as is often the case in historiography, it is these periodicals which are most typically the product of the age and most characteristic of the spiritual climate of the time. One cannot estimate the readership of the more substantial pamphlets, books, essays and other works of criticism, such as those of Thomas Phillips, Lewis Edwards, Ieuan Gwynedd and Henry Richard, but one can be certain that the readership of the periodicals was much greater and socially more diverse. It is this combination of writings at different levels, the books and pamphlets of the educated élite and the fugitive effusions of the humbler, less well-educated writers, that explains the spiritual power released by the Reports and the very profound effects they had in the shaping of the nation in the nineteenth century. It is in this context that the question can be raised: to what extent and in what ways did the publication of the Reports affect the political life of the country?

In some respects the times were propitious not, as we shall see, for political action as such but for something which must always precede political action and which politics, properly so called, presupposes. There must be in existence, or coming into existence, a public opinion, a receptiveness to new ideas, agreement as to their importance and a readiness to organize behind them for there to be movement of a political kind. There were factors in that rapidly changing world that were conducive to such a development. The increasingly buoyant publishing industry was one.[119] Publishing had not yet taken off into sustained growth as was to be the case after the repeal of the 'taxes on knowledge' a few years later, but already in the mid forties it was becoming easier than at any earlier period to sustain magazines, though it was still crucially necessary for most of them to have the support of one or more of the religious denominations or friendly societies. Newspapers, likewise, were now more numerous, becoming more competitive and more reliant on circulation figures than on the patronage of powerful interest groups.[120] *The Principality*, a weekly newspaper published at Haverfordwest and then at Cardiff where it was edited by Ieuan Gwynedd, appeared in 1848 and played a leading role in the formation and mobilization of opinion regarding the Blue Books.[121] This was precisely the time when publishing houses were moving away from the relatively stagnant west of the country to the mining and manufacturing areas on the Glamorgan and Monmouthshire coalfield. Merthyr Tydfil and Aberdare, already important centres of printing, now became the heart of publishing in south Wales.

This happened for two main reasons. The first was that it was in the coal and iron towns that the bulk of the population was now to be found with the flow into them of new immigrants continuing unabated. By comparison with the places from which their populations were drawn they were rich and prosperous, places where surplus wealth was becoming available in sufficient quantities to support cultural institutions, such as the eisteddfod, which succoured books and publishing.[122] Secondly, they were also rapidly being linked by railway to London and the great provincial cities of England and to the rest of Wales. These things were happening; men could foresee, as they thought, the slant and direction of material progress, and many of the criticisms of the Commissioners on the poor state of secular education were addressed to those who had eyes to see. 'Chwarau teg i Lingen a

Symons, nid celwydd y cwbl a ddywedant am anwybodaeth y Cymry, ac nid gwir yr oll a ddywed eu gwrthwynebwyr mewn hunan-amddiffyniad. Mae rhan fawr o'r genedl yn warthus am ddiffyg dysg a gwybodaeth.' (Fair play to Lingen and Symons, not everything they said about the ignorance of the Welsh was a lie, and not everything their opponents said in self-defence was the truth. A large part of the people are disgracefully lacking in education and knowledge.)[123] It was about this time too that Jelinger Symons, now an HMI, wrote a tract extolling the potential wealth of Wales and pointing to the need for an educated and enlightened people to exploit it.[124] This was a theme which quickly took on a Welsh dress.

The level of political awareness and understanding was raised by the rapid unfolding of astonishing events from February onwards on the continent of Europe. The year 1848 was the year of revolutions, and the reception of the education Reports was played out against a background of political upheavals of unprecedented extent and importance. In France and Italy, Germany and Austria there were popular risings against despotic monarchies. Democratic constitutions and governmental institutions were being devised in state after state in order to enshrine the new-found liberties and rights of oppressed peoples. It was the year when nationalism swept the Continent and liberalism threatened even the papacy, that bastion of reactionary power.[125] Many of the writers who reflected upon these events saw in them a cosmic significance, signs of the millennium and the approach of the apocalypse.

> Tymmor gofidiau brenhinhoedd a phen-cadbeniaid yw'r flwyddyn hon; ac y mae yn dra difyrus i feddwl am danynt. Maent wedi cael eu dydd . . . Bernir gan rai fod yr angel y flwyddyn hon yn dechreu tywallt y chweched phiol, a bydd ei thywalltiad 'yn paratoi ffordd brenhinoedd y ddaear.'[125]
> (This is the time of troubles for kings and generals: and it is highly entertaining to contemplate. They have had their day . . . Some judge that this year the angel is beginning to pour out the sixth phial, and its outpouring will 'prepare the way of the kings of the earth'.)

But the editor ends the article with an analysis of political developments in Britain. Our Queen, he writes, is safe on her throne: she need not flee nor go in fear of her subjects: but there is reason to believe that her ministers corrupt her relations with the people. Some of their measures are unacceptable, including their scornful rejection of the Chartist Petition which had been signed by 5,400,000.

> Nid diogel un gorsedd ond a sylfaenir mewn cyfiawnder. Mae eisiau diwygiad seneddol, oblegid nid llaes y bobl a glywir yn Nhŷ y Cyffredin, ond llais y pendefigion.
> (Only the throne established in justice is safe. Parliamentary reform is necessary, for it is not the voice of the people that is heard in the House of Commons but the voice of the aristocracy.)

Such articles appeared frequently in the course of 1848 and 1849, and they are evidence that revolution on the Continent was sharpening the political awareness of the Welsh people and focusing their attention on politics.

In any case this enhanced sense of involvement in great political changes had been growing in the course of the decade. Despite the tragedy of Newport at the end of the previous decade Chartism was still very much alive and in pursuit of its original aims as embodied in the rules of the Charter Association but repudiating, for the most part, the strategies of its 'physical force' wing. This meant change by constitutional means and that, in turn, involved exercising whatever rights men already possessed, however meagre they might be. The campaigns of the Anti-Corn Law League, more especially in north Wales but with increasing success also in south Wales, had worked towards the same end.[127] Dissenting ministers, shop-keepers, industrialists large and small, and lawyers and professional men who had supported the frequent petitioning campaigns of the League, studied its literature and rejoiced in its great victory, were already involved in local politics, in poor-law administration and in the public health struggles then beginning.[128] The very antipathy between the two movements, their mutual hostility, had contributed hugely to this change in attitudes, this creation of a new climate of opinion. People who read the political and news pages of the periodicals, however inconsiderable the information they contained, who agreed or disagreed with the comments and reflections of editors and correspondents on current events, and who were persuaded to support petitions to Parliament and other high authorities felt themselves to be participating in the political process. And this was new.

It is this sense of gradually unfolding changes in attitudes and in people's perceptions of their situation which explains why reactions to the Reports should have taken the form they did. It was not difficult for critics of the Commissioners to dissect their reports and to expose their ignorance, their sophistries, their built-in bias against Nonconformists; nor was it difficult to illustrate the un-believable arrogance, prejudice and stupidity of some of the Assistant Commissioners. 'Pe chwyliasent holl golegau y byd, dilys yw na chawsant neb yn fwy anaddas at y gorchwyl.'[129] (Had they searched all the colleges of the world they could scarcely have found men less suited for the task.) All this was done, as we have already remarked, with clinical efficiency in numerous pamphlets, while newspapers and denominational magazines, with their own special interests to defend, printed detailed criticisms of evidence relating to particular places known to their readers. In this way and by these means the initial reaction of disbelief had, by the end of the year, been replaced with feelings of outrage and resentment, even of hatred, and a conviction that the Commissioners' attacks on the Welsh people, their language and culture, were deliberate policy on the part of government. Lewis Edwards, weightiest because the fairest of critics, came to the conclusion that the explanation lay not in a deliberate, preconceived determination on the part of the three Commissioners to traduce the Welsh people by lying about them, for they were all honourable gentlemen; but rather it reflected the natural tendency of those who feel strongly in favour of one side of a case to forget or ignore what is favourable to the other side. One of the favourite policies of Members of Parliament at the present time, he wrote, was the determination to bring education into the hands of central government, and Wales was the ideal part of the country to start with. In the past there have been minor skirmishes about the role of government in education, but the decisive engagement, the Battle of Waterloo, was to be fought here in the Principality. And to prepare the ground the Commissioners were sent to collect evidence and to make a case. 'Cyfreithwyr y llywodraeth oeddynt, yn chwilio am dystiolaethau dros y llywodraeth, erbyn y daw yr achos ymlaen yn llys y Senedd, ac fel y cyfryw y dylem edrych arnynt.'[130] (They were government lawyers come to search for evidence for the government before the case comes up in the court of Parliament, and as such we ought to regard them.) This explanation gained very wide currency: the author of *Artegall, or Remarks on the Reports*, for example, describes them as 'the partial inferences of advocates, the special pleadings of Counsel for the prosecution, in the cause of

QUALIFICATION OF WITNESSES.

EVIDENCE GIVEN.

THE UNLUCKY VISIT.

PICTURES FOR THE MILLION OF WALES.

Nos. 5, 6,

QUALIFICATION OF WITNESSES.
THE SERVICE OF KEY-HOLE AND CREVICE.

EVIDENCE GIVEN—THE PARSON AND COMMISSIONER
TRANSACTING PUBLIC BUSINESS.

Parson.—This is tolerable wine, Mr. Commissioner—my Church-warden is a good fellow, he will pay for this out of the next church rate. With regard to your queries —it is evident to you, from the fact of my drinking parish wine, with a Queen's Commissioner, that there is no religion in this parish, or, at least, that we have no *communicants.* I assure you, I found no religion here, and (he added mentally, while the other was drinking his glass), *I brought none with me.*

Commissioner. Have the goodness to give me such an account of the morals and manners of the Welsh as I require for the use of their lordships.

Parson. All the women of Wales are prostitutes when they have opportunities—and of opportunities they have enough in their prayer meetings. The men and the women are drunken, when they can afford it, and, in order to afford it, they are continually lying, and cheating, and thieving.

Com. I thank you, Rev. Sir, that's exactly what I want. Of course you have a right to assume and say that such is the case when the people are so provoking as to repudiate the church, and turn their backs upon the successors of the apostles, proving themselves, by choosing their own religion, so awfully disaffected against their superiors in Church and State.

Parson. It is no assumption either—it is a part of the sacred (secret?) duty of some of the clergy, assisted by the parish clerks, to watch the proceedings of the people in their houses after dark, by peeping through chinks and key holes ; and I have had the pleasure frequently of seeing the women change their under garments—and, *they had but one room !* the men *must* have been there.

Com. I was cautioned by old Gathercoal Scuttleworth not to look him in the face, nor expect my reward, without bringing sufficient evidence to him that Dissenters are all immoral, and their meetings for devotion and instruction nurseries for crime ; I am therefore under great obligations to you, Sir, and other rev. gentlemen, who are willing to let such evidence appear under your names. I beg to propose as a toast, *The Bishops and Clergy.*

Y MODD Y CEISIA AC Y CA Y LLYWODRAETH WHIGAIDD ACHWYNIADAU YN ERBYN Y BOBL, GAN YR OFFEIRIAID.

Y darlun cyntaf (No. 5.) a ddengys y modd y bu i'r offeiriad gasglu ei wybodaeth am arferion y bobl yn eu tai wedi nos. Efe a ddywed y bydd y merched yn newid eu crysau yn ngwydd y dynion, a'r dynion yn ymolchi yn ngwydd y merched ; ac y mae'n awgrymu (yn y Saesneg) y bydd pob peth yn cael ei wneud weithian yn ngwydd y Person a'r Clochydd, er mawr ddifyrwch a digrifwch i'r frawdoliaeth gysegrlân ! Dywed mai un o ddyledswyddau yr " Olynwyr " yw talu ymweliadau yn y tywyllwch i ysbio trwy dyllau ac agenau am ddefnydd chwedlau.

Yn yr ail ddarlun (No. 6.) gwelir y Person yn yfed gwin gydâ'r Commissioner, ar draul y Dreth Eglwys, yr hon y bwriedir ei gosod ar y plwyf (trwy help y Dissenters *cynffuniog*) o ddeutu y Pasg. " Nid oes dim crefydd—(sef nebi gymmuno) yn y plwyf," medd efe wrth y dyn a'r wig,—" ac ni ddygais inau ddim gydâ mi o Feirion," medd efe *wrtho ei hun.* "Y mae'r defaid wedi myned oll yn eifr—i'r Capel yr â'r bobl, gan wrthod eu gweinidogion awdurdodedig—ânt i'r Capel i gadw 'gweddi dywyll,' fel cynt, a mwy o lawer, a hyny dan y ffug o adduli ac addysgu ; ond eu dybenion yw creu cyflensderau i buteinio, ac i ddangos eu doniau yn gweddio. Mi welais i â'm llygaid fy hun, a llygaid y clochydd, yr holl gwrdd gweddi yn myn'd i'r daflod o'r Capel, ac yn aros yno drwy'r nos. Yr iaith Gymraeg ydyw'r drwg, y hi sydd yn gwnend y bobl yn Ymneillduwyr, ac Ymneilldnaeth sydd yn dyfetha eu moesau, a'u llysgoleigdod. Y mae'r Cymry mor farbaraidd fel y gwnant *reidiau heb gyfleusderau ! !* ac os na allant gael tŷ o amryw stafelloedd y maent yn foddlon i fyw mewn *un* stafell !—a fu erioed y fath *anrybod-aeth?* O Benarlâc, i Gaerlleon-ar-Wysg, ar hyd y terfyn lle nad oes dim ond yr Eglwys lân, a'r Saesneg fendigaid, y mae pawb yn ddysgedig, yn gyfoethog, ac yn foesol ; ond yn Nghymru Gymreig, tan ddylanwad y weddi dywyll, y mae pawb yn bob peth gwaeth nâ'u gilydd.

Y dyn a'r wig.—Diolch yn fawr i chwi, Barchedig Syr, am eich tystiolaeth werthfawr—a dyma iechyd da i Lord John Russell.

No. 7.

THE UNLUCKY VISIT.

ANOTHER SCENE IN A SCHOOL.

Commissioner. Well master Syntax, old boy, how do ye come on ?

Teacher. Have you any particular business with me ?

Com. Particular business ? Yes I think I have—aint I a royal Commissioner, sent to examine the competency, or rather the incompetency, of such fellows as you? Now give me an account of yourself, and of your school.

Teacher. I think you have had a glass too much this morning ; and your visit to us in such a state is most unlucky, for you, and those who sent you.

Com. O, an unlucky visit, Eh ! I shall put you and your imps down in the royal report as a parcel of fools, and I'll prove you to be nothing better. Now can you tell who was the father of Zebedee's children ? What are those boys laughing at?

Teacher. They are thinking how well they could give a lesson of morality, and decent behaviour, to a Queen's Commissioner.

Com. We in England are none of your Teetotallers and Methodists —a glass of grog does no harm at all, it makes a fellow a little merry, that's all.

Teacher. The education government proposes for us is intended to put down Methodism and Temperance I suppose ?

Com. Yes, and the Welsh language, and every thing else that is Welsh. By destroying the Welsh they will destroy disssent—you'll be all right then young chap—you will not then make a long face at seeing a man a little merry with drink. Wales is to be made of the same religion as Herefordshire.

Here the Teacher rises and peremptorily orders the rude, but candid intruder out of the school, who retires amidst a storm of shouts of " Hold him up."

Cardiff: Printed by D. Evans, at the " Principality Office."

Cartoon by Hugh Hughes. (*National Library of Wales*)

Shuttleworth *versus* Wales', and concludes that 'the Commissioners
were sent forth with instructions to make a case which they
diligently and faithfully laboured to accomplish.'[131] Bishop
Thirlwall scouted this idea as being highly improbable. In the
nature of things, no evidence could possibly be adduced in its
support, and certainly not through minute examinations of the
reports themselves — examinations 'which might extract a
quintessence of poison out of the Bible itself'.[132]

But such arguments as Thirlwall's, for all their cogency, miss the
point, which was that such inherently political explanations were
widespread and being reached independently by men of humbler
station and fewer pretensions than these élite writers. For example,
the columns of *Seren Gomer* are full of letters (a much favoured way
of getting into print) making the same accusations. Clearly,
indignation and resentment were stimulating political discussion.

At the heart of the discussion was the consenting, if not active,
role of the clergy of the Established Church in the preparation of the
reports. For a long time you have laboured, now more so than ever
before, declared Lewis Edwards addressing Church of England
clergy, to fill the minds of the rich with a prejudice against the
Nonconformists. No language is too low for you to use, nor sin too
awful to accuse them of. Despite the fact that many of your kith and
kin are Nonconformists to whom you owe whatever of religious
knowledge you possess, in whose Sunday schools you learned to
read, whose sweet hymns you learned by heart, you do not hesitate
to call your mothers and sisters whores, and you care not that your
nation is being traduced in newspapers throughout the kingdom.
What is praiseworthy in our nation the clergy claim for the Church
and contrariwise, what is evil you attribute to Nonconformity even
though it is acknowledged on all hands that good order and respect
for the law is the fruit of their devoted labour. He quotes against
them that most terrifying condemnation of the Pharisees; 'Canys yr
ydych yn cau teyrnas nefoedd o flaen dynion: canys chwi nid ydych
yn myned i mewn, a'r rhai sydd yn myned i mewn nis gadewch i
fyned i mewn.' (For ye shut up the kingdom of heaven against men:
for ye neither go in yourselves, neither suffer ye them that are
entering to go in.) But as certain as the unchanging laws of God your
treason will one day rebound on your heads. To build a church on
lies and deceit is the surest way to destroy it, and he warns them that
admirers of the satirist Twm o'r Nant are preparing to publish a

magazine in which the clergy's cant and hypocrisy, their lies and hatred will be exposed for all to see.[133]

These brief references to Lewis Edward's writings cannot convey the passionate resentment, the deep dislike, the bitterness and the anger in the original, and perhaps nothing illustrates better the almost unbelievable change wrought by the reports of the Commissioners in the minds of the leaders of Nonconformist thought. This was the authentic language of Dissent, but the author was the calm, scholarly head of a Calvinistic Methodist college devoted to raising the standard of public debate within his denomination and between denominations, the tendency of whose mind was to eschew unseemly controversy, especially such as might involve the denomination in political affairs. Prudence and restraint were his watchwords, but necessarily the attack on the Church, defensive though it might be, was implicitly an attack on the establishment and a declaration of political intent. In fact, of all the writers in Wales in that crucial year, Lewis Edwards was the most explicitly political. His second *Traethodydd* article ends thus:

> Allow me to remind you that our rulers are as likely to take notice of our speeches and resolutions as they are to the braying of asses unless we succeed in influencing elections. All that is required is to have a few people establish a reform association in a suitable place: and that place in my opinion is Liverpool. Nothing can withstand our countrymen in that city once they have determined to act. There must be a well-qualified man to give his whole time to the work. Two hundred votes, more or less, are all that are required to upset the balance in most of the Welsh constituencies. And I should not be surprised to learn that in Liverpool alone a hundred have bought the right to vote in each of the Welsh counties. In every county there are large numbers who would gladly join; but few of them think it worthwhile to act at present, since their individual votes are unlikely to achieve much one way or the other. There must be a general movement; and if the matter were taken up in earnest, it would not be too much to anticipate that a conscientious Nonconformist would be returned to Parliament from every county and borough in Wales.[134]

The contribution of Henry Richard,[135] at that time the minister of Marlborough Congregational Church in London, took the form of a lecture, one of a series of lectures on education being given under the auspices of the Congregational Board at Crosby Hall. His subject was 'The Progress and Efficacy of Voluntary Education, as exemplified in Wales'. It was widely reported in the Nonconformist press and published soon after. Richard's biographer points out that it might more fitly have been entitled 'A Vindication of the Welsh people from the Aspersions of the Education Commissioners'.[136] This was the lecture which established his reputation as the foremost champion of Wales in England, and its eloquence placed him in the first rank of Dissenting ministers in London. It is also, in effect, the first draft of the book which was to launch his political career as 'the member of Wales'. *Letters on the Social and Political Condition of the Principality of Wales*, published in London in 1866 (and in an enlarged edition under the title *Letters and Essays on Wales* in 1884), has a similar structure. First he surveys the history of education in Wales from the Age of the Saints to the end of the eighteenth century, followed by a description of the moral state of the country on the eve of the Methodist Revival. He then examines the progress of education in Wales by comparing the statistical returns from 1803 to 1847 in order to illustrate the levels of literacy and the reading habits of the common people. He gives a brief outline of Welsh literature and publishing in order to reveal its overwhelmingly religious character and its effect on the character of the people, especially with regard to their intense religiosity. He produces statistical evidence from the criminal returns to reinforce written evidence as to the extraordinarily law-abiding character of the people, despite what he describes as the aberrations of the Rebecca Riots and the disgraceful but untypical episode of the Chartist disturbances.

Yet the Blue Books proclaim 'that there is not a more ignorant, depraved, idle, superstitious, drunken, debauched, lewd, and lying population on the face of the earth', and he can well understand the verdict of the English newspapers that 'Wales is fast settling down into the most savage barbarism', 'sunk in the depths of ignorance', 'their habits those of animals, and will not bear description'. How can it be, he asks, that 'the effect which the faithful and earnest preaching of the Gospel of Jesus Christ will produce on the moral character of a community . . . can be suddenly belied and reversed?'[137] 'It is *not* true.' There is no doubt that Henry Richard's analysis of the Reports was the most devastating of all, not merely because of its forensic acuteness and eloquence but by reason also of its social realism. For example, he questions the Commissioners' logic and finds their powers of observation to be deficient in their unpleasant assumption that a want of cleanliness and decorum in the living arrangements of the lower classes is proof of their moral degeneracy.

> If they live together in small cottages, in a manner which is at variance with our notions of propriety and comfort, it is because they cannot help it. Their poverty, and not their will, consents. I say it is not fair to the poor to forget the mighty difficulties with which they have to contend.[138]

Like most of the writers we have referred to Henry Richard subscribed to the conspiracy theory elaborated by Lewis Edwards. His pamphlet was addressed to 'fellow Christians and fellow Dissenters to defeat the conspiracy which is assuredly forming against freedom of religion and education in Wales', and like Edwards he believed that the Church of England was at the heart of it.[139] But there were differences also between the two leaders which are important if we are to understand the political implications of this episode. Lewis Edwards writes like a man newly convinced of a truth, Richard like a divine already in possession of the truth. Lewis Edwards was a Calvinistic Methodist, a denomination whose adherents were customarily prejudiced in favour of the old Church, Henry Richard a Congregationalist, educated in the 'Dissidence of Dissent, the Protestantism of the Protestant Religion', one for whom the wickedness of established churches was axiomatic. Lewis Edwards, like most of his denomination, was an advocate of political action only when compelled by circumstances, and he believed in the natural bonds of social deference. Henry Richard held that politics was of the essence of Christianity and that therefore the believer was called upon to be active in pursuit of justice and liberty. The convergence of two such different philosophies as embodied in these very remarkable men was testimony not only to the importance of the moment but was also an unmistakable indication of the change taking place in the nature of Welsh politics and of the direction in which it would move in the future.

This political change became apparent in the lives of these two men, both of whom, incidentally, were born in north Cardiganshire within a few miles of each other and educated in the same school in Llangeitho. Lewis Edwards continued with his educational and literary labours, now heavier and more urgent than ever before, opening up windows onto the world of classical thought, bringing modern languages and the classics of English literature into the homes of the common people, presenting history, ancient and modern, to the growing readership, and beginning a new era in the study of theology. His influence in his denomination grew enormously in the following years: the future belonged to him because it was he who was educating the new generations of ministers, preachers and schoolmasters for what was already the largest denomination in Wales. It is impossible to exaggerate the importance of his role in the work of politicizing the common people which was then beginning in earnest. Educating them, as Lewis Edwards was doing, was to lay the essential foundations for Nonconformist Liberal Wales. When the time of action came the new political classes would know how to judge of issues and how to discriminate between rival policies.[140]

Henry Richard's part in this process was to be more direct and involved. He gave up the pastorate of his chapel in May 1848 in order to become secretary of the London Peace Society, and by 1853 he had also given up the title of 'Reverend'. He had long been associated with the circle of London Dissenters and familiar, through them, with political pressure groups in the metropolis and the provinces, and he was well known to the élite of English Nonconformity. The secretaryship of the Peace Society greatly extended the fields of his activities and enlarged the circle of his political friends. In particular, his relationship with Cobden became close and through him with some of the leading Radical politicians in the House of Commons.[141] All the societies he now belonged to were primarily political, they shared the same religious language and rhetoric, all were dependent upon their supporters for their incomes (though all could boast very wealthy men as members), all looked to Parliament for the realization of their particular programmes, and to that end all advocated parliamentary reform and the extension of the suffrage. Apart from the Peace Society the society nearest his heart was the Liberation Society which had been formed four years earlier by his friend Edward Miall.[142] It was through this society that Henry Richard was to make his impact on Welsh politics.

But political action of the kind advocated by Lewis Edwards or, indeed, by existing London and provincial reform societies, assumed a level of maturity which was not yet present in Wales in the 1840s and early 1850s. There were no permanent reform organizations in existence, not even that most elementary form of political organization, the constituency registration society. This is why Lewis Edwards looked to Liverpool where politics was a continuing activity, a permanent interest for its large and prosperous electorate. In fact, when a reform movement began in earnest in the mid 1850s it was launched in Liverpool by the Liverpool Welsh.[143] So far as constituency politics were concerned only a small, almost infinitesimal, minority had any rights they could exercise, and in most places those rights were severely limited in practice by social conventions as old and as rigid as the system itself. The Reform Act of 1832 had not interfered with the deferential relations which normally characterized both industrial and rural communities, and though it had increased the aggregate numbers of voters it had reduced the proportion of lower-class voters in most of the ancient corporate towns to which most people looked for political initiatives. Virtually the only constitutional right the majority of people had was the right to petition Parliament, but this also was restricted by law and convention, and was an expensive procedure requiring mature organization and planning. The old Welsh denominations and individual chapels understood these limitations only too well, and the most effective petitioning, so far as the mobilization of opinion was concerned, was that organized by powerful interests and pressure groups such as the anti-slavery movement, the National Charter Association, the Anti-Corn Law League and the Liberation Society. But however exciting and stirring the demonstrations at which petitions were agreed it was still activity at a distance and far removed from the ideal of democratic participation in the representative system.

The only area in which effective political action could be taken by relatively large numbers of persons was in local government. Considerable numbers of voters were involved in the government of corporate towns which were also centres of industry and trade, such as Carmarthen, Swansea, Cardiff and Newport in the south and Caernarfon in the north. As such places expanded and their industries became more diversified so also there developed in them new social classes which rapidly came to challenge and finally to dislodge the stratified structures of the *ancien régimes* by which they had been governed. Where before the local gentry had ruled the roost there were now aggressive industrialists and professional men, agents, tradesmen and shopkeepers, all of them eager to take part in the government of their towns, jealous of their reputations, prepared to invest in new town halls and amenity buildings.[144] In lesser places, and in towns which did not possess any form of government beyond that of the parish, there were fewer opportunities for participation, but even in these rising prosperity brought more and more people into government if only to vote once every three years for Guardians of the Poor. Some industrial parishes, in the mining areas in particular, were more deprived in these respects than others — for example, the iron towns and mining villages of the south Wales coalfield — and all were worse off than the ancient boroughs where comparatively large numbers of men voted as freemen. Public health legislation, beginning with the Public Health Act of 1848, permissive at first but soon obligatory on all local authorities, introduced a new machinery of elections and greatly extended the arena of public controversy.[145] Here again the electorate was restricted to certain classes of ratepayers, but the possibility of taking part in political decisions was more open than ever before, even to the unenfranchised. It was in this area of local politics, and at a time when issues of the greatest public importance were being discussed, that the political implications of 'Brad y Llyfrau Gleision' first became apparent.

This was at Aberdare immediately following the publication of Lingen's Report. An Appendix, it will be recalled, printed Revd John Griffith's opinion as to the moral condition of his parish which included the astonishing statement that 'there is no religion whatever in my parish', and the atrocious testimony as to the morality of the women of the place. Revd Thomas Price, Baptist minister and one of the rising figures in local government especially in the field of education and public health, thereupon called a public meeting, which was chaired by the colliery proprietor David Williams, Ynys-cynon ('Alaw Goch') and attended, so it was reported in *The Principality*, by about 2,500 persons. There were other Welsh colliery owners and ministers of religion with Price on the platform — there were sixteen chapels in Aberdare at the time — including David Davis, Maes-y-ffynnon, who was to become as active as Price in local and national politics, so much so that he earned the sobriquet 'the Gladstone of Wales'. There was also a miner, Mr W. Lewis, who was to become prominent in working-class politics. A number of resolutions were passed condemning Griffiths and Lingen (though acknowledging that a better system of education was required), calling upon Sir John Guest, the MP for Merthyr Tydfil, to contradict the aspersions contained in the Reports should they be raised in Parliament, arranging for the evidence of Griffiths and Booker to be translated into Welsh and circulated throughout the parish, and finally resolving that a copy of the resolutions should be sent to the Committee of Council on Education, to Lord John Russell, *The Principality*, the *Cardiff and Merthyr Guardian*, and *The Times*.[146] It would be a great error to regard this episode as a storm in a teacup. In fact, it was a highly portentous event: it marked the beginning of a change in the nature of politics in the fastest-growing, most Welsh part of the constituency, the emergence of key personalities, the alliance of colliery and chapel, and the articulation of new political doctrines without reference to the old political élites.

There were similar meetings in other parts of Wales, in Troedyr-aur, Cardiganshire, and in Brynmawr in Breconshire, for example, and many other places addressed memorials to the government. The new climate of opinion created by the Blue Books was favourable for the planting of the seeds of a new kind of radicalism in Wales, and the year 1848 saw a surge in popular support for the Liberation Society especially in those parts of the country where opinion had been most aroused. It was then that Edward Miall made his first visit to Wales and that local agents were appointed to prepare the soil and sow the seed which was to bear such rich fruit twenty years later.[147]

The key figure in these developments was Henry Richard. As we have seen, he had understood the political implications of the Commissioners' Reports from the beginning, and during the next twenty years he brilliantly exploited his popularity as a patriotic Welshman. It was on behalf of his 'vilified Fatherland' that he appealed to his English audience in 1848, to prevent his countrymen, a 'simple, warm-hearted, but defenceless people' from being 'first overwhelmed with calumny, and then, under cover of that, . . . oppressed by a yoke of conscience'.[148] This was the rhetoric which, strange as it is to our ears, roused the nationalism latent in the response to the Blue Books, identified its enemies, shaped and moulded it, and channelled it in constitutionally defined political directions. 'Demand these things as a nation', was his consistent cry. He recognized better than any of his contemporaries the electoral possibilities of the vast and growing network of chapels throughout the land and in the great provincial centres of England.

With his friend Edward Miall he concentrated the attention and the ample resources of the Liberation Society on Wales and, as we have seen, he wrote the key political text in the formation of Welsh Nonconformist Liberalism. This book provided Welsh people, on the basis of a coherent view of history and a comprehensive analysis of their present social situation, with a political programme which everyone could understand and in the fulfilment of which all could share. He gave them a political language.

By the 1860s the events of 1848 had become memories in the minds of those who had experienced them, and a history to be learned and understood for the young. Much had been forgotten in the intervening years: many episodes which contemporaries had regarded with pride, many struggles against what had been seen as injustice no less heroic than those 'old, unhappy, far-off things, And battles long ago'. The violent background of the Rebecca Riots, like the revolutionary drive and ruthlessness which had characterized Chartism and the early struggles of trade unions, had been painted out, lost to the consciousness, obliterated from the social memory. But many things remained to all appearances unchanged. More so than in the past the culture of the chapels persisted, and it was within this cultural continuum that the leaders we have examined could make themselves understood. In the great Merioneth election of 1868 Lewis Edwards took a leading part in the formation of a Reform Society in Bala and in making it an instrument to protect the tenant farmers who had been threatened with eviction if they persisted with their intention of voting against the Conservative candidate, whom they regarded as a Puseyite and an enemy to true religion. It was in this situation of suffering and tragedy that his desire back in 1848 that the people should begin to organize politically came to be realized.[149]

For his part Henry Richard had a wider field to operate in, not less than the whole of Welsh Nonconformity and the British political scene. From the early 1860s onwards he presented himself as the defender of Welsh Nonconformity against its detractors, in Wales as in England, as one standing 'in the breach, to defend the character of my countrymen against severe assaults made on their intelligence and morality'. It was this stance, along with his unflagging work for the cause of peace (itself sufficient to keep him in the public eye and to endear him to generations of Welshmen), his determined views on the disestablishment of the Church of England in Wales as the only effective means of putting an end to the injustice and social inferiority which Nonconformists had been compelled to suffer throughout their history, and his unwavering radical position on parliamentary reform, which gave him a moral authority such as no other Welsh politician possessed. Such was his authority that in the general election of 1868 he issued an *Address to the Welsh People* exactly as if he were a party leader issuing his manifesto.[150] And, of course, in a very real sense this is what he was, his words understood in all parts of the country and his party cry, 'Trech gwlad nag arglwydd' (Mightier the people than the lord), as clearly heard in Cardiganshire as in Merthyr Tydfil. The experience of 1848 was at the heart of what he had to say, not as a rhetorical device but as a shaping influence in his political thought. The landed proprietors, in alliance with the Church, had been part of that old conspiracy against the ordinary people, their language and their culture, which he and Lewis Edwards and others had identified. Now was the time to bring them to book. 'We are the Welsh nation, not you. This country is ours, and therefore we claim to have our principles and sentiments and feelings represented in the Commons' House of Parliament.' This was the core of the argument: 'The nation's soul, character and conscience have never yet been represented.' The members returned from Wales have 'felt no sympathy with your principles, felt no pride in your national history, felt no jealousy for your national religion, reputation and fame: and when you were assailed again and again in the House of Commons and in the English press, out of the thirty two men who represented you . . . not one man has ever stood up to defend his calumniated countrymen'.[151] The language was resonant of the language he had used twenty years previously. Its use in 1868 inaugurated a new period in Welsh social and political history, and 'Brad y Llyfrau Gleision' had become an inspiration rather than a symbol of defeat, a weapon rather than an instrument of shame.

Notes

1 The Observers and the Observed

[1] *Bristol Times*, Saturday 7 February 1852. Among the 'maniacs' in the county asylum at Briton Ferry was a certain Revd Benjamin Jones (no doubt, a sufficiently anonymous name) who attributed his malady to preaching and drinking. The writer commented on this remark as 'a random stroke of sanity: . . . for all who know the Welsh, know how the lower orders of them, at least, in the mining districts, mix up religion and liquor. From the public-house to the chapel, from the chapel to the public-house, are, I am told, in many places, the alternations of an entire Sunday, and so perfectly are the popular requirements understood, that a public house on the opposite way, almost invariably follows the erection of a new place of worship, and the topics are nearly the same in both places, for you hear theology as actively discussed at the tables of the tap as from the pulpits of the preaching house. The 'Revd' Benjamin Jones, therefore, who had been a hard preacher and a hard drinker, in telling the causes of his own insanity, also revealed the failings of a large class.'

[2] *Baner ac Amserau Cymru*, 7 Mawrth 1860.

[3] *Sermon, preached before the District Committee of the SPCK . . . for the part of the Diocese of Llandaff situate in the county of Glamorgan* (Cardiff, 1830).

[4] *Yr Adolygydd*, III (1850), p.19.

[5] *Anecdotes of the Life of Richard Watson, Bishop of Llandaff: written by himself* (2nd edn., London, 1818), p.502. On Watson see *DNB* and J. H. Overton, *The English Church in the Nineteenth Century, 1800–1833* (London, 1894). The conventional view of Watson was that he neglected the spiritual interest of his diocese in pursuit of more profitable preferment through politics and

> 'Ex cathedra' at orthodoxy laugh,
> And rise to Lambeth from decayed Llandaff.

Quoted in Edward Mahon Roose, *Ecclesiastica: or, the Church, her Schools and her Clergy* (London, 1842), p.300. The most recent life of Bishop Watson is T. J. Brain, 'Richard Watson, Bishop of Llandaff, 1717–1816' (unpublished Ph.D. dissertation, University of Wales, Aberystwyth, 1982), which shows, on the contrary, that Watson though non-resident, like most other eighteenth-century bishops, was nevertheless as conscientious in his ecclesiastical duties as contemporaries expected him to be. He was attacked not for failing in his duties but for his unorthodox theological opinions and his pronounced liberal political teachings.

⁶ 'Happy, indeed, is it for the lowly and sequestered peasant, in such times as these, if he hears little of what is stirring in the busier world. Enviable is his lot, if, secluded in his native mountains, and unacquainted with any but his own aboriginal language, the wretched effusions of impiety and sedition daily issuing from the presses of the metropolis are to him almost, if not altogether, inaccessible. In this respect, many parts of the Principality may have reason to rejoice in retaining their vernacular tongue, inasmuch as it has afforded them some security, at least, against one of the most pestilent evils.' *A Charge delivered to the Clergy of Llandaff . . . in 1821* (London, 1821), p.16. See also *Sermons and Charges of William van Mildert . . . to which is prefixed a memoir of the author by Cornelius Ives* (London, 1838). But see Appendix to Bishop Ollivant's *Primary Charge* (for which see note 12 below) where he quotes from *Y Diwygiwr* (Ebrill 1851) to show that this was no longer the case.

⁷ *A Charge . . . September 1827 at the Primary Visitation by Charles Richard Sumner, now Bishop of Winchester* (London, 1828). For Sumner see *Life of Charles Richard Sumner, DD, Bishop of Winchester*, by George Henry Sumner (London, 1876). Pp. 114–33 deal with his brief stay in Llandaff.

⁸ G. H. Sumner, op. cit., p. 131. The bishop may have spent only a short time in the diocese but it seems to have made a permanent impression on him and to have been a powerful motive in his drive for church extension. His biographer (his son) quotes the recollections of an acquaintance: 'he could not divest himself of his Welsh associations, and found in his deep interest for that people, that however separated he had indeed a Welsh heart.'

⁹ Gwyn A. Williams, *The Welsh in their History* (London, 1982); David J. V. Jones, *The Last Rising: The Newport Insurrection of 1839* (Oxford, 1985). Also Ivor Wilks, *South Wales and the Rising of 1839: Class Struggle as Armed Struggle* (London, 1984).

¹⁰ For this see the present author's essay 'Ecclesiastical economy: aspects of church building in Victorian Wales' in R. R. Davies *et al.*, *Welsh Society and Nationhood: Historical Essays Presented to Glanmor Williams* (Cardiff, 1984).

[11] William van Mildert — the first bishop to reside in the diocese — occupied the see between 1819 and 1826. In roughly that decade — 1820–9 — a total of 100 places of worship were built in the diocese, 39 of them in the archdeaconry of Glamorgan and 61 in the archdeaconry of Monmouth. See Wilton D. Wills, 'Ecclesiastical reorganization in the Diocese of Llandaff, 1830–1870' (unpublished MA dissertation, University of Wales (Swansea) 1965), p. 40.

[12] *Charge . . . at his Primary Visitation in September 1851 by Alfred, Bishop of Llandaff* (London, 1851), p. 27. The *Charges* of this great churchman are a primary source for the understanding of social developments in the south Wales coalfield in the second half of the century.

[13] See, in general, T. Ferguson, 'Public health in the nineteenth century', *Population Studies*, XVII (1963–4), Part 3, March 1964; F. B. Smith, *The People's Health 1830–1910* (London, 1979); Anthony S. Wohl, *Endangered Lives: Public Health in Victorian Britain* (London, 1983). M. J. Cullen, *The Statistical Movement in Early Victorian Britain* (London, 1975) studies the preoccupations and bias which informed the work of the statisticians, including, of course, the Annual Reports of the Registrar-General.

[14] These themes are discussed in greater detail in chapter 2 below. The quotation is taken from John Simon, *Public Health Reports*, 2 vols., ed. E. Smeaton (London, 1887).

[15] The quotations are from *Report to the General Board of Health . . . into . . . the sanitary condition . . . of Merthyr Tydfil* by R. W. Rammell (London, 1850), *Report on the Sanitary Condition of Merthyr Tydfil* by William Kay (Merthyr Tydfil, 1854) and from correspondence between Dr Holland and the General Board of Health in 1853 in PRO MH13/125. For further references see Ieuan Gwynedd Jones, *Communities: Essays in the Social History of Victorian Wales* (Llandysul, 1987), pp. 239–62.

[16] Contrary to what the editor believes, Welsh historians are fully aware of the existence of this invaluable source and have been using it for the past thirty years or more.

[17] For the authorship of the Letters see *The Unknown Mayhew: Selections from the 'Morning Chronicle' 1849–50*, edited with Introductions by E. P. Thompson and Eileen Yeo (London, 1971), pp. 9–10, and P. E. Razzell and R. W. Wainwright (eds.), *The Victorian Working Class: Selections from Letters to the 'Morning Chronicle'* (London, 1973), pp. xiv–xv.

[18] Compare Lingen's 'miniature men'.

[19] The evidence for this is overwhelming and to be found not only in what was said and written but, more importantly, in what was assumed to be the case. For some discussion of this see my essay 'Religion and society', in *Explorations and Explanations: Essays in the Social History of Victorian Wales* (Llandysul, 1981), pp. 217ff. and 'The religious frontier' in

Communities, op. cit., *passim*. See also, in general, E. T. Davies, *Religion in the Industrial Revolution in South Wales* (Cardiff, 1965), C. B. Turner, 'Revivals and popular religion in Victorian and Edwardian Wales', (unpublished Ph.D. dissertation, University of Wales (Aberystwyth), 1979), and R. Tudur Jones, *Ffydd ac Argyfwng Cenedl, Cyfrol I* (Abertawe, 1981), esp. chapter 2.

[20] *Hanes Diwygiadau Crefyddol Cymru o Ddechreuad Cristionogaeth yn y Wlad hyd y Dywigiad Diweddaf* gan y Parch. Henry Hughes, Bryncir (Caernarfon, n.d. (1906)), p. 249. Not all observers held that there was a close correlation, or developmental pattern, between revivals and changing economic and social conditions. For most people revivals were evidence that the hand of God was moving among the people to bless them, and in this respect Wales was especially blessed. She was known as 'Gwlad y diwygiadau' (the land of revivals), and Christmas Evans warned his readers not to forget these powerful outpourings of the Spirit. 'Nid swn cloch yn unig oedd y weinidogaeth, ond yr oedd hefyd ynddi sugn y pomgramadau. Gwelwyd oedfaon fel corwyntoedd y dehau yn plygu derw Basan trwy yr holl goedwig fel brwyn.' (The ministry was not merely a bell [i.e. to awaken or proclaim] but contained within it also was the juice of the pomegranate [to comfort, sweeten and heal]. Services were like forests through which southern hurricanes blew, bending the oaks of Basan before them like rushes.) *Y Traethodydd*, II (1846), p. 6. Christmas Evans believed that it was the absence of revivals which accounted for the relative weakness of religion in England as compared with Wales. See William Morgan, *Cofiant, neu Hanes Bywyd Christmas Evans* (Caerdydd, 1839).

[21] There was a strong ritualistic connection between the friendly societies and chapels and churches which religious leaders endeavoured to strengthen at the expense, so they hoped, of the public houses where the societies invariably met and whose landlords were paid a 'wet rent' for the use of their premises. Annual feasts usually began in chapel for a sermon and ended in the pub for a bibulous meal. The connection between the chapels and the Rechabites, a teetotal friendly society founded by the temperance movement in 1835, was complete. The only indigenous Welsh friendly society, the Ivorites, was often torn between the chapel-orientated mores of its leaders and the requirements of its members. Dr Thomas Price, of Calfaria Baptist Chapel, Aberdare, who attained the highest offices both of the Oddfellows and of the Ivorites, perhaps owed his great popularity and influence to the fact that he was anything but teetotal. There is no satisfactory history of the friendly society movement in Wales. In general see P. H. J. H. Gosden, *The Friendly Societies in England, 1815–75* (Manchester, 1961). There is a great deal of valuable background information in Dot Jones, 'Did friendly societies matter? A study of friendly society membership in Glamorgan, 1794–1910', *Welsh History*

Review, 12 No. 3 (June 1985), pp. 324–49, and the same author's 'Self-help in nineteenth century Wales: the rise and fall of the female friendly society', *Llafur, the Journal of the Society for the Study of Welsh Labour History*, 4 No. 1 (1984), pp. 14–21. For the Ivorites see Elfyn Scourfield, 'Cymdeithasau cyfeillgar yn Ne Cymru yn ystod y ddeunawfed ganrif', (unpublished Ph.D. dissertation, University of Wales (Swansea), 1984). For Thomas Price see *Bywgraffiad y Diweddar Barchedig Thomas Price, MA, Ph.D., Aberdar* gan y Parch. Benjamin Evans ('Telynfab'), (Aberdar, 1891).

[22] For publishing in Aberdare see Brynley F. Roberts, 'Argraffu yn Aberdar', *Journal of the Welsh Bibliographical Society*, XI Nos. 1–2 (1973–4).

[23] Printed in *Gemau Margam, sef y Cyfansoddiadau Buddugol yn Eisteddfod Agoriad Neuadd y Gweithwyr, Taibach, Hydref 21, 1872. Dan Nawdd Cymdeithasau Dyngarol* (Aberafan, 1873). This was revised and republished under the title *Cenedlyddiaeth: Traethawd Arobryn Cystadleuol, yn Eisteddfod Taibach, Sir Forganwg, yn y flwyddyn 1873* gan Benjamin Griffiths (Index), (Caerdydd, 1882).

[24] This is a huge theme which has scarcely as yet begun to be tackled by literary and social historians. There is a great need for a history of the local eisteddfod to complement the splendid pioneering work of Professor Hywel Teifi Edwards on the National Eisteddfod. See his *Gwyl Gwalia: Yr Eisteddfod Genedlaethol yn Oes Aur Victoria 1858–1868* (Llandysul, 1980).

[25] The most comprehensive and valuable treatment of these related themes is Sian Rhiannon Williams, op. cit. This work contains an exhaustive bibliography. Consult also, among other essays in the volume, 'Kilsby Jones, Darwin a Rhagluniaeth' in E. G. Millward, *Cenedl o Bobl Ddewrion: Agweddau ar Lenyddiaeth Oes Victoria* (Llandysul, 1991).

[26] On this see 'The religious frontier' in *Communities*, op. cit., pp. 211 ff.

[27] But see Millward, op. cit., on this important aspect of Welsh literary development.

2 The People's Health in Mid-Victorian Wales

[1] PRO MH 13/3.i: James Lewis, MD to the General Board of Health (hereafter GBH), dated from Maesteg, 15 December 1857. See A. H. Williams, 'Public health and local history', in *The Local Historian*, 14 No. 4 (1980). Mrs Margaret Thomas read an earlier draft of this paper and I am grateful for her comments.

[2] Twenty-Fifth Annual Report of the Registrar-General (hereafter ARRG) for 1862 (1864), Table: Density of Population and Annual

Mortality 1841–50, 1851–60, with 20-year Mean Annual Rates of Mortality, Supplement, lvii, lviii. Cf. the statistically more refined studies by E. H. Greenhow, 'On a standard of public health for England', *Journal of the Statistical Society of London*, XXII (1859), 253–67. On the methodologies used and the reliability of the statistics generally consult M. J. Cullen, *Statistical Movement in Early Victorian Britain: The Foundations of Empirical Social Research* (London, 1975).

³ Select Committee on Public Health Bills 1855, *Parliamentary Papers* (hereafter *PP*) 1854–5, XIII (244) *passim*, especially the evidence of Toulmin Smith.

⁴ 25th ARRG, op. cit., lvii-lviii. The following is the list for Wales extracted from his series and ranked in ascending order.

16 deaths per 1000	Lampeter	Cardigan	*23 per 1000*
Builth	Dolgelley	Presteigne	Wrexham
	Llanelly	Ruthin	Pontypool
17 per 1000	Aberaeron	Llanfyllin	
Pwllheli	Festiniog	Llanrwst	*24 per 1000*
Corwen		St Asaph	Newport
Anglesey	Aberystwyth		
Haverfordwest	Pembroke	*20 per 1000*	
		Carnarvon	*25 per 1000*
	19 per 1000	Llandovery	Abergavenny
18 per 1000	Chepstow	Montgomery	
Newcastle Emlyn	Swansea	Carmarthen	
Narberth	Conway	Hay	*27 per 1000*
Bala	Monmouth		Crickhowell
Knighton	Llandilo Fawr	*22 per 1000*	
Rhaiadr	Bridgend	Neath	*28 per 1000*
Tregaron	Machynlleth	Cardiff	Merthyr Tydfil

⁵ Second AARG (1839), *PP* 1840, XVII (276), 50. See also reports of the Local Government Board Inspectors on the working of the Public Health Act of 1872: Report of Andrew Doyle on No. 8 District (dated 23 October 1872), *PP* 1875, XL (134), 768 ff.

⁶ Ruth Glass, 'Urban images', in G. A. Harrison and J. B. Gibson (eds.), *Man in Urban Environments* (London, 1976), 349.

⁷ Census of Great Britain, 1851, Vol. 1, Report, xlv ff.

⁸ Census of 1861. General Report, Vol. III, 100–1, for the Table showing proportions of populations in town and country in each Registration County. See especially the rules adhered to in the construction of the Table, p. 100. The town populations were estimated as follows:

Wales (the Registration Division) 32.0%: Monmouthshire 30.7%: Anglesey 24.3%: Brecknock 13.1%: Cardiganshire 13.7%: Carmarthenshire 23.0%: Caernarfonshire 23.9%: Denbighshire 17.8%: Flintshire 27.0%: Glamorgan 54.9%: Merioneth 5.7%: Montgomeryshire 30.4%: Pembrokeshire 33.7% and Radnorshire 27.9%.

⁹ See, in general, Harold Carter, *The Towns of Wales: A Study in Urban Geography* (Cardiff, 1966), and more specifically, idem, 'Transformations in the spatial structure of Welsh towns in the nineteenth century', *Transactions of the Honourable Society of Cymmrodorion* (1980), which studies Neath, Merthyr Tydfil and Aberystwyth, and Harold Carter and Sandra Wheatley, *Merthyr Tydfil in 1851: A Study of the Spatial Structure of a Welsh Industrial Town*, Board of Celtic Studies Social Science Monograph Number 7 (Cardiff, 1982). See also C. Roy Lewis, 'A stage in the development of the industrial town: a case study of Cardiff, 1845–75', *Trans. Institute of British Geographers*, New Series No. 2 (1979), 129–52.

¹⁰ Census of 1851, Report, xlvii.

¹¹ *Llais y Wlad*, 5 Tachwedd 1875.

¹² 65th ARRG, Part 1, 1904, xxxiv: *PP* 1904, XIV.

¹³ On under-registration see M. J. Cullen, *The Statistical Movement in Early Victorian Britain: The Foundation of Empirical Social Research* (London, 1975), esp. pp. 32–3, and D. V. Glass, 'Under-registration of births in Britain', *Population Studies*, V (1951–2).

¹⁴ Supplement to 25th ARRG, 1864, v. Letter . . . on Mortality during the 10 years 1851–60, by William Farr. 'The still born children . . . are not registered: and a certain number of infants that breathe for a short time are, it is believed, to save the burial fees, interred as the still born are buried, and so escape registration.'

¹⁵ The figures are 6,926 of children under 5 years out of a total of 18,555 or 37.3%. The proportion was 49.9% for the registration counties of Monmouth, Glamorgan and Carmarthen. According to Dr Greenhow's Report of 1858 on deaths from diarrhoeal diseases in Merthyr Tydfil 1848–58 *excluding deaths from cholera in the two epidemics* of 1849 and 1854 which occasioned the deaths of a total of 2,138, more than one-third of all deaths were of infants under 1 year and more than two-thirds under 5 years. The death rate per 1,000 live births of infants under 1 year was computed at 385.4, 1 year to 5 years 370.3, 5 years to 6 years 128.5: Second Annual Report of the Medical Officer of the Privy Council [hereafter ARMOPC], *PP* 1860, XXIX (201), pp. 118–21.

¹⁶ For statistics consult Dr Greenhow's 'Report on the circumstances under which there is an excessive Mortality of Young Children among certain manufacturing populations', *PP* 1862, XXII, 187 ff and the Annual Reports of the Registrar-General. The Sixty-fifth ARRG (1904), *PP* 190

XIV is devoted to this problem. See also W. P. D. Logan, 'Mortality in England and Wales from 1848 to 1947', *Population Studies*, IV (1950–1).

[17] *Report on the Sanitary Condition of Merthyr Tydfil* by William Kay, MD, published by the Local Board of Health (Merthyr Tydfil, 1854), p. 16. See also 'The sanitary history of Merthyr Tydfil' by Thomas Jones Dykes, *British Medical Journal* (1885), p. 192.

[18] See Margaret Pelling, *Cholera, Fever and English Medicine* 1825–1865 (Oxford, 1978), especially 97–8.

[19] Seventh ARMOPC 1864, *PP* 1865, XXVI, Appendix 9s, 496 ff.

[20] *PP* 1854, LXIII (145), 'Return of the number of medical practitioners'. Cf. W. P. D. Logan, 'Mortality in England and Wales from 1848 to 1947', *Population Studies*, IV No. 2 (September 1950), 132, who points out that among the medical practitioners who certified the causes of death in 1848 were a few who had received their medical training towards the end of the eighteenth century. By 1861 there were 523 medical practitioners in Wales of whom 69 were qualified as MD, 52 with qualifications as physicians, the rest being apothecaries. See *Medical Directory* for 1861. By 1881 the total of practitioners was 594; see *Medical Directory* for 1891. For appointments of MOHs up to the end of 1873 see Fourth Annual Report of the Local Government Board [hereafter ARLGB], 1874–5, *PP* 1875, XXXI, 38–9.

[21] 'Return of the number of Medical Practitioners', op. cit.

[22] For the legislation see Sir John Simon, *English Sanitary Institutions Reviewed in their Course of Development and in Some of their Political and Social Relations* (1890).

[23] A. H. Williams, 'Public health', op. cit.

[24] G. Penrhyn Jones, 'Cholera in Wales', *Nat. Lib. Wales J.*, 10 (1957–80), 281–300.

[25] ARLGB for 1891–2, *PP* 1892, XXXVII, 107 for the expenditures quoted and for annual sums sanctioned in the period 1871–91 — the latter aggregating £50,043,590.

[26] These and other details are based on an analysis of the sums sanctioned in PRO MH13 (A. H. Williams, op. cit., *passim*).

[27] Seventh ARMOPC 1864, *PP* 1865, XXVII, 129 ff.

[28] Eighth ARMOPC 1865, *PP* 1866, XXXIII, 470 ff. Dr Simon's introduction to this Report (pp. 12 ff) is of great importance.

[29] Seventh ARMOPC 1864, op. cit., 129 ff.

[30] Royal Commission into the Housing of the Working Classes, First Report, *PP* 1884–5, XXX (4402), Qs. 12, 974–13, 119.

[31] Ibid., Qs. 12,982–4. For a detailed and well-informed discussion of housing in Merthyr Tydfil see also 'Labour and the poor. The mining and manufacturing districts of South Wales', Letter VI, *Morning Chronicle*, 8 April 1850.

[32] For conditions in Flint and the north Wales coalfield see Ieuan

Gwynedd Jones, 'Church building in Flintshire in the mid-nineteenth century', *Journal of the Flintshire Hist. Soc.*, XXXIX (1979–80). For Bethesda, see Geraint Davies, 'Bethesda: the growth and development of a slate quarrying town' (unpublished Ph.D. thesis (Aberystwyth), 1984).

[33] Eighth ARMOPC, op. cit., 476–7.

[34] For Cardiff see *Sixth Annual Report on the Sanitary Condition of Cardiff* by H. J. Paine, MRCS (Cardiff, 1859), and *Cardiff Local Board of Health Special Report on other Sanitary Works executed in the years 1856, 1857, 1858*, by T. Waring, CE, Surveyor to the Board (Cardiff, 1859); and for Swansea Tom Ridd, 'The development of municipal government in Swansea in the nineteenth century' (unpublished MA thesis (Swansea), 1955).

[35] Eighth ARMOPC, op. cit., 548. For an assessment of the quality and effectiveness of the local administration in Cardiff up to 1850, see D. C. James, 'The genesis of sanitary reform in Cardiff', *WHR*, 11 (1982). The series of papers by Peter H. Thomas on 'Medical men of Glamorgan' in Stewart Williams (ed.), *Glamorgan Historian*, vols. 1–9 (1963–73) and Vol. 11 (1975) contain useful references and information. See also Peter E. Jones, 'Bangor Local Board of Health 1850–83', *Trans. Cymm. Soc.*, 37 (1976) and R. D. Till, 'Public health and the community in Neath 1835–60', *WHR*, 5 (1971).

[36] See Henry Wren to the Merthyr LBH, dated from the constabulary office 7 May 1857, A. H. Williams, op. cit., 1015–1. On Merthyr in general see Tydfil Davies Jones, 'Poor law and public health administration in the area of Merthyr Tydfil Union, 1834–94' (unpublished MA thesis, University of Wales, 1961).

[37] See 'The Cotton Famine' and 'Dr Edward Smith's Report on the Nourishment of the Distressed Operatives' in Fifth ARMOPC (1862), *PP* 1853, XXV, 16–21 and 320–456: see especially the section on 'Economic and Nutritive Value of Food', ibid., 345 ff. Dr Smith subsequently published *The Present State of the Dietary Question* (1864) and *Practical Dietary for Families* (1865). In addition to the reports by Dr Hunter discussed below, there were reports on the environmental causes of excessive mortality by Dr Greenhow on ironstone and coal mining and iron manufacture in Abergavenny (i.e. the district which at that time included the industrial towns and villages east of Merthyr on the northern rim of the coalfield) and Merthyr Tydfil. See Third ARMOPC 1860, *PP* 1861, XVI, *passim* and Fourth Annual Report 1861, *PP* 1862, XXII, 160–6. A very illuminating report by a non-medical man is that by John Jenkins, an assistant commissioner for the Education Commission of 1861. See *Reports of the Assistant Commissioners on the State of Popular Education* 1861, vol. 2, 437–634. As he was a south Walian it is perhaps not surprising that he found the peasantry of north Wales inferior to those of south Wales!

[38] Sixth ARMOPC (1863), *PP* 1864, XXVIII, 223–4. Royston Lambert, *Sir John Simon 1816–1904 and English Social Administration* (London, 1963), 340.

[39] Fifth ARMOPC (1862), *PP* 1863, XXV, 345 ff.

[40] Royston Lambert, op. cit., p. 340; John Burnett, *Plenty and Want: A Social History of Diet in England from 1815 to the Present Day* (London, 1966), 121 ff.; Dereck J. Oddy and Dereck S. Miller (eds.), *The Making of the Modern British Diet* (London, 1976). On Wales see R. Elwyn Hughes ac Eleri Jones, 'Edward Smith a bwyd y Cymro', *Y Gwyddonydd*, XVIII, 2 (1980). I am grateful to Miss Sian Gruffydd for discussing some aspects of this topic with me.

[41] ARMOPC, op. cit., 232.

[42] Ibid., 269. For a discussion of the purely nutritional aspects see R. Elwyn Hughes, art. cit.

[43] Sixth ARMOPC (1863).

[44] David Jenkins, *The Agricultural Community in South Wales at the turn of the Twentieth Century* (Cardiff, 1971). On the farm labourers in general see the excellent chapter 6 in David W. Howell, *Land and People in Nineteenth Century Wales* (London, 1977).

[45] Sixth ARMOPC (1863), 277–8 for Dr Smith's definitions of these foods, and see S. Minwell Tibbott, 'Sucan and llymru in Wales', *Folk Life*, 12 (1974), 31–40.

[46]

	Carbonaceous Foods	Nitrogenous Foods
England	40,673 grams	1,594 grams
Wales	48,354 grams	2,031 grams
Scotland	48,980 grams	2,348 grams
Ireland	43,366 grams	2,434 grams

[47] *Report of the National Eisteddfod of Wales, held at Chester . . . 1866* (Carnarvon, 1866), 20.

[48] 'Conditions of nourishment', Sixth ARMOPC (1863), 15. Cf. the quotation from Thomas Wright in James H. Treble, *Urban Poverty in Britain 1830–1914* (London, 1979), 151, and William Farr's opinion that 'the want of food implies the want of everything else — except water — as firing, clothing, every convenience, every necessary of life, is abandoned at the imperious bidding of hunger. Hunger destroys a much higher proportion than is indicated by the registers.' First ARRG (1839), 106.

[49] 'Report on the death rate of the population in parts of south Wales', Seventh ARMOPC (1864), *PP* 1865, XXVI, Appendix 9s, 496 ff. See also David W. Howell, op. cit.

[50] Ibid., 498.

[51] 'Letter to the Registrar General on the causes of death by William Farr', 24th ARRG for 1861.

[52] Reports of the Local Government Inspectors on the working of the Public Health Act of 1872. No. 8 District. Report of Andrew Doyle. *PP* 1875, XL (134), 778.

[53] On cholera see Margaret Pelling, *Cholera, Fever and English Medicine 1825–1865* (Oxford, 1978); R. J. Morris, *Cholera 1832: The Social Response to an Epidemic* (London, 1976); Michael Durey, *The Return of the Plague: British Society and the Cholera 1831–2* (Dublin, 1979). For cholera in Wales see G. Penrhyn Jones, 'Cholera in Wales', *NLWJ*, 10 (3) (1957–8).

[54] Harold Carter, 'Transformations in the spatial structures of Welsh towns in the nineteenth century', *Ante* (1980), 175–200. See also Harold Carter and Sandra Wheatley, 'Some aspects of the spatial structure of two Glamorgan towns in the nineteenth century', *WHR*, 9 No. 1 (1978), 32–56, and the same authors' 'Residential patterns in mid-Victorian Aberystwyth', in Ieuan Gwynedd Jones (ed.), *Aberystwyth 1277–1977* (Llandysul, 1977), 46–84. For Cardiff see C. Roy Lewis, 'A stage in the development of the industrial town: a case study of Cardiff, 1845–75', *Trans. Inst. of British Geographers*, New Series, 4 No. 2 (1979), 129–52.

[55] *Traethawd ar Gynydd Darfodedigaeth ac Anhwylderau Corfforol Ereill a Rhai a Achosir trwy Ymwrthod a Chig-fwyd ac Ymborth Briodol.* Gan Robert Edwards (Asaph Gwaenydd), Caernarfon [d.d. (1870)]. Cf. also *Y Llysieu-Lyfr Teuluaidd . . .*, gan R. Price, Cwmllynfell, a E. Griffiths, Abertawy (Abertawy, 1849), t.6.

[56] 'Perthynas meistr a gweithiwr' gan Waldo (i.e. y Parchedig John Rowlands, Cwmafon), *Y Gwyliwr*, 12 Chwefror 1869.

[57] For example, 'Tŷ y gweithiwr a'i drefniad', gan Weithiwr, *Y Beirniad*, VIII (1867), tt. 124 ff; 'Cartrefi y gweithwyr', gan Gweithiwr, *Yr Haul*, XV (1871), t. 219; *Agoriad Anneddau (Ventilation of Dwellings); neu Eglurhad darluniadol rhwng anadlu Awyr Bur a Mwynhau Iechyd* [d.d. (1849)].

[58] For the details see Hywel Teifi Edwards, *Gŵyl Gwalia: Yr Eisteddfod Genedlaethol yn Oes Aur Victoria 1858–1868* (Llandysul, 1980), 53 ff., especially 63 and 67–8. B. L. Davies, *Hugh Owen 1804–1881* (Cardiff, 1977) and idem, 'Sir Hugh Owen and education in Wales', *Ante* (1971), 191–223 does not deal with this important aspect of Owen's work. Most perceptive is Gwyn A. Williams's essay, 'Hugh Owen', in *Pioneers of Welsh Education* (Swansea, n.d. [1962], 72–3).

[59] 'Tai Gweithwyr', gan y Parchedig J. Davies, Aberaman, *Y Beirniad*, IV (1863), tt. 197–203. See also 'Y Gweithiwr', *Y Cylchgrawn*, III (1853), t. 135 where the author declares that a clean and convenient house, a good wife, fresh air, plenty of light, pleasing furniture and a sufficiency of the necessities of life constitute the best 'board of health'.

[60] 'Cartref y gweithiwr', gan Owen Jones, Maentwrog, *Y Dysgedydd* (1875), t. 288. Cf. 'Trefniad cegin y gweithiwr', *Yr Ymofynydd* (1859), t. 60, where a shelf of books is included among the essential articles of

furniture for the living room. Cf. also 'Llenyddiaeth y gweithiwr', gan y Parchedig J. H. Evans, *Yr Eurgrawn Wesleyaidd*, LVII (1865), tt. 16–19. The most remarkable work of this kind was *Coginiaeth, a Threfniadaeth Deuluaidd: cyfaddas i anghenion Gwragedd Gweithwyr Cymru*, gan Mrs S. A. Edwards, Ty'n-y-Cefn, Corwen, traethawd Gwobrwyedig Eisteddfod Llundain, 1887 (Dinbych, 1889). Mrs Edwards budgeted for a total of £35 for furnishing and equipping a four-roomed house for a newly married couple, distributed as follows: £6.16s.10d. for bedroom 1, £5 for bedroom 2, £3.5s.10d. for the kitchen, £2.11s.5d. for the scullery, £3.18s.0d. for books, £3.6s.2d. for household linen and £5.11s.4½d. for food, £1.0s.4½d. for miscellaneous small items, leaving £3.10s.0d. to be invested in the savings bank. It is significant that about 13 per cent of the actual expenditure proposed should be on books.

[61] 'Ond pan yr edrychwn ar lenyddiaeth Gymraeg, gellir ei galw yn llenyddiaeth y gweithwyr. Y mae yn hollol yn nwylaw y gweithwyr a gweinidogion yr efengyl, a'r gweinidogion hynny, gan mwyaf, wedi bod unwaith yn weithwyr llengar. Nid yn anaml y mae ein hargraffwyr gweithiol, a rhai o alwedigaethau ereill, yn myned a'r prif wobrwyon am draethodau yn ein heisteddfodau. A phe buasai ein heisteddfodau wedi cyhoeddi eu cynyrchiadau, buasai gennym gyfoeth o ffrwyth meddwl y dosbarth gweithiol.' J. H. Evans, yn *Yr Eurgrawn Wesleyaidd*, LVII (1865), t. 19. ('But when we examine Welsh literature we can regard it as the literature of the workers. It is entirely in the hands of workers and ministers of the gospel, and those ministers, for the most part, having at one time been workers with a literary bent. Often our working printers, and men from some other occupations, take the chief prizes for essays in our eisteddfodau. And if our eisteddfodau had published their work we should now possess the riches of the mind of the working class.')

[62] Sir John Simon, *English Sanitary Institutions* (1890).

[63] Cf. Nigel Naunton Davies on his ancestor Revd Henry Davies, Capel y Cymer, Ystradyfodwg, in J. Cule (ed.), *Two and a Half Centuries of Medical Practice: A Welsh Medical Dynasty* (Llandysul, 1975).

[64] 'Y gwahanol driniaethau i adfer iechyd', gan y Parch E. Davies, *Yr Eurgrawn Wesleyaidd* (1866), t. 187. See also the same author's *Cynghorion a Chyfarwyddiadau, er Cymorth i Bobl Gyffredin Werthfawrogu, Cadw, ac Adfywio Iechyd* (Llanrwst, 1840).

[65] *Y Llysieu-lyfr Teuluaidd . . .*, gan R. Price, Cwmllynfell, ac E. Griffiths, Abertawy (Abertawy, 1849). For other titles see John Cule (ed.), *Wales and Medicine: A Source-list for Printed Books and Papers showing the History of Medicine in Relation to Wales and Welshmen* (Aberystwyth, 1980).

[66] 'Crach-feddygon' in *Brutusiana* (1855), t. 97.

[67] See A. H. Williams, op. cit.

[68] Roughly 250 urban districts in England and Wales were surveyed. See

Transactions of the Sanitary Institute of Great Britain, VIII (1886–7), p. 210, for 'An account of an investigation into the classes who administer the Public Health Act'. For a discussion of this investigation see Anthony S. Wohl, op. cit., chapter 7, especially pp. 167–8. See also E. P. Hennock, *Fit and Proper Persons* (London, 1973), and Derek Fraser, *Urban Politics in Victorian England: The Structure of Politics in Victorian Cities* (Leicester, 1976).

[69] A. H. Williams, op. cit., *sub* Bridgend and Llanelly.

[70] See Ieuan Gwynedd Jones, 'Merthyr Tydfil: the politics of survival', *Llafur,* 2 (1) (1976), and the same author's *Health, Wealth and Politics in Victorian Wales* (Swansea, 1979).

[71] A. H. Williams, op. cit., 1539 ff.

3 Language and Community in Nineteenth-century Wales

[1] *The Literature of Wales* reprinted from the *Eclectic Review*, edited by Thomas Price DD (London, n.d. (1851)). The article reaches this conclusion after arguing that though in point of power and expressiveness 'it transcends most of the old and all the modern tongues', the advance of English, which has been taking place since the conquest of Wales by the Saxons, is now so rapid and irresistible that its demise is inevitable. This is because English, 'being the emporium of the best works and latest discoveries in science and art, besides being the language of the laws and literature of the country, as well as the avenues to distinction, preferment, and power', places the monoglot Welshman under distinct disadvantages. Its continuance is an unmixed evil insofar as it preserves and fosters animosity and rancour among different races, perpetuates feud and national strife, hinders good feeling and friendly intercourse, and restricts social and commercial relations. 'The abolition of that language [Welsh] therefore, how repugnant soever to the feelings and long-cherished associations of Welshmen, would be to him the greatest boon.' The power, expressiveness and purity of the Welsh language had in previous centuries been precisely the most powerful argument for preserving and developing it.

[2] For further discussion of this and the following points see above pp. 105 ff.

[3] J. E. Southall, *The Welsh Language Census of 1901* (Newport, 1904). See also *Yr Iaith Gymraeg: 1785, 1885, 1985! neu, Tair Miliwn o Gymry Ddwy-ieithawg Mewn Can Mlynedd,* Cyfres o Lythyrau gan D. Isaac Davies, B.Sc. Gyda hanes sefydliad Cymdeithas yr Iaith Gymraeg (Dinbych, 1886). On this latter see J. Elwyn Hughes, *Arloeswr Dwyieithedd — Dan Isaac Davies* (Caerdydd, 1984).

[4] For Edwards see the entry in *The Oxford Companion to the Literature of Wales,* p. 164. Add to the books listed Geraint H. Jenkins, *Literature,*

Religion and Society in Wales 1660–1730 (Studies in Welsh History, Cardiff, 1978), and Glanmor Williams, *Grym Tafodau Tân* (Gomer, 1984) and the same author's *Religion, Language, and Nationality in Wales* (Cardiff, 1979), chapter 1.

⁵ *Yr Adolygydd* (The Critic), III (1850).

⁶ Erasmus Saunders, *A View of the State of Religion in the Diocese of St David's. About the beginning of the 18th Century. With some Account of the Causes of its Decay, together With Considerations of the Reasonableness of augmenting the Revenues of Impropriate Churches* (London, 1721. Reprinted Cardiff, 1949).

⁷ For the Methodist view of religious history see Glanmor Williams and Geraint Jenkins above, and the numerous histories published in the last century: for example, John Hughes, *Methodistiaeth Cymru: sef Hanes Blaenorol a Gwedd Bresennol y Methodistiaid Calfinaidd yn Nghymru; O Ddechreuad y Cyfundeb hyd y Flwyddyn 1850*, 3 cyfrol (Wrexham, 1851). See also Derec Llwyd Morgan, *Y Diwygiad Mawr* (Gomer, 1981), and the essay 'Hanes byr Ebeneser Niwbwrch (1785–1985)' in idem, *Pobl Pantycelyn* (Llandysul, 1986), pp. 131ff.

⁸ Dr Thomas Rees was the author of *History of Protestant Nonconformity in Wales, from its Rise in 1633 to the Present Time* (London, 1861 and 2nd edn. 1883). On Thomas Rees see the biography by his friend, the historian John Thomas, *Cofiant y Parch. T. Rees, DD, Gan John Thomas, DD, Liverpool* (Dolgellau, 1888).

⁹ For Parry (1833–1911) see his autobiography in *Cyfrol Goffa: Hanner Canrif o Lafur Gweinidogaethol Parch. Abel J. Parry, DD, Rhyl* (Colwyn Bay, n.d.), pp. 17–158.

¹⁰ *Y Traethodydd*, 1 (1846).

¹¹ There were pressure groups at work to ensure this. Among the most interesting and effective was the Association of Welsh Clergy in the West Riding of York under the leadership of the Revd Joseph Hughes (Carn Ingli), perpetual curate of Meltham, Yorks., who was its secretary. Its annual reports and petitions against the appointments of non-Welsh-speaking Englishmen to Welsh bishoprics and livings, which were given wide publicity in the Welsh periodicals, especially in *Yr Haul (The Sun)*, the Church of England monthly, are summarized by Sir Joseph Bradney in *Journal of the Welsh Bibliographical Society*, III (July 1929), pp. 243–53. There was a tremendous upsurge of interest in the question on the publication in 1850 of the official return 'Numbers of Services performed in each Church and Chapel in Wales', *PP*, 1850, XLII (226), which distinguished between English and Welsh services. The review in *The Principality*, 15 March 1850, ended, with typical bombast: 'There is no Welsh Church. There was; but there is not.'

¹² Quoted in T. Morgan, *Life and Works of Thomas Thomas DD* (Carmarthen, 1925), p. 96.

[13] When Parry applied for a place in Pontypool Baptist Academy in 1854 he was interviewed in English, and though he had only preached in Welsh and never prayed in English, he was nevertheless obliged to preach his acceptance sermon in English. As he explains in his autobiography, the only English he knew was Liverpool street English, and that would not do in Magor! It is not surprising that he broke down under the strain. See *Cyfrol Coffa.*, op. cit.

[14] For Kilsby Jones see 'Atgofion am Ysgol Neuaddlwyd' in Parch. Vyrnwy Morgan, *Kilsby Jones* (Wrexham, n.d.), pp. 352–73. The original essay is in *Y Traethodydd*, III (1848), pp. 373–84.

[15] *Y Traethodydd*, XIX (1864), pp. 384 ff.

[16] For these and further references see my 'The religious frontier in nineteenth century Wales', *Communities: Essays in the Social History of Victorian Wales* (Llandysul, 1987), pp. 211–36.

[17] Quoted in the *Monmouthshire Merlin*, 29 Nov. 1834. Cf. his speech at the Gwent and Dyfed Eisteddfod in Cardiff, August 4 1834, as reported in the *Cardiff and Merthyr Guardian*. See also *Seren Gomer*. Lady Charlotte Guest, who was present, refers to this 'most exciting' speech in her diaries: see the Earl of Bessborough (ed.), *Lady Charlotte Guest: Extracts from her Journal* (London, 1950), p. 33. This kind of sentiment, fanciful as it might now appear, was very common among supporters of the eisteddfodau organized by Cymreigyddion y Fenni, for whom see, in general, Prys Morgan, *The Eighteenth Century Renaissance* (Llandybïe, 1981), pp. 136 ff. In a speech later in the year Thomas Price is reported to have said about the Welsh language that it had withstood all oppositions and persecutions, and yet maintained its silken robes unblemished by any impurity: and that he was very confident that it was not impossible that a Welsh elegy would yet be sung on the passing of the English language. He added that he hoped to see this desirable consummation before his own death, but that this was unlikely! See Mair Elvet Thomas, *Afiaith yng Ngwent* (Caerdydd, 1978), p.6 for quotations from *Seren Gomer*. The whole of the chapter is relevant.

[18] E.G. Ravenstein, 'On the Celtic languages of the British Isles: a statistical survey', *Journal of the Royal Statistical Society*, 42 (1879).

[19] See *The Gwyneddion; or an Account of the Royal Denbigh Eisteddfod, held in September 1828* (Chester, 1830).

[20] Quoted in *Y Geninen*, 1 (1883), p. 19. It was D. Griffiths ('Clwydfardd') who deplored the readiness of certain of his contemporaries deliberately and as a matter of educational policy to sacrifice the Welsh language. See *Carnarvon and Denbigh Herald*, 5 February 1859.

[21] *Y Geninen*, op. cit., p. 20.

[22] *Y Geninen*, op. cit., p. 176.

[23] *Y Diwygiwr*, 1851, p. 64. This was a very common notion indeed. For example, a petition addressed to the 1847 Education Commissioners by the

Dissenters of Llanfair Caereinion attributed the fact that 'Offa's Dyke is like Sodoma [*sic*] and Galilee [*sic*] of the Gentiles in ungodliness and ignorance' to the failure of parents to teach Welsh to their children and as a consequence to deprive them of the privileges of Welsh Sunday Schools. *Reports of the Commissioners of Inquiry into the State of Education in Wales,* Part III, North Wales. Appendix H, p. 338. In his evidence to the Education Commission of 1861 Revd Michael D. Jones declared that in all rural places 'that have ceased to be Welsh by the adoption of the English language to the exclusion of the native idiom . . ., the people everywhere seem to become debased by losing their nationality. The English parts of Wales are notoriously backward.' (*Report of Commission (Duke of Newcastle) on the State of Popular Education in England,* Vol 6, Minutes of Evidence, p. 623). Thus also the opinion of a writer at the opposite end of the country: 'Language is the key to the character of a nation . . . Look for a moment at those districts where the Welsh language has been supplanted by the English tongue, the inhabitants have degenerated in body and mind, and . . . religion is a shadow of religion.' (*Star of Gwent,* 30 October 1869). Evidently it was believed that the Welsh language was a defence against lax morals even in English towns (*Y Traethodydd,* XVI (1860), p. 244). Quotations such as these could be multiplied to emphasize not the objective validity of the alleged social facts but the strength of the widespread and deeply held subjective belief.

[24] The quotation is from an address given by him to the English Presbytery of the Welsh Calvinistic Methodists as reported in the *Liverpool Courier,* 7 January 1892. See also *Athrofa Y Bala: ei Sylfaeniad a'i Hagoriad: yn cynnwys hefyd y pregethau a draddodwyd ar adeg ei hagoriad* (Bala, 1868), p. 13–16 for the paper by Revd John Parry, Classical Tutor at the College. He said [my translation] that our [i.e. the Welsh Calvinistic Methodists'] relations with England are growing ever closer, so much so that we can no more escape the influence of her literature and theology than we can her customs, her commerce and her language. Her literature is growing increasingly infidel [*anffyddiog*], and her theology increasingly under the influence of tradition on the one hand and of rationalism on the other. What a mercy that it is not thus in Wales!

[25] *Y Geninen,* Hydref 1896. 'Y pwlpud a sefyllfa crefydd yng Nghymru'.

[26] Ibid. (1883), p. 20.

[27] *Gwyneddion,* op. cit., pp. 14–15.

[28] *Cofiant y Parchedig John Jones, Talsarn,* gan Owen Thomas (Wrexham, n.d. (1874)), vol 2, p. 721–3.

[29] T.M. Jones ('Gwenallt'), *Llenyddiaeth Fy Ngwlad: Sef Hanes y Newyddiadur a'r Cylchgrawn Cymreig* (Treffynnon, 1893), pp. 64–5.

[30] The quotations are from an essay 'Ar Deilyngdod y Gweithiwr, ynghyd a'r gofal a ddylai fod ganddo am dano ei hun' (The Merits of the Worker,

with the care for himself that he should have) by Dafydd Howel ('Llawdden'), *Yr Haul*, 1853, pp. 94–7, 133–5, 165–8. Llawdden (1803–1903), son of a Welsh Calvinistic preacher, took holy orders in 1855 and ended up as Dean of St Asaph. He was a poet, an evangelical preacher, popular among Nonconformists, a non-political nationalist, a keen eisteddfodwr, and renowned for his efforts 'to discipline the taste, direct the culture, and elevate the imagination of his countrymen'. Clearly, he started out on this crusade at an unusually early age and with a set of ideas that scarcely changed thereafter. T.R. Roberts, *Eminent Welshmen 1* (Cardiff and Merthyr, 1908), p. 170–1.

[31] The Revd John Griffith, Rector of Merthyr and previously Vicar of Aberdare, could see this happening, and deplored it. He wrote, 'It is a fearful evil to think that rich and poor should each have a distinct language. My earnest desire is to see the Welsh-speaking classes raised in everything above their present level' (*Cardiff and Merthyr Guardian*, 21 April 1849: also ibid., 9 March 1850). These articles appeared in the aftermath of the publication of the *Reports of the Commissioners of Inquiry into the State of Education in Wales* in 1848, for which see above, p. 147.

[32] Fabian Tract No. 1, *Why are the Many Poor?* (1884) was translated under the title *Paham mae y Lluaws yn Dlawd?* (?1891) as Tract No. 38. Note, 'Lluaws' also means 'majority'. Tract 78, *Socialism and the Teaching of Christ* by the Revd John Clifford (1898) appeared as Tract No. 87, *Sosialaeth a Dysgeidiaeth Crist* (June 1899).

[33] Jonathan Parry informs me that the following SDF tracts were translated: *The Gospel of Discontent* (1892), *An Address to Workers on Strike* (1898) and *What is the Use of a Vote: What Social Democrats Want* (1892).

4 Margam, Pen-hydd and Brombil

[1] This is the text of a lecture delivered at the Glamorgan History Society's Autumn Day School held on 11 November 1989.

[2] W. De Gray Birch, *A History of Margam Abbey* (1897); Frederic Evans, *'Tir Iarll' (the Earl's Land, comprising the Ancient Parishes of Llangynwyd, Bettws, Margam, and Kenfig* (Cardiff, 1912); James O'Brien, *Old Afan and Margam* (Aberavon, 1926); A. Leslie Evans, *The Story of Kenfig* (Port Talbot, 1960); A. Leslie Evans, *The Story of Taibach and District* (2nd edn., Port Talbot, 1982); Neville Granville, *Cefn Cribwr: Chronicle of a Village* (Barry, 1980); Hilary Thomas, 'Margam estate management, 1765–1860', *Glamorgan Historian, VI* (1969), 13–27.

[3] This is based on John Bateman, *The Great Landowners of Great Britain and Ireland* (4th edn., 1883, reprinted Leicester, 1971), for which see Brian Ll. James, 'The great landowners of Wales in 1873', *National Library of*

Wales Journal, XIV (1966), 301–20, and David W. Howell, *Land and People in Nineteenth-century Wales* (London, 1977), pp. 20ff.

⁴ See 'A survey and valuation of estates of Margam in the County of Glamorgan belonging to C.R.M. Talbot, surveyed by order of the trustees . . . 1814', Glamorgan Record Office D/D Ma/E/1.

⁵ On the beauty of the Margam woods, see Dafydd Morgannwg, *Hanes Morganwg* (Aberdâr, 1874), *sub* Margam.

⁶ For industrialization in general, see *Glamorgan County History V: Industrial Glamorgan* (Cardiff, 1980); A. Leslie Evans, *Taibach*; and Granville, *Cefn Cribwr.*

⁷ There are various estimates. I have relied upon W.D. Rubinstein, *Men of Property: The Very Wealthy in Britain since the Industrial Revolution* (London, 1981), p. 252. That the estate was in bad order in 1890 was the opinion of Mr Rees Thomas, Hall Farm, Pyle, who gave evidence on behalf of the Margam tenants before the Welsh Land Commission; see Royal Commission on Land in Wales and Monmouthshire, Minutes of Evidence, Vol. 2, Qs 26,136–26,180, esp. Qs 26,163–4.

⁸ See Poll and Canvass Books for the 1820 Glamorgan Election, NLW, Penrice and Margam MS 10,232, Check and Canvass Book, *sub* Havod y Porth.

⁹ On the railway interest of Talbot, see, in general, *GCH*, V, and E.T. MacDermot, *History of the Great Western Railway,* vol. 1 (1927).

¹⁰ Anthony Trollope, *Phineas Redux* (World's Classics ed.), vol. 1, p. 214.

¹¹ This according to John Vivian Hughes, *The Wealthiest Commoner* (Port Talbot, 1978). But see John Davies, *Cardiff and the Marquesses of Bute* (Cardiff, 1981) for the record of the second Marquess as Lord Lieutenant.

¹² On this election, see Ieuan Gwynedd Jones, *Communities: Essays in the Social History of Victorian Wales* (Llandysul, 1987), pp. 295–6.

¹³ See J. Vincent and M. Stenton (eds.) *McCalmont's Parliamentary Poll Book of All Elections, 1832–1918* (Brighton, 1971), pp. 118–19, and M. Stenton (ed.), *Who's Who of British Members of Parliament,* vol. 1 (1976), p. 371.

¹⁴ *Hanes Bywyd Siencyn Penhydd neu Mr Jenkin Thomas* (3ydd arg., 1860), t.1. Extracts from this and the same author's *George Heycock a'i Amserau* (1867) are to be found in Henry Lewis (gol.), *Morgannwg Matthews Ewenni* (Caerdydd, 1953). See also J.J. Morgan, *Cofiant Edward Matthews, Ewenni* (Wrecsam, 1922). For his other writings, see W. Llywel Morgan (gol.), *Gweithiau y Diweddar Barch. Edward Matthews, Ewenni* (Dolgellau, 1911). There is a useful essay in Ioan Williams, *Capel a Chomin: Astudiaeth o Ffugchwedlau Pedwar Llenor Fictoraidd* (Caerdydd, 1989).

¹⁵ In 1814 these were Penhydd Waelod, 72 acres and £26.4s.4d annual value; Penhydd Issa 138 a. and £37.1s.8d.; Penhydd Genol 1353 a. and

£177.14s.7d. A poll book of 1820 names Pennydd Waelod, Bwlch Pennydd, Pennydd Ganol and Pennydd Issa. NLW Penrice and Margam MS 10, 232.

[16] The size of farms in 1814 was as follows: under 50 acres — 51; 51 to 100 — 24; 101 to 150 — 9; 151 to 200 — 6; 201 to 250 — 5; 251 to 300 — 3; 301 to 350 — 4; 351 to 400 — 2; 401 to 450 — 1; 451 to 500 — 1; 501 to 600 — 0; over 600 — 2. The whole estate aggregated 16,786 acres and an annual value of £7,047.

[17] Margam Moors was valued at £1,215. See 'Survey and valuation of Margam'. It was the policy of the estate to let all tenants have one acre on the Moors for hay; see Welsh Land Commission, op. cit., Q.25,985 (evidence of Mr Knox, the agent).

[18] This is based on an analysis of the Enumerators' Returns, Census of 1851, PRO HO 107/22462, comparing Brombil, Blaen Mallog, Tonmawr, Lôn Tan Groes and dwellings to the west of the park with Morfa Mawr village, Groeswen, Constant and Taibach.

[19] *Siencyn Penhydd*, pp. 2–4.

[20] For Griffith Llewellyn the agent, see Hilary Thomas, art. cit. Griffith Llewellyn held a number of farms in the Brombil valley. See 'Survey and valuation.'

[21] Welsh Land Commission, op. cit., Q.24, 776.

[22] The diet of small farmers and their indoor labourers consisted of, for breakfast, bread and butter or cheese, tea; for dinner, bacon and vegetables, or broth with vegetables. On Sundays perhaps poultry or fresh meat. For supper, bread and cheese or butter, tea. As the old saying has it, 'un enllyn ynghyd'.

[23] Welsh Land Commission, op. cit., Qs 24, 777, 24, 847, 24, 848.

[24] On these recreations, see *Siencyn Penhydd* (also in Henry Lewis, op. cit.); *Trans. Aberafan and Margam Historical Society*, 4 (1930), pp. 2ff; J. O'Brien, op. cit. There is an excellent study of sport in society by Gareth Williams in *GCH*, VI: *Glamorgan Society, 1780–1980* (Cardiff, 1988), ch.XVIII.

[25] Welsh Land Commission, op. cit., Q.26, 170, for the agent's optimistic description.

[26] For the grange economy, see F. G. Cowley, *The Monastic Orders in South Wales, 1066–1349* (Cardiff, 1977), pp. 76ff.

[27] Thomas Gray, 'Notes on the granges of Margam Abbey', *Journal of the British Archaeological Society* (December 1903), reprinted as a pamphlet.

[28] *Trans. Aberafan and Margam Historical Society*, III (1929).

[29] Gray, op. cit.

[30] *Trans. Aberafan and Margam Historical Society*, I (1924), p. 39 and III (1929), p. 81.

[31] See the delightful description of the situation by W.J. Llewellyn in ibid., IV (1930), p. 25.

[32] For this and other churches in the district, see Ieuan Gwynedd Jones and David Williams (eds.), *The Religious Census of 1851: A Calendar of the Returns Relating to Wales*, vol. 1: *South Wales* (Cardiff, 1976). Also, NLW, Church in Wales cited below.

[33] Llangan where the deeply admired Revd David Jones officiated was the favoured church. See John Hughes, *Methodistiaeth Cymru,* cyfrol III (Wrexham, 1854), t.57. But the whole chapter, after due allowance for the author's fictive propensities, is relevant to my argument.

[34] Church in Wales, LL/C/153X. For the Church Building Society grant of £500 (a massive grant under the circumstances) see Lambeth Palace Library, ICBS M Box 2 (1825–7), and ICBS Annual Report for 1826, p. 123.

[35] See *Religious Census*, p. 221. Talbot gave £500 invested in 4% consols to augment the income of the joint benefice. See LL/C/153X.

[36] For Aberafan with Baglan, see NLW, Church in Wales LL/SR/1; for St Catherine's Baglan (consecration dated 7 March 1882), see LL/C/18; for consecration of Michaelstone-super-Avon dated 10 June 1856, see LL/C/168X, and for the restoration and rebuilding of Llangynwyd in consequence of its ruinous and dilapidated condition, see LL/F416, dated 9 July 1891.

[37] Evans, *Taibach.*

[38] For the wider background consult *GCH*, V. There is much interesting detail in Evans, *Taibach.*

[39]

TABLE

The Population of Margam and District, 1801–1891

Parish	1801	1811	1821	1831	1841	1851	1861	1871	1881	1891
Tythegston	283	324	334	404	794	1152	1678	1490	1638	1578
Pyle	406	443	444	475	803	991	1192	883	938	880
Kenfig	249	242	222	276	297	285	278	270	264	221
Margam	1809	1803	2047	2902	3526	4747	5528	5205	5708	6274
Llangynwyd	403	436	485	826	1817	2565	2187	2154	2444	—
Aberafan	275	321	365	572	1290	2380	2916	3396	4681	6086
Lower Michaelstone	137	101	207	793	2132	5421	5322	5318	4924	5280
Upper Michaelstone	95	131	188	257	399	653	861	602	569	829

Source: Census Reports

[40] Evans, *Taibach*.

[41] There is a list of explosions in Dafydd Morganwg, op. cit., tt. 63–4; also R. Morgan, 'Taibach', t.37. Morfa colliery was notorious for its phantoms, ghost trains drawn by ghastly white horses and lights reminiscent of 'cannwyll corff' (corpse candle); see 'Local mining superstitions', *Trans. Aberafan and Margam Historical Society*, IV (1930), p. 74. See also Gareth Phillips, 'Paternalism on trial', *Morgannwg*, XXXI (1987), pp. 46–65.

[42] *Siencyn Penhydd*, t.28.

[43] This is discussed in relation to Swansea by the present author in his essay 'The making of an industrial community', in Glanmor Williams (ed.), *Swansea: An Illustrated History* (Swansea, 1990). See also Harold Carter on the same phenomenon in relation to the development of Neath, in 'Transformation in the spatial structures of Welsh towns in the nineteenth century'. *Trans. Cymmrodorion*, 1980, pp. 175–200.

[44] *Parliamentary Papers*, 1854 LXIII (360)

[45] Morgan, 'Taibach', tt. 34 and 53; Evans, *Taibach*, pp. 60ff.

[46] Built on land given by Talbot in 1840; Morgan, 'Taibach', t.50. This author does not mention the truck shops, for which see Evans, *Taibach*, p.66.

[47] PRO MH13, Aberavon 1854–69. This correspondence between the local authority and the General Board of Health has been transcribed by A.H. Williams under the title 'Public Health in Mid-Victorian Wales' (1983). Copies of this unpublished work can be consulted in the libraries of the University Colleges.

[48] Morgan, 'Taibach', t.48.

[49] MH 13.

[50] This is based on an analysis of the Enumerators' Returns, Census of 1861.

[51] Morgan, 'Taibach', tt.36–7.

[52] Enumerators' Returns, 1861.

[53] Morgan, 'Taibach', t.36.

[54] *Gemau Margam*, t.62; Benjamin Griffiths (Index), *Cenedlyddiaeth* (Caerdydd, 1882).

5 1848 and 1868: 'Brad y Llyfrau Gleision' and Welsh Politics

[1] I have relied, for the most part, on L.J. Williams, *Digest of Welsh Historical Statistics* (Cardiff: Welsh Office, 1985), Vol. 1, Table 13, Population of Towns.

[2] Ibid., Table 11, Birth Rates, and Table 14, Migration.

[3] Census Reports. See also L.J. Williams, op. cit., Table 3, Age and Marital Condition.

[4] *Sermon Preached before the SPCK* (Cardiff, 1830).

[5] See J. Stuart Maclure (ed.), *Educational Documents: England and*

Wales 1816–1967 (2nd edn., London, 1968) prints useful extracts from some of the leading sources mentioned in this paper. Leslie Wynne Evans makes extensive use of Parliamentary Papers in his *Education in Industrial Wales 1700–1900* (Cardiff, 1971). Sheila M. Owen-Jones, 'Religious influence and educational progress', *Welsh History Review [WHR]*, 13 No. 1 (June 1986), pp. 72–86, makes excellent use of National Society Reports as well as Parliamentary Papers, and H.G. Williams, 'Longueville Jones and Welsh education: the neglected case of a Victorian HMI', *WHR*, 15 No. 3 (June 1991), pp. 416–42 is an important study of the whole subject. E.G. West, *Education and the Industrial Revolution* (London, 1975) is a stimulating study of the general field, W.A.C. Stewart and W.P. McCann, *The Educational Innovators 1750–1880* (London, 1967) and Harold Silver, *The Concept of Popular Education* (London, 1965) I have found very valuable. The best introduction to the subject is Gillian Sutherland, *Elementary Education in the Nineteenth Century* (Historical Association, 1971).

⁶ *Census of Great Britain, 1851. Education. England and Wales. Report and Tables* (London: HMSO, 1854). The civil servant responsible for the Census (under the Registrar-General) was Horace Mann, who was also responsible for the Religious Census. See his 'The resources of popular education in England and Wales: present and future', *Transactions of the Royal Statistical Society* (March 1862), pp. 50–71.

⁷ For an official view as to its reliability see the evidence of R.R.W. Lingen, Secretary of the Committee of Council of Education before the Newcastle Commission, *PP*, 1861, XXI, Part VI, Minutes of Evidence, Q.200.

⁸ This is discussed below, pp. 113–15.

⁹ For Kay-Shuttleworth see Frank Smith, *The Life and Work of Sir James Kay-Shuttleworth* (London, 1923); B.C. Bloomfield (ed.), 'The autobiography of Sir James Kay-Shuttleworth', in *Education Library Bulletin*, Supplement 7; and Robert Johnson, 'Educational policy and social control in early Victorian England', *Past and Present*, 49 (Nov. 1970), pp. 100ff. and Robert Colls, ' "Oh happy English children!" Coal, class and education in the north east', ibid., 73 (Nov. 1976), pp. 74–99.

¹⁰For biographical notes on the Inspectors see J.E. Dunford, 'Biographical details of HM Inspectors of Schools appointed before 1870', *History of Education Society Bulletin*, No. 28 (Autumn 1981), pp. 8–23. For Hugh Seymour Tremenheere, see E.L. and O.P. Edwards (eds.), *I Was There: The Memoirs of H.J. Tremenheere* (Eton, 1965).

¹¹For Allen, see Dunford, op. cit., and *DNB*. He was the son of the Revd D. Bird Allen, Rector of Burton-in-Rhos, Pembs.: his brother was Vicar of Castlemartin and, later, Dean of St David's Cathedral. John Allen, like his brother, was educated at Westminster and Trinity College, Cambridge: he was examining chaplain to the Bishop of Chichester. He took an active part

in church expansion: for his views on the rebuilding of one church see the essay on the rebuilding of Llanrhystyd Church in Ieuan Gwynedd Jones, *Communities: Essays in the Social History of Victorian Wales* (Llandysul, 1987), pp. 58–9.

[12] For Fletcher see Dunford, op. cit., and *DNB*.

[13] For Revd Harry Longueville Jones see Dunford, op. cit., and *DWB*. Also H.G. Williams, 'Longueville Jones and Welsh education: the neglected case of a Victorian HMI', *WHR*, 15 (June 1991), p. 416.

[14] For Henry Mayhew, author of *London Labour and the London Poor* (reprinted New York, 4 vols., 1968), see E.P. Thompson and Eileen Yeo (eds.), *The Unknown Mayhew* (London, 1971). For the essays of the *Morning Chronicle* correspondents see P.E. Razzell and R.W. Wainwright (eds.), *Selections from the Morning Chronicle: The Victorian Working Class* (London, 1971). The Letters on Wales are to be found in their entirety in J. Ginswick, *Labour and the Poor in England and Wales 1849–1851. Vol. 3: The Mining and Manufacturing Districts of South Wales and North Wales* (London, 1983).

[15] See G.A.F. Best, *Temporal Pillars: Queen Anne's Bounty, the Ecclesiastical Commissioners, and the Church of England* (Cambridge, 1964), and Owen Chadwick, *The Victorian Church*, Part 1 (2nd. edn., London, 1970). I have dealt with some of the Welsh background and evidence in my *Explorations and Explanations: Essays in the Social History of Victorian Wales* (Llandysul, 1981), chs. 1 and 2, and in *Communities*, op. cit., chs. 1–5. See also E.T. Davies, *Religion in the Industrial Revolution in South Wales* (Cardiff, 1965).

[16] D.J.V. Jones, *Chartism and the Chartists* (London, 1971), p. 39.

[17] On this see C. Birchenough, *History of Elementary Education in England and Wales* (London, 1938), and Chadwick, op. cit., ch. V. For the Voluntaryist case see Clyde Binfield, *So Down to Prayers* (London, 1977), pp. 80 ff.; B.L. Manning, *The Protestant Dissenting Deputies* (Cambridge, 1952); J. Murphy, *State, Church and Schools in Britain 1800–1900* (London, 1971). There are key documents in David M. Thompson (ed.), *Nonconformity in the Nineteenth Century* (London, 1972).

[18] *Minutes of the Committee of Council on Education* (hereafter *Minutes*) 1839–40. The *Minutes* were Parliamentary Papers but were also published in separate volumes annually.

[19] Sir Thomas Phillips, *Wales: The Language, Social Condition, Moral Character, and Religious Opinions of the People, considered in their relation to Education* (London, 1849), p. 50.

[20] Hansard, 3rd series XLIX, 119, 2 August 1839.

[21] *Minutes* 1839–40, p. 16, and Appendix II, p. 154 'On the state of elementary education in the mining districts of south Wales'.

[22] This was later published as a pamphlet *The Population of Pontypool and the Parish of Trevethin* (London, 1840).

[23] *Minutes* 1839–40, Appendix II, op. cit., pp. 154ff.

[24] See the present author's essay 'Ecclesiastical economy: aspects of church building in Victorian Wales', R.R. Davies *et al.*, *Welsh Society and Nationhood: Historical Essays Presented to Glanmor Williams* (Cardiff, 1984), pp. 216–31.

[25] For the 'Circular to Twenty-nine Mining proprietors in Monmouth', dated 25 March 1840 see *Minutes* 1840–1, p. 15.

[26] 'Memorial of Sir Thomas Phillips', dated 12 November 1840, ibid., p. 16.

[27] Ibid., p. 16–17.

[28] *Minutes* 1846, pp. 422 ff.

[29] See Dunford, op. cit.

[30] *Minutes* 1845, II, p. 199.

[31] Hansard, 3rd Series, LXXXVI, 869, 19 May 1846.

[32] 'Education in the mining and manufacturing district of south Staffordshire. Report to the Council of the Statistical Society by its Secretaries', *Journal of the Statistical Society of London*, X (1847), p. 237. See also the massive report by Joseph Fletcher, 'The Moral and Educational State of England and Wales', ibid., Sept. 1847, pp. 193 ff.

[33] *Minutes* 1847, p. 93.

[34] Ibid., p. 94.

[35] *Minutes* 1839–40, Appendix 11.1.

[36] 'First report . . . Employment of Children . . in Mines and manufactories', *PP*, 1842, XV, pp. 353–6.

[37] Mitchell's report on the West Midlands District, *Minutes* 1848/49/50 (1850), p. 313.

[38] 'Addysg yng Nghymru', reprinted in *Traethodau Llenyddol*, p. 409.

[39] *Minutes* 1848–9, p. 313.

[40] *Minutes* 1847, p. 60.

[41] *Journal Stat. Society*, op. cit., (1847). For the purposes of his study Fletcher divided England and Wales into eight geographical districts distinguished by their predominating industries. Each of these he further divided into two portions according to the least and most instruction available in each. The sixth group consisted of the *'agricultural and mining districts chiefly occupied by a Celtic population in the western parts of South Britain'*, [my italics] i.e. Cornwall, Monmouth, south Wales and north Wales. He noted that, except for Cornwall, most of this district was 'receiving little more than Sunday school instruction in the Bible, in Welsh, owing to the obstacle of language'. He compared this with the northern agricultural/mining district which it closely resembled, except that *'the latter are chiefly of Scandinavian descent* [my italics]. Their dialects are often

far from being intelligible to a cultivated ear, but contain most of the Saxon roots of the language, and therefore offer comparatively little obstacle to the progress of instruction, especially in reading the authorized version of the Scriptures, which adheres as much as possible to these roots.' Racial or ethnographic explanations of social differences were very influential at this time.

[42] *Minutes* 1845, i, p. 81.

[43] Ibid., p. 93.

[44] Allen reported that children in Norwich were known by numbers hung around the neck or worn on the forehead. *Minutes* 1845, I, p. 106.

[45] Ibid., p. 93. On the myth of rural innocence see David J. V. Jones, *Rebecca's Children: A Study of Rural Society, Crime and Protest* (Oxford, 1989).

[46] *Reports of Commissioner (Mr Tremenheere) on the Operation of the Mines Act and on the State of the Mining Population in England, Scotland and Wales, 1844–49*, Report for 1846, pp. 30–49. These reports are exhaustively studied from different points of view in Leslie Wynne Evans, op. cit., David J.V. Jones, *The Last Rising* (Oxford, 1985), Ivor Wilks, *South Wales and the Rising of 1839* (London, 1985), and especially by Sian Rhiannon Williams, 'Rhai agweddau cymdeithasol ar hanes yr iaeth Gymraeg yn ardal ddiwydiannol Sir Fynwy yn y bedwaredd ganrif ar bymtheg' (unpublished Ph.D. dissertation, University of Wales (Aberystwyth) 1985).

[47] Report for 1846, op. cit.

[48] Hansard, 3rd Series, LXXXIV, pp. 845–60, 10 March 1846. The remainder of the sitting was spent debating a motion by T.S. Duncombe, the Radical member for Finsbury, for the prerogative of mercy to be extended to Williams, Frost and Jones, the Chartists who had been condemned for their part in the Newport Rising in 1839.

[49] Hansard, 3rd Series, LXXXVI, 869, 19 May 1846.

[50] *Yr Haul*, 1840, tt. 347–9.

[51] Hansard, 3rd Series, LXXXIV, 845–59, 10 March 1846.

[52] Ibid., pp. 860–4. The Irish system of national education was supported by government grants and regulated by a Board which made it possible for children of parents of all religious persuasions to receive secular education together, religious instruction being provided on school premises by the denominations before or after ordinary school. The member mainly responsible for this scheme, Thomas Wyse (Lib. Waterford City), spoke to the effect that the Irish experience demonstrated 'the great improvement which of late years had taken place in the tastes, habits and feelings of the Irish people', and much of this he attributed to 'the organized system which had recently been established and which might be termed . . . "national" '. For details of the system see James Murphy, op. cit.

[53] Compare *Y Dysgedydd*, 1846, pp. 122–30. The *Drysorfa* was of the opposite opinion: 'O Newyddion Gwladol ni roddais ond ychydig iawn:

canys yr wyf yn gryf o'r farn fod y cyfryw bethau yn iselad mawr i'r Cyhoeddiad' (Of political news I have given but little: for I am strongly of the opinion that such matters greatly debase the publication) (the editor's (Revd John Roberts of Liverpool) introduction to the 1846 volume, p. iv). More typical was the Revd David Rees, editor of the Independent *Y Diwygiwr*, who announced his intention of expanding rather than reducing his coverage of political and parliamentary affairs: *Y Diwygiwr*, XII (1847), p. vi.

[54] *Report of the Commission of Inquiry into the State of Education in Wales . . . In Three Parts. Part I, Carmarthen, Glamorgan and Pembroke. Part II, Brecknock, Cardigan, Radnor and Monmouth. Part III, North Wales* (London, 1847).

[55] *Report*, Part II, p. 1 and p. 269.

[56] For Thomas Thomas (1805–81) see *DWB* and T. Morgan, *Life and Work of T. Thomas, DD* (Carmarthen, 1925) which is a slight work but useful for its quotations from contemporary sources relating to this archetypal Welsh Nonconformist. For Ieuan Gwynedd, see *DWB sub* Evan Jones. Some of his writings on education are reprinted in Brinley Rees, *Ieuan Gwynedd: Detholiad o'i Ryddiaeth* (Caerdydd, 1957). The meetings were reported in the monthlies and in the local weekly newspapers. The two Resolutions passed at the Pontypool meeting are quoted in Morgan, op. cit., pp. 83–4.

[57] For Symons's negotiations see Report, Part 2, p. 272.

[58] For example, *Y Diwygiwr*, Editor's Address for 1847, esp. p. vi.

[59] E.g. *Seren Gomer*, 1846, t. 358.

[60] Ibid.

[61] *Minutes* 1847–8, p. xvi.

[62] See *Minutes* 1847–8, p. xvi, 'Representations agreed to at a meeting of the Welsh Education Commmittee of the National Society on 6 May 1848 . . . and communicated to the Lord President on 12 May by a deputation consisting of Bishops of St Davids and St Asaph and Sir Thomas Phillips.' Ibid., p. xxvii, 'Memorandum from the Calvinistic Methodists of Brecon', and p. xix, 'Memorandum from the Friends of Civil and Religious Liberty in the town of Carmarthen', dated 17 May 1848. The Brecon memorandum, like the others, pleaded for an adaptation of the Minute to suit the special circumstances of Wales 'and thereby enable the ancient and loyal race of the Cymry to maintain their rightful position among the nations'. See also the Bishop of St David's *Charge*, 1848.

[63] *Y Drysorfa*, Mawrth 1833, tt. 77–8, and the comment t. 182.

[64] For a fuller discussion see, *Explorations and Explanations*, op. cit., p. 217.

[65] Census of Great Britain: Education. Report and Tables (1854); Table R, p. clxxxvi. The total is made up as follows: north Wales 1,389 Sunday schools with 132,967 scholars, and south Wales 1,382 schools and 136,411

scholars. Note: unlike those for England, which refer to registration counties, the figures for Wales relate to these two divisions of the country and not to individual counties.

[66] Ibid., Table 23, p. lxxvi.

[67] Ibid., Table 18, p. lvi.

[68] Ibid., Table 22, p. lxx.

[69] *Y Traethodydd* (The Expositor) 1845. The essay was by Revd John Hughes, Liverpool, and henceforth a regular contributor to the quarterly. He was the author of *Methodistiaeth Cymru* (3 vols., Wrecsam, 1851–6).

[70] *Seren Gomer*, Ebrill 1848, tt. 110–12. Cf. also ibid., Ebrill 1847, pp. 110–12. This was in the form of an Address, drawn up at the request of a general meeting of Nonconformists in Llandeilo, and sent to the editors of all periodicals. It should be remarked that scarcely a month went by without articles on, or other references to, education in *Seren Gomer*. This was generally the case with most of the periodicals. Education was a major concern and not something awakened by the government.

[71] *Bywyd a Llythyrau y diweddar Barch. Lewis Edwards, DD*, gan Thomas Charles Edwards (Liverpool, 1901), t. 207.

[72] *Charge. Third Visitation 1848* (London, 1848), p. 53. He said that 'too much stress is commonly laid on religious knowledge and devotional excitement in comparison with moral habits and discipline'. This rather superior attitude was common among Anglicans. In this connection it is interesting to note that Bishop Thirlwall was the patron of the project to bring out a translation of *Chamber's Information for the People*. Volume 1 was published under the title, *Addysg Chambers i'r Bobl. Gan Ebenezer Thomas 'Eben Fardd'* (Pwllheli, 1849). See Charles Ashton, *Hanes Llenyddiaeth Gymreig* (Liverpool, 1908), p. 588, and T.M. Jones ('Gwenallt'), *Llenyddiaeth fy Ngwlad* (Treffynnon, 1893), pp. 64–5.

[73] Alfred Ollivant, *Charge. Primary Visitation* (London, 1850), p. 26.

[74] Report, Part III, pp. 337–57.

[75] Report, Part I, Appendix, p. 236.

[76] Ibid., Part II, p. 52.

[77] Ibid., Part II, pp. 50–5 for Symons's views on Sunday schools.

[78] Ibid., Part I, pp. 2–3.

[79] Ibid., Part II, pp. 310–11.

[80] Ibid., Part I, p. 3.

[81] Ibid., Part III, pp. 59–60 and Appendix pp. 322–30.

[82] For James Rhys Jones see *Kilsby Jones* gan y Parch. Vyrnwy Morgan (Wrexham, n.d.), an adulatory biography typical of its period but which contains many of Kilsby's lectures and writings. For a devastatingly critical view see E.G. Millward, 'Kilsby Jones, Darwin a Rhagluniaeth' in *Cenedl o Bobl Ddewrion: Agweddau ar Lenyddiaeth Oes Victoria* (Llandysul, 1991), tt. 158–65. See Daniel Evans, *Life and Works of William Williams MP*

(Llandysul, 1939), p. 202, which states categorically that Kilsby was the translator but without divulging the source for this information.

[83] For John Jones ('Tegid') see *DWB*, and Bedwyr Lewis Jones, 'Yr offeiriad llengar', in Dyfnallt Morgan (gol.), *Gwŷr Llen y Bedwaredd Ganrif ar Bymtheg* (Llandybïe, 1968). See also the entry in Meic Stephens (ed.), *The Oxford Companion to the Literature of Wales* (Cardiff, 1986), pp. 310–11.

[84] *Adroddiadau Dirprwywyr i Gyflwr Addysg yn Nghymru* (Llundain, 1848), t. iii and Reports, Part I, p. 41.

[85] *Adroddiadau*, 'Rhagymadrodd y Cyfieithydd'.

[86] Ibid., t. ii.

[87] Ibid., tt. ix–xi.

[88] Prys Morgan, 'Dyro olwg ar dy eiriau', *Taliesin*, 70 (1990), tt. 38–45.

[89] R. Elwyn Hughes, *Nid am Un Harddwch Iaith: Rhyddiaith Gwyddoniaeth yn y Bedwaredd Ganrif ar Bymtheg* (Caerdydd, 1991).

[90] Lewis Edwards, 'Ysgolion ieithyddol i'r Cymry', *Traethodau Llenyddol*, t. 23.

[91] Report, Part I, p. 7, and Appendix, p. 285, for the evidence of Revd Archer Evans, Carmarthen.

[92] Report, Part II, seriatim.

[93] Brinley Rees, op. cit., contains, along with selections from his Welsh writings, *A Vindication of the Educational and Moral Condition of Wales in reply to William Williams late MP for Coventry* (Llandovery, 1848), pp. 77–104. See also his *Facts, Figures, and Statements in illustration of the Dissent and Morality of Wales* (London, 1849).

[94] For full references to his writings on the subject of education in his *Diwygiwr* see Iorwerth Jones, *David Rees y Cynhyrfwr* (Abertawe, 1971). One of his essays on the Blue Books is included in Glanmor Williams (ed.), *David Rees Llanelli: Detholion o'i Weithiau* (Caerdydd, 1950), tt. 32–6.

[95] Owen Owen Roberts, *Addysg yn Nhogledd Cymru* (Caernarfon, 1847). There was an English version of this pamphlet. For Roberts see *DWB*.

[96] Lewis Edwards contributed two weighty articles to *Y Traethodydd* in 1848, both of which are reprinted in *Traethodau Llenyddol*, tt. 374–405 and tt. 406–21. Lewis Edwards wrote extensively on the theme of education, usually in a non-controversial manner, and printed numerous articles by other authors.

[97] See below for Henry Richard's writings.

[98] For Thomas Price ('Carnhuanawc') see *DWB*. He was the leading Celtic scholar of his time and the author of *Hanes Cymru* which appeared in fourteen parts between 1836 and 1842. For his life and work see Mair Elvet Thomas, *Afiaith yng Ngwent* (Caerdydd, 1978) and John Davies, *Hanes Cymru* (London, 1990), tt. 372–3. For his contribution to the controversy

see E.I. Williams, 'Thomas Stephens and Carnhuanawc on the "Blue Books" of 1847', *Bull. Board of Celtic Studies*, IX (1938), pp. 271–3.

[99] The instructions were included in the epitome of the Reports, p. iv.

[100] *Charge* 1848, p. 52. 'I am inclined to regret that the instructions to the commissioners contained a clause which led and almost forced them to speculate upon it, and to invite the expression of opinions on the state of morals in particular neighbourhoods. To me it appears that such an investigation had little to do with the main object of the inquiry.'

[101] Report, Part II, p. 57.

[102] Ibid., p. 62.

[103] Report, Part III, p. 61.

[104] Ibid., p. 63.

[105] Ibid., p. 66.

[106] Ibid., p. 67.

[107] Ibid., p. 67.

[108] Ibid., p. 68.

[109] Ibid., p. 68.

[110] Report, Part I, p. 28.

[111] Ibid., p. 114.

[112] Ibid., p. 237.

[113] Ibid., pp. 478–92.

[114] Report, Part II, p. 294.

[115] For John Griffith see Wilton D. Wills, 'The Revd John Griffith and the survival of the established church in nineteenth century Glamorgan', *Morgannwg*, XIII (1969), p. 75. Also, for the religious climate of the time, the same author's 'The clergy in society in mid-nineteenth century south Wales', *J. Historical Society of the Church in Wales*, 29 (1974), pp. 27–43. For the religious condition of his parish see E.T. Davies, op. cit. and Ieuan Gwynedd Jones, 'The building of St Elvan's Church, Aberdare', in *Communities*, op. cit. The evidence John Griffith gave before the Episcopal and Capitular Revenues Commission is important: see *PP* 1855, XX (1175), Minutes of Evidence, Qq. 2853–2964. See also Letters of John Griffith, Vicar of Aberdare 1847–59, Cardiff Free Library MSS 3–508. A lively, well-informed account of religious affairs from a Nonconformist point of view is to be found in *Bywgraffiad y diweddar Barchedig T. Price, MA, Ph.D., Aberdar*, gan y Parch. Benjamin Evans ('Telynfab') (Aberdâr, 1891).

[116] For Booker see Charles Wilkins, *History of the Iron, Steel and Tinplate Trades* (Merthyr Tydfil, 1903), pp. 242–8, and Arthur H. John and Glanmor Williams (eds.), *Glamorgan County History*, V: *Industrial Glamorgan* (Cardiff, 1980), *passim*.

[117] Report, Part I, p. 485.

[118] The latest and best account is by Prys Morgan 'From Long Knives to

Blue Books', in *Welsh Society and Nationhood*, op. cit., pp. 199–215, and John Davies, *Hanes Cymru* (1990), tt. 376–9. See also the thorough study in Sian Rhiannon Williams, op. cit. Since this essay was written the following collection of essays has appeared: Prys Morgan (gol.), *Brad y Llyfrau Gleision: Ysgrifau ar Hanes Cymru* (Llandysul, 1991).

[119] For Welsh periodicals see T.M. Jones ('Gwenallt'), *Llenyddiaeth Fy Ngwlad* (Treffynnon, 1893); Aled Gruffydd Jones, 'Y wasg Gymreig yn y bedwaredd ganrif ar bymtheg', *Cof Cenedl*, III (Llandysul, 1988), tt. 89–116. *Y Drysorfa* sold 3,000 copies monthly in 1846 and this had risen to 5,000 by 1847: its price in that period came down from 6 pence to 4 pence, according to an editorial in 1847. Consider the comment in *Yr Ymofynnydd* (The Inquirer) 1848, p. 17: 'Y mae dydd yr argraff-wasg wedi dyfod i Gymru . . . Er fod y Saesneg yn ymdaenu drwy'r wlad, mae'n debyg bod mwy o ddarllenwyr Cymraeg yn awr nag a fu oll. Y mae dydd y "dim ond pregethu" ar fyned heibio. Fe *fyn* ddynion ddarllen; ac fe a'r cyhoeddiadau bychain lle nad all pregethwr fyned, a gwnant lawer o'i waith drosto.' (The day of the printing-press has arrived in Wales . . . Even though English is spreading throughout the land it is likely that there are more readers of Welsh than ever before. Gone are the days of preaching only. Men *insist* on reading; and the small publications go where no preacher can, and they do much of his work in his stead.) For the general background see Richard D. Altick, *The English Common Reader: A Social History of the Mass Reading Public 1800–1900* (London edn., 1963).

[120] E.D. Rees, 'South Wales and Monmouthshire newspapers under the Stamp Acts', *WHR*, 1 no. 3 (1962), pp. 301–24.

[121] On the *Principality* see ibid., pp. 317–18.

[122] This is well illustrated in Brynley F. Roberts, 'Argraffu yn Aberdar', *J. Welsh Bibliographical Society*, XI, Nos. 1–2 (1973–4).

[123] *Seren Cymru* (Mai 1848), t. 153.

[124] Jelinger Symons, *The Industrial Capacities of South Wales* (London and Tenby, 1855), reprinted from *The Cambrian Journal*, 1854. In this pamphlet the author advocated the development of Milford Haven as a major Atlantic port, served by a new railway from London via a bridge over the Severn at Aust and running along the northern edge of the south Wales coalfield — roughly the line of the coach road. Education had a key role to play in the imperial exploitation of Wales which these engineering feats would make possible: 'I need hardly remark how largely moral elevation and social decencies contribute to industrial vigour and the value of skilled labour.' He quotes passages from his own report in 1847 to illustrate how lacking these desirable qualities were, and calls upon the wealthy industrialists to undertake ameliorative, paternalistic measures (pp. 21–2).

[125] See in general the *New Cambridge Modern History*, X. *The Zenith of European Power: 1830–70*, esp. chaps. IX on nationalism by J.P.T. Bury

and XV by Charles Pouthas on the revolutions of 1848. The most recent and profoundly penetrating work is E.J. Hobsbawm, *Nations and Nationalism since 1870* (Cambridge, 1990). For Wales see Glanmor Williams's collected essays on this and related themes, *Religion, Language and Nationality in Wales* (Cardiff, 1979). Marian Henry Jones, *Hanes Ewrop 1815–1871* (Caerdydd, 1982), gives particular attention to these topics and their Welsh implications, and her 'Wales and Hungary', *Trans. Hon. Soc. Cymmrodorion*, 1968, part 1 (1969), pp. 7–27, is essential reading for the growth of nationalism in Wales.

[126] *Seren Cymru* (Mai 1848), t. 156. Millenarian explanations of current events were very popular and influential at this time; they indicate a deep-set distrust by common people of more conventional explanations. See, for example, *Y Frwydr Fawr rhwng Cenhedloedd y Ddaear* (Dinbych, 1853) and its sequel *Attodiad i'r Frwydr Fawr* (Dinbych, 1853). On millenarianism in general see J.F.C. Harrison, *The Second Coming: Popular Millenarianism 1780–1850* (London, 1979).

[127] See Ryland Wallace, *'Organise! Organise! Organise!' A Study of Reform Agitations in Wales 1840–1886* (Cardiff, 1991), pp. 12–34, and Ieuan Gwynedd Jones, 'The Anti-Corn Law Letters of Walter Griffith', *Bull. Board of Celtic Studies*, XXVIII, Part 1 (Nov. 1978), pp. 95–128.

[128] For Public Health see above chapter 2.

[129] *Traethodau Llenyddol*, op. cit., t. 410.

[130] Ibid., t. 413.

[131] *Artegall; or Remarks on the Reports of the Commissioners of Inquiry into the State of Education in Wales* (2nd edn., London, 1848), intro. p. 3. The author was Jane Williams ('Ysgafell'), historian, writer and biographer of Carnhuanawc. See *DNB* and *DWB*.

[132] *Charge* 1848, pp. 49–50. The bishop wrote of the work (in a footnote on page 48) that it had 'been warmly greeted by parties whose praise should make a well-meaning man uneasy and mistrustful of himself'.

[133] *Traethodau Llenyddol*, pp. 419–21.

[134] Ibid., p. 421.

[135] See Charles S. Miall, *Henry Richard MP, 1812–88* (London, 1889), Lewis Appleton, *Memoirs of Henry Richard, the Apostle of Peace* (London, 1889), Eleazer Roberts, *Bywyd a Gwaith y diweddar Henry Richard* (Wrexham, 1902) and Ieuan Gwynedd Jones, *Henry Richard 1812–88, Apostle of Peace* (Fellowship for Reconciliation, Llangollen, 1988).

[136] Charles S. Miall, op. cit., p. 23.

[137] Henry Richard, *On the Progress and Efficiency of Voluntary Education, as Exemplified in Wales* (Crosby Hall Lectures, 1848), p. 134. See also Margaret Venables George, 'An assessment of the contribution of Henry Richard to education' (unpublished University of Wales MA dissertation, (Swansea) 1975), 135; ibid., pp. 212–13.

[138] Henry Richard, op. cit. p. 203.

[139] For Lewis Edwards see Trebor Lloyd Evans, *Lewis Edwards: Ei Fywyd a'i Waith* (Abertawe, 1967). For his editorial policy read his letters to contributors in *Bywyd a Llythyrau y diweddar Barch. Lewis Edwards, MA, DD* gan Thomas Charles Edwards (Liverpool, 1901).

[140] Ieuan Gwynedd Jones, 'The dynamics of Welsh politics', in *Explorations*, op. cit.

[141] See Cobden Papers, BL Add. MSS 43647–78. Another close associate and friend was Joseph Sturge whose biography he wrote under the title *Memoirs of Joseph Sturge* (London, 1864). There is much background to Richard's political education and life in Alex Tyrrell, *Joseph Sturge and the Moral Radical Party in Early Victorian Britain* (London, 1987). For his relations with the wealthy Liberal Nonconformist philanthropist Samuel Morley, and the way some of his carefully calculated giving was directed towards Wales, see Richard's memoir of him in Edwin Hodder, *The Life of Samuel Morley* (London, 1887), pp. 293–301.

[142] For Edward Miall see Binfield, op. cit.

[143] For the political life of Liverpool and the Liverpool Welsh see Derek Fraser, *Power and Authority in the Victorian City* (Oxford, 1979): Colin G. Pooley, 'Welsh migration to England in the mid-nineteenth century', *Journal of Historical Geography*, 9 No. 3 (July 1983), p. 287; J.R. Jones, *The Welsh Builder on Merseyside* (Liverpool, 1946); and R. Merfyn Jones and D. Ben Rees, *Liverpool Welsh and their Religion* (Liverpool, 1984).

[144] Recent studies include those on Swansea: see Glanmor Williams (ed.), *Swansea: An Illustrated History* (Swansea, 1990); Ralph A. Griffiths (ed.), *The City of Swansea: Challenges and Change* (Alan Sutton, 1990); and Cardiff: Neil Evans, 'The Welsh Victorian city: the middle class and civic and national consciousness in Cardiff, 1850–1914', *WHR*, 12 no. 3 (June 1985), pp. 350–87. For north Wales, see A.H. Dodd, *The Industrial Revolution in North Wales* (2nd edn., Cardiff, 1951), R. Merfyn Jones, *The North Wales Quarrymen 1874–1922* (Cardiff, 1981) on Blaenau Ffestiniog and Bethesda, and for the port towns Lewis Lloyd, *The Port of Caernarfon* (Caernarfon, 1989) and idem, *Pwllheli: The Port and Mart of Llŷn* (Caernarfon, 1991). Key studies include E.P. Hennock, *Fit and Proper Persons: Ideal and Reality in Nineteenth-Century Urban Government* (London, 1973), and Derek Fraser, *Urban Politics in Victorian England: The Structure of Politics in Victorian Cities* (Leicester, 1976).

[145] See above ch. 2.

[146] The key sources are in *Bywgraffiad Barchedig T. Price Aberdar*, op. cit., and see my essay 'Dr Thomas Price and the election of 1868 in Merthyr Tydfil', in *Communities*, op. cit., pp. 262–321.

[147] See Ryland Wallace, op. cit.

[148] Richard, op. cit., p. 224.

[149] See 'Merioneth politics in the mid-nineteenth century' in *Explorations and Explanations*, op. cit., p. 141 for Lewis Edwards's speech.

[150] This Address appears in virtually all the Welsh periodicals and local newspapers.

[151] This is quoted from his eve-of-the-poll speech reported verbatim in the *Aberdare Times*, 11 November 1868.

Index